Historical Dictionary of
Algeria

Alf Andrew Heggoy
with Robert R. Crout

African Historical Dictionaries,
No. 28

The Scarecrow Press, Inc.
Metuchen, N.J., & London
1981

Library of Congress Cataloging in Publication Data

Heggoy, Alf Andrew.
    Historical dictionary of Algeria.

    (African historical dictionaries ; no. 28)
    Bibliography: p.
    Includes index.
    1. Algeria--History--Dictionaries. I. Crout,
Robert R., joint author. II. Title. III. Series.
DT283.7.H43   965'.003'21   80-24126
ISBN 0-8108-1376-9

TABLE OF CONTENTS

Appendices (continued)

LIST OF MAPS

EDITOR'S FOREWORD

Algeria was the last country in North Africa to attain independence and was long assumed to have a shallow historical background and weak national identity.   Nevertheless, it has turned out to be one of the most dynamic states in the region. It quickly assumed a leadership role on the Maghrib, Arab, African and international scene.   This occurred both under the flamboyant Ben Bella and the most withdrawn Boumedienne, although policies varied and were projected differently.   And Algeria can be expected to play a significant part under any leadership, due to such natural assets as its considerable size and wealth, its strategic location in Africa and opposite Europe, but especially due to its will to make up for the late start by pressing ahead with economic development and nation building.

Yet, not much is known about Algeria.   Its past has been explored less extensively than the greater dynasties to the east and west.   Much of what happened during the revolution still remains to be fathomed.   The actions, or relative importance, of the historic leaders and the thousands who lived in the shadows and were unknown or known through their war names, are not clearly defined.   Even in the new post-independence regimes, the party and military circles have been sufficiently closed to limit the flow of information. Thus, despite its international prestige, Algeria is very poorly understood by outsiders.

This explains the significance of the present book. For, it delves into the oft-forgotten historical roots reaching back to Berber and earlier foundations and showing the long succession of invaders from the Romans, to the Arabs, to the French.   It provides a wealth of details on the revolutionary period.   And it is no less informative about the present state and party structures.   A number of annexes go beyond this by listing chronologically the many greater and lesser figures who have ruled over Algeria.

Professor Alf Heggoy is certainly well-placed to write

this volume in the series of African Historical Dictionaries. Born and partially educated in Algeria, he did his post-doctoral research work in North Africa, and has returned periodically to Algeria. A specialist on French and North African affairs, he can deal competently with both strains of recent history. He has written numerous papers and articles over the years and his earlier book Insurgency and Counter-insurgency in Algeria will soon be joined by a Social and Intellectual History of Algeria. Professor Heggoy was ably supported by Robert Crout. Crout earned his Ph. D. at the University of Georgia in 1977. Since then, he has published a number of articles on French Colonial History. He is presently an editor of the Lafayette papers at Cornell University.

Jon Woronoff
Series Editor

AUTHOR'S PREFACE

In transliterating Arabic names, I have not used the standard rules set forth in the Library of Congress Cataloguing Service, "Bulletin 49" (Washington D. C. , 1958). Instead, I have used the spelling of such names most commonly found in literature about Algeria. Thus, for example, I have an entry for Ben Badis, not for Ibn Badis. I have done so because most non-specialists reading about Ben Badis would not know that the proper transliteration would be Ibn Badis. The spelling of many Arabic names was fixed in our Latin alphabet by French colonial officials who were not necessarily linguists. In general, publications of the independent Algerian government have continued to use the spellings used by the former imperial masters. To do anything else would simply be an unnecessary complication. Also, for reasons of clarity and simplicity, I have avoided the use of diacritical marks. Thus, for example, I have used Abd al-Qadir rather than 'Abd al-Qadir. Where there might be some confusion, or when more than one form of the name appeared in published literature, I have made secondary entries sending the user back to the primary one.

In alphabetizing the dictionary, I have considered Ben, Ibn, Abu, Bou, etc. ... as part of the name. Thus, Ben Allah and Ben Ali are both to be found listed under "B, " not under "A, " and Abu Zaiyan is listed under "A, " not under "Z. " Prefixes such as al- or el-, however, have been ignored. Therefore, al-Ghumari is listed under "G, " not under "A, " and el-Mokrani will be found under "M, " not under "E. "

While every effort has been made to be as complete as possible, some entries are less informative than others, and some entries may be missing altogether. Such lapses are, in part, a reflection of the state of the art. Very little is, in fact, known about many of the Algerians who have only recently risen to prominence. In general, however, this dictionary should be most useful as a first-reference for anyone reading about Algeria in English. I should also point out that, with but a few exceptions, Europeans have not been included in this dictionary. To have included too many French public figures might well have drowned the Algerians, might have tended to make this an historical dictionary of French colonial Algeria rather than an historical dictionary of Algeria.

In closing, let me thank my colleague Robert R. Crout for contributing about twenty-five percent of the entries and for helping with proof-reading and other chores that are a necessary part of preparing a manuscript. Martin L. Mickelsen contributed the entries on "Allied Invasion of Algeria, " "Maison-Carrée Mutiny, " "Naval Battle of Mers-el-Kebir, " "Reform Ordnance of December 1943 and March 1944" and "Vichy Algeria"--all entries about which he knew a great deal because of his research on de Gaulle. Gratitude is also owed to Paul Minor, my graduate research assistant who helped in various tasks.

Alf Andrew Heggoy

INTRODUCTION

The Natural Setting and the Economy

The Democratic and Popular Republic of Algeria is the second largest African country with an area of 2,381,741 square kilometers. Most of that vast country, however, is desertland and approximately ninety-five percent of the nearly eighteen million Algerians live within a one-hundred-mile belt bordering on the Mediterranean Sea, or roughly within ten to twelve percent of the total area, in that portion of the land lying north of the arid Sahara. This portion of the country has a Mediterranean climate. With a 620 mile shore, the country's terrain is extremely varied. Even the narrow northern plain is often broken up by mountains, many of which slope directly into the sea. On the whole, northern Algeria is dominated by two mountain ranges that run east-west from Tunisia to Morocco. Northernmost is the Tell Atlas which rises from the coastal plain and is flanked by a high plateau to the south. This high plateau of dry undulating steppe, in turn, gives way to the Saharan Atlas which mark the beginning of the Sahara.

The Tell Atlas mountains extend up to 4,000 feet in altitude, while the Saharan Atlas, which are a continuation of the Moroccan High Atlas, loom up to 7,000 feet above sea level. Both mountain ranges descend toward the east and ultimately merge imperceptibly into the coastal plains of Tunisia. The Saharan Atlas form an almost continuous chain, while the Tell Atlas are irregular and thus tend to compartmentalize northern Algeria into isolated geographic regions.

East of Algiers, the capital which sits on the coast halfway between the Moroccan and Tunisian borders, the coastal regions generally receive more than thirty-two inches of rainfall per year. Another area just to the south, but extending up to the coast west of Algiers, receives between twenty-four and thirty-two inches. A third region, bordering those already mentioned but also encompassing most of the coastline between Algiers and Oran, receives only from six-

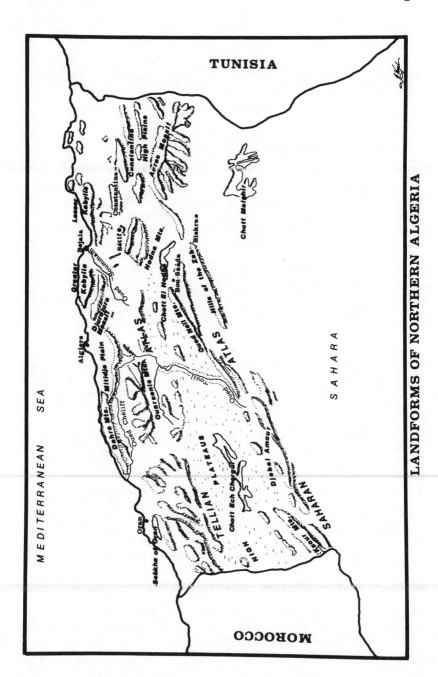

teen to twenty-four inches per year.   From Oran to the
Moroccan border more arid conditions prevail.   As in the
High Plateaus further south, this region averages from eight
to sixteen inches of rainfall per year, making it unsuitable
for agriculture but able to support extended pastoralism.
The Saharan Atlas, averaging a mere four to eight inches,
comes close to qualifying as desert.   Of course, the Sahara
itself receives virtually no precipitation at all.   Including the
land in the Sahara, Algeria is the second largest territory
in Africa.   Indeed the Algerian land mass is somewhat larger
than the entire area of the United States east of the Missis-
sippi, almost as extensive as the combined areas of Alaska
and Texas, and more than four times larger than France.
Yet, because so much of its land is agriculturally unproduc-
tive, Algeria must import a larger percentage of its food-
stuffs.

        While as much as sixty percent of the Algerian popu-
lation is still engaged in agriculture, most of that number
depends upon subsistence farming by traditional means of
cultivation for their livelihood.   Despite the predominance of
a pastoral economy, Algeria also contains some large-scale
farms which utilize modern machinery and produce cash
crops such as citrus, olives and figs.   However, most of
these farms are privately owned.   Other crops such as tobacco, wheat, barley, oats, and grapes, are generally produced on lands formerly owned by extremely wealthy settlers
and large companies.   After Algeria gained its independence
in 1962, these colonial landowners fled to France, leaving
their farms to the Algerians who had worked them as hired
hands.   These farms were then spontaneously organized
through self-management committees after the new government declared them "vacant" and seized their titles in the
name of the Algerian people.   After 1963 Algerian bureau-
crats took the self-management farms in hand and organized
them into agricultural cooperatives.   Before Algeria can once
more feed itself the government must extend the modern agricultural sector and oversee the modernization of the traditional sector.   At this time, however, the Algerians are fo-
cusing more on rapid industrialization than upon modernization of agriculture.

        To pay for this industrialization, the Algerian leader-
ship is counting on oil reserves which, at present rates of
exploitation, may well be depleted within two decades.   Although the country contains vast reserves of natural gas,
these too will eventually run dry.   Both oil and gas reserves

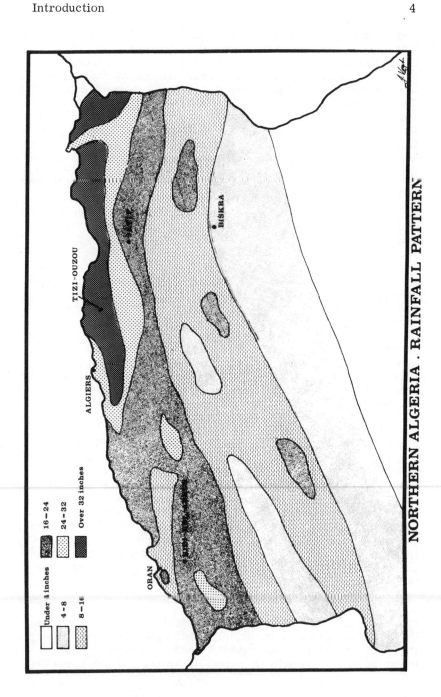

NORTHERN ALGERIA . RAINFALL PATTERN

are of very high grade. An extensive network of roads and
pipelines have already been built to bring these resources to
markets. Because these limited resources are not renew-
able, the country faces an inevitable economic crisis which
will be compounded by Algeria's very high birth rate. The
crisis is inevitable, that is, unless the country manages to
create a modern industrial economy. Algeria views it as
necessary to create a diversified industrial sector, a need
that led the government to commit the equivalent of nearly
twelve billion dollars (U. S.) to the development plan for 1974-
1977.

History Before the French Conquest

Algeria's history has, in many ways, reflected the country's
geography. Except for its Mediterranean coastline, the republic has no natural borders. For as long as there has
been recorded history, there have been inhabitants in North
Africa whom outsiders named Berbers. These people call
themselves Imazigen which, roughly translated, means noble-
men. When Carthage began to dominate Africa's Mediterranean shoreline around 1000 B. C. , it ruled the area that
would eventually become Algeria. Later (145 B. C.), the
area of present day Tunisia was seized by the Romans, at
about the same time as the first distinct independent state in
the central regions of Northwest Africa appeared. This state
was Numidia, under the control of the fascinating Berber
leader Massinissa (d. 148 B. C.). Although Massinissa's successors were clients of Rome, there was a political entity in
the geographic area occupied by modern Algeria. The last
two Massyle kings (descendants of Massinissa) were Juba II
(25 B. C. --23 A. D.) and Ptolemy (23 B. C. --40 A. D.). Thereafter, colonizer followed colonizer with only brief periods of
independence for the central regions of what the Arabs were
to call the Maghrib--roughly, the area of modern Tunisia,
Algeria, and Morocco. In the fifth century, the conquerors
were the Vandals, who were in turn replaced by Byzantines.
Colonization by Carthaginians, Greeks, Romans, Vandals, and
Byzantines did not really change the Berbers.

     The next wave of invaders did make a difference, how-
ever. In the early seventh century, Arabs who had recently
converted to Islam began their conquest of what would here-
after be known as the Maghrib. Over the next several centuries practically all the Berbers who inhabited the central
Maghrib became Muslims. The language and culture that are

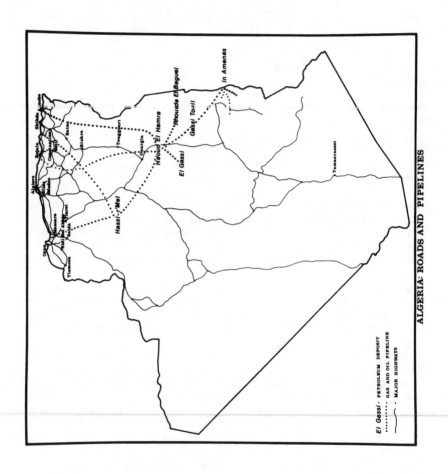

ALGERIA: ROADS AND PIPELINES

El Gassi - PETROLEUM DEPOSIT
········· - GAS AND OIL PIPELINE
⌒ · MAJOR HIGHWAYS

nearly indistinguishable from Islam became that of roughly
seventy-five percent of the people of "Algeria." A colloquial
form of Arabic, the language in which the Muslim holy book,
the Qur'an, is written, became the "national" language of the
vast majority of Algerians. Only twenty-five percent remained
Berbers, but even they became Muslims.

Since the seventh century, therefore, Algeria has been
inhabited mostly by Muslims. For as much of this time, it
has been neither a state nor a nation. Instead, it has been
an area between two states--Tunisia and Morocco. Under
the sway of the former it was drawn towards Cairo, and under the latter towards Granada and the shining Ibero-Islamic
civilization that flourished there. Like a see-saw Algeria
was first under the control of the more stable state to the
east, and then under the tutelage of Morocco--and back and
forth it went, helpless to control its own destiny. Still, the
ill-defended but culturally distinct area between Tunisia and
Morocco maintained its ethnic identity. Over the centuries
there were occasional dynasties centered in "Algeria," among
them the Hammamids (1007-1163) whose capital was Bejaia
and the Zayyamids (1236-1554) whose central city was Tlemcen.
However, it was not until the coming of the Barbarossa brothers, Aruj and Khayr al Din, that the embryonic Algeria gained
institutional stability. Turkish officials and privateers, they
conquered Algiers and created an autonomous state that owed
theoretical allegiance to the Sublime Porte of Istanbul. Since
deys ruling in Oran, Constantine, and Titteri owed allegiance
to the successors of the Barbarossa brothers, the deys of
Algiers, Algeria was in effect a quasi-independent state from
the early 1500s until the French attacked it in 1830, thoroughly
dismantled the government and embarked upon a long and
drawnout conquest of Algeria.

National Awareness in the Nineteenth Century

The evidence clearly indicated that an Algerian state or, at
the very least, an embryonic Algerian nationalism existed at
the time the French penetrated the Maghrib. When the French
attacked Algiers, for example, peripheral tribes from areas
that routinely refused to pay taxes to the central authorities
sent soldiers to help defend the capital. With the Turks gone,
Abd al Qadir managed to create a successor Islamic state.
While the Algerian state might be defined negatively, simply
as a coalition of all the area's inhabitants who did not wish
to see a government of "infidels" imposed on Muslim lands,

this state did control roughly two-thirds of the inhabited land
area of Algeria and a like proportion of the Arab and Berber
inhabitants of the land.   Understanding modern statecraft, Abd
al Qadir attempted, unsuccessfully, to gain diplomatic recognition from England and from Spain.   Although this recognition was refused and though Abd al Qadir encountered difficulty in obtaining modern weapons, he and his followers
stoutly resisted the French for fifteen years, until 1845.   That
Abd al Qadir and his armies resisted French penetration so
long can be understood only by realizing the nationalistic sen-
timents of the Algerians.   To view them as merely religious
and xenophobic resisters is to embrace a deeply rooted fal-
lacy which has long been the standard of Eurocentric colonial
historiography.

        Algeria's heroic resistance to French penetration did
not end with the capture, imprisonment, and exile of Abd al
Qadir, however, and the French were compelled to fight on
until 1859 in order to subdue their intractable foes.   Indeed,
France continued to struggle against a steady stream of regional rebellions for another one-hundred-three years.   Among
the most troublesome to the French were the Awlad Sidi
Shaykh revolt in Orania in 1864, the Kabyle uprising of 1871,
and the Setif rebellion of 1945.   In retrospect, then, it is
clear that the Algerians never completely ceased their armed
resistance against the imperial invader until 1962, when Algeria finally achieved political independence.

The French Colonial Period

From 1830 to 1962, Algerians continued to resist foreign
domination.   When armed resistance did not work, they resisted through passive means.   Nevertheless, the French
gained and maintained the upper hand during most of this
period of Algeria's history, even though this authority was
sometimes maintained by cruel means, particularly in the
early colonial period.   In one incident, a whole tribe, seek-
ing refuge from the foreign army in a local grotto, was
fumigated to death.   More commonly, villagers who refused
to acknowledge the authority of France saw their crops burnt,
their fruit trees cut down, and their domesticated animals
taken away by French soldiers.   Pacification--cruel policies
are often described with words that sound humane and civi-
lized--usually went hand-in-hand with colonization.

        Colonization policies, reduced to essentials, meant

taking land and property from Algerians and transferring
them to immigrant settlers from Europe. By 1860, most of
the fertile coastal plains of Algeria "belonged" to Europeans
with the Algerians themselves pushed back into marginal
farmlands of the mountains. Such revolts as the one by the
Kabyles in 1871 furnished colonial authorities with the necessary excuses for further confiscation of land and the conse-
quent extension of colonization.

        France's Third Republic declared most of northern
Algeria an integral part of the nation and divided the country
into three departments. Unlike any other group of French
departments, however, Algeria had a governor, clearly a
colonial office. Another anomaly was the fact that, at first,
only Europeans could vote--although France had established
universal manhood suffrage in 1871. Algerian males were
not allowed to vote until 1919. Even then, only 421,000 of
them gained access to the ballot box. Universal manhood
suffrage did not come to Algerians until even later, in 1958.
Before that date Algerians voted in a second electoral college, the first being reserved for Europeans, an insignificant
number of naturalized Frenchmen of Algerian origin, and
Algerian Jews who had become French citizens by government fiat, the Cremieux decree of 1871. There were other
differences between France's metropolitan and African departments. In 1900 a "Financial Delegation" was created to give
Algeria a large degree of administrative and fiscal autonomy.
By law, two thirds of the delegation were elected by "Europeans." The other third were "Muslims" appointed by the
French colonial authorities. After 1919, the second electoral
college was allowed to elect one half of the 120 delegates in
this peculiar parliamentary body. Sixty Algerian delegates
represented ninety percent of the population; their European
colleagues, only ten percent.

        An integral part of France, Algeria had, nevertheless,
its own currency which, though different, was on par with
the metropolitan franc. Travellers between Marseilles and
Algiers, presumably two French ports, had to go through
customs. Quite clearly, there were two categories of citizenship in the Algerian departments, another anomaly not found
in any other group of French departments. There were also
special laws and regulations that applied only to Algerian
subjects, not to European settlers, such as the infamous
"code de l'indigénat."

        French colonialism did bring a modicum of moderniza-

tion to Algeria, but clearly not for the benefit of Algerians.
Ports, railroads, roads, and eventually airports were built.
But these served Algerian interests only incidentally; they
were clearly built to serve settler interests and, sometimes,
strategic purposes. Even before World War 1, there were
considerable economic advances to be noted in Algeria, particularly in agriculture and, to a lesser extent, in manufacturing. But the advantages gained were concentrated in European hands; Algerians themselves shared in these riches, but
only marginally. What was true in the political and economic
realms also prevailed in the social, both before and after
the war of 1914. Although France passed laws prescribing
mandatory elementary education in 1881, very few Algerian
children ever gained access to French schools. Practically
all settler children got access to schools, but never more
than fifteen percent of appropriately aged Algerians attended
these same colonial schools before 1954. In fact, French
authorities accommodated more Algerian children in colonial
schools between 1954 and 1962 than between 1830 and 1954.

     Political, economic and social disabilities suffered by
Algerians in the French colonial period of their history eventually transformed their nationalism. But before discussing
modern Algerian nationalism, which began as a reaction to
second class status for Algerians in their own country, it is
essential to stress the fact that a national sentiment rooted
in Abd al Qadir's resistance movement was always present.
French historiography tended to stress the religious and
xenophobic attributes of Abd al Qadir's Algerian state. In
contrast, Arab and Berber oral traditions kept alive a vision
of Abd al Qadir as a patriot and as an authentic national hero.
The most recent scholarly interpretation of this fascinating
Berber leader and Arabic scholar stresses the essential political characteristics of Abd al Qadir, a man who knew how
to use the institutions and social forces of his own world and
time to resist the French conquest and pacification of Algiers.
The religious aspects of his rule were just one of the means
of assuring legitimacy for the state he created to stave off
the French.

Early Algerian Anti Colonialism

Given the popular view as well as the more recent critical
and analytical understanding of Abd al Qadir's role in Algerian history, one should not be too surprised to discover that
one of the first rumblings of modern Algerian nationalism

centered on the person of one of his grandsons, Khaled Ben
el Hachemi. He won election to the Algiers municipal council
in 1919, the first time some male Algerians were allowed to
vote. His platform proposed the cessation of foreign immigration to Algeria, Algerian access to French citizenship with
the maintenance of Muslim status, the abolition of mixed communes, compulsory education in Arabic and French, and equal
representation for Europeans and Algerians in the colony's
various assemblies. Although his program clearly reflected
associationist tendencies--he was not calling for French evacuation of Algeria, but asking that Algerians and Algerian culture be treated as equal to Frenchmen and French culture--
he was quickly forced into exile. In spite of claims to the
contrary, France did not want Algerians to become equals;
if the French government could accept this proposition, European settlers in Algeria obviously would not.

After Emir Khaled's failure, other proto-nationalists--
men such as Ferhat Abbas and Dr. Ben Djelloul in the 1930s
--continued to work for essentially assimilationist or associationist programs. Only gradually did it dawn on Algerian
political elites, generally men who had gained something from
the French presence in Algeria, that reforms within the
French system would not lead to equality for Algerians. Reforms such as the Clemenceau Law of 1919, which gave the
vote to some Algerian men for the first time, or the Blum
Violett Proposal of 1936 (which never passed but which would
have allowed Algerians to become French citizens without
giving up their personal Islamic status), came too late, gave
too little, or were not accepted by French legislators.

Nevertheless, Ferhat Abbas and other liberal Algerian
leaders persevered in efforts to achieve equality for Algerians within the French system. In December 1942, for example, Abbas headed a group requesting the creation of a
constituent assembly elected by universal suffrage according
to the national self-determination clause of the Atlantic Charter. The evidence, however, shows that Abbas still thought
of reforms within a French framework. When the first request met with a lack of response, Abbas and his group demanded immediate reform, particularly the acceptance of
Arabic as an official language in Algeria and the eventual
creation of an Algerian state in some sort of federal union
with France. The French, prodded by General de Gaulle,
finally reacted to growing discontent among Algerian subjects
by announcing a new statute for Algeria in March 1944. But
this was only a weak compromise that satisfied no one. Some

60,000 additional Algerians would become French citizens,
but the Algerian share of seats in an assembly was limited
to only forty percent, and further discussion about the creation of an Algerian state was ruled out. The country would
continue to be three overseas departments of France. Only
then did Abbas create the AML, a political party dedicated
to the creation of an autonomous Algeria federally linked to
France. Control of events were, in any case, already slip-
ping out of the grasp of liberal Algerian politicians. Extrem-
ists on both sides were taking over: reactionary settlers presided over the killing of up to 50,000 Algerians in the repression that followed the Setif uprising of 1945, then blatantly
manipulated the 1948 elections to suit themselves; radicals
in the most radical of Algerian parties, the MTLD-PPA which
Messali Hadj no longer controlled as effectively as he had
earlier.

Origins of Modern Algerian Nationalism

Before the outbreak of Revolution in 1954, there existed three
important Algerian political groupings. One was composed
of moderate politicians generally associated with Ferhat Abbas.
While this group was eventually driven to demand the right
of national self-determination and the application of the Atlantic Charter to Algeria, the moderates always worked within
the French system and did not become outright nationalists
until after the beginning of the war of national liberation. A
second grouping was a party created among North Africans
in France and only "imported" into Algeria when it was already a full-blown institution. This was the ENA (North
African Star) which, under various acronyms, was always
Messali Hadj's party. Beginning in 1926 with financial assistance from the French Communist Party, the ENA quickly
broke with its parent and went its own way. The leader's
mark on the ENA was clear: drafted into the French army,
then demobilized, he had stayed on in France. While barely
managing a proletarian existence on the edges of France's
industrial economy, Messali Hadj had been attracted to the
Communist Party, which he joined. But before becoming a
Communist, Messali Hadj had been a member of the Tlemcen
lodge of the Derkawa Brotherhood, which was a sufi order.
For as long as Messali Hadj controlled the ENA and its many
successor organizations, this radical proletarian party combined Marxist organization with Pan-Arabic and Pan-Islamic
ideology. It was also uncompromisingly anti-colonial and
nationalist and, by its very intransigent stand, it forced the

more moderate politicians into increasingly radical positions.
To refuse to move in a radical direction would have made
middle-class parties irrelevant in the eyes of an ever increas-
ing number of Algerians.

Before World War II, the ENA had become the PPA
(Algerian People's Party) which was outlawed by the Vichy
regime. In 1945, it reappeared as the MTLD (Movement for
the Triumph of Democratic Liberties). But below the surface,
the illegal PPA continued while, in even deeper clandestinity,
the OS (Secret Organization) drafted members from among
the most radical followers of Messali Hadj. The Supreme
Leader himself did not approve of the OS, an institution created by the young hawks who were themselves impatient with
what they saw as the leaders' timidity. Dedicated revolutionary nationalists who had long since lost all faith in the pos-
sibility of achieving any acceptable goals within the French
system, the OS members were all men who would organize
the CRUA (Revolutionary Committee for Unity and Action) and
the Front for National Liberation in 1954.

The third of the three most important Algerian political groupings of the pre-revolutionary period was the Association of Algerian Reformist Ulama founded by Abd al Hamid
Ben Badis in 1931. Unlike the various institutions created
by Ferhat Abbas and Messali Hadj, the Ulama did not claim
to be a political party. Instead, Ben Badis and his followers
claimed to be a religious and cultural association. But their
program had crystal-clear implications. They founded schools
in which all teaching was done in Arabic, a fact that was in
clear violation of French colonial laws on education. They
created a Muslim scouting organization within which young
boys learned to recite a telling motto: "Islam is my religion;
Arabic is my language; Algeria is my fatherland." They
published Ech Chihab and El Basair, two Arabic periodicals
in which the Ulama preached pan-Arabic and pan-Islamic doctrines. In spite of disclaimers, the Ulama were preparing
a generation of young Algerians to think of Algeria without
France. Already in 1936, Ben Badis was writing:

> " ... we have observed that the Muslim Algerian na-
> tion has come into being and exists. This nation
> has its own history ... it has its own religious and
> linguistic unity, its culture and its tradition. We
> then say that this Muslim Algerian nation is not
> France, cannot be France and does not want to
> be France."

Nevertheless, Ben Badis was not as politically radical as
Messali Hadj. The leader of the Ulama would accept an
Algeria in a French Commonwealth and pointed to the relationship between Canada and England to explain what he had
in mind.

       It was not theologians in the Ulama group or the mod-
erates who surrounded Ferhat Abbas who launched Algeria's
war of national liberation. It was not even the radical Messali Madj who, by 1954, was in enforced exile in France and
engaged in a bitter struggle to maintain control of the MTLD.
It was, instead, those young hawks in Messali Hadj's party
who created the OS over his protest in the late 1940s. In
spite of careful compartmentalization of the OS, French colonial authorities stumbled on this organization and decapitated
it by arresting practically all of the national leaders. But
Ben Bella eventually escaped as did other imprisoned OS
leaders. The French had, in any case, not dismantled every
unit. Some were not discovered and remained intact and
ready to swing into action, which they did at the stroke of
midnight on October 31, 1954. So did a motley group of
other separatists, deserters from the French army and some
plain outlaws. They were quickly recast, however, into a
truly national insurgency force which the French authorities
would not be able to completely destroy. Although colonial
military strength quickly jumped from around 50,000 men to
well over half a million, and although the war lasted eight
years, the ragtag army which started the war, probably no
more than 500 men at the beginning, maintained itself and
grew. Finally, France tired of the war and withdrew, end-
ing a one hundred thirty-two year imperial venture in Algeria.

The War of National Liberation

The War of National Liberation was long and bloody. In
this struggle, neither side was really well organized at the
start. The French had just over 50,000 soldiers garrisoned
throughout Algeria although it had long been established that
around 84,000 men were needed to maintain law and order in
the colony. On the other hand, the insurgents were fewer
than five hundred in November 1954, and this number grew
only gradually to an eventual 25,000 men in the ALN's (Army
of National Liberation) internal army. Neither side had, at
first, created appropriate institutions needed to fight or to
resist the War of National Liberation.

The radical nationalists who seized the initiative in
1954 maintained their momentum and quickly created the
bureaucracies and other institutions needed to keep the insurgency alive. At the Soummam Congress which was held
in Algeria itself under the nose of a growing French military
presence, the internal leaders of the FLN-ALN defined their
party's political objectives and created the first governmental
institutions of an independent socialist Algerian Republic. They
created a thirty-four member National Council of the Algerian
Republic (CNRA) and a five man Executive and Coordinating
Committee (CCE) to manage revolutionary policies between
meetings of the larger body. The delegates at the Soummam
Congress also set the policy that led to urban terrorism and
to the battle of Algiers (1956-57).

French authorities had meanwhile adjusted to the insurgency situation and their increasingly severe repressions
of the Algerian population eventually forced the ALN to return
to guerilla actions: the nationalists failed to liberate a portion of the national territory and to progress from guerilla
warfare to more standard warfare which, theoretically, they
had expected to do. By early 1958, a military stalemate had
been established within Algeria: the French, by building
border barriers of electrified wire and mine fields, had made
it difficult for the ALN to receive supplies or reinforcements
from outside the country. On the other hand, French troops
of close to a half-million men could not effectively control
all of Algeria or come to grips with freedom fighters now
operating in small guerilla groups that could strike at will.

Although military operations continued after 1958, and
although the loss in lives and property continued to be heavy,
the essential struggle between France and Algerian Nationalists was to be a political one for the balance of the war.
When the French government seemed to waver, to be willing
to consider an Algeria that would not be an integral part of
France, the more extreme European settlers took to the
streets to attempt to force continued French control. These
events of May 1958 marked the end of the Fourth French
Republic and ushered in de Gaulle's Fifth Republic. The
Nationalists of the FLN-ALN also reacted, creating the Provisional Government of the Algerian Republic (GPRA) under
the leadership of the moderate Ferhat Abbas. While the
fighting was not over, it was soon supplemented with secret
negotiations between France and Algerian Nationalists, talks
that eventually led to the signing of the Evian Agreements on
March 18, 1962. Ten days later, a transitional administration

was created. Under the presidency of Abderrarman Farès,
it was composed of FLN members, other Algerians, and
Europeans, who supervised the transition of power from
France to representatives of the GPRA.

Independence and the Transition of Power

On July 3, 1962, de Gaulle proclaimed Algeria independent
following a referendum on July 1 in which ninety-one percent
of the Algerian voters opted for independence. It would take
several more months, however, to achieve peace. Nearly
one million European settlers fled Algeria in 1962. This left
the country sorely short of technical and professional people
since such jobs had been largely monopolized by the dominant
European minority which now migrated to France. To com-
plicate the situation even further, the shaky unity maintained
by the FLN-ALN during the War of National Liberation broke
up as various political and military national elites began to
compete for power. The GPRA under the leadership of Ben
Khedda wished to take over. But they were immediately challenged by Ferhat Abbas, who had only recently been dropped
from the presidency of the GPRA, and by GPRA members
who had been held in French prisons--Ben Bella, Mohammed
Khider, Mohammed Boudiaf, Ait Ahmed and Rabah Bitat.
Also competing for power were the highest placed leaders of
the ALN and various wilaya commanders who had led the
fight against France from within Algeria. With but a few
exceptions, the latter liked neither the ALN leaders based in
Morocco and Tunisia, nor the politicians of the GPRA.

   Ben Khedda got to Algiers first. But Boumedienne
refused to obey orders from Ben Khedda and the ALN remained loyal to Boumedienne. The latter came to terms
with Ben Bella and the two crossed into Algeria and set up
headquarters at Tlemcen on July 11, 1962. Ben Bella had,
meanwhile, created a Political Bureau which, he claimed,
represented the FLN and rivaled the GPRA. As the ALN
troops moved toward Algiers, they had to fight several pitched
battles with wilaya elements. All-out civil war was avoided
only because of the intervention of mass demonstrations organized by the UGTA. After some considerable political ma-
neuvering, an Algerian Assembly with constituent powers was
elected; it met on September 25, 1962, and elected Ferhat
Abbas as its president. The next day, Ben Bella was elected
Prime Minister. He immediately organized a cabinet staffed
by his own partisans, by associates of Boumedienne, and by
a few "historic leaders."

The Ben Bella Years

Once in power, Ben Bella moved to consolidate his power.
His government outlawed the PCA (Algerian Communist
Party), Messali Hadj's PPA (Algerian People's Party) which
had been the MNA (Algerian National Movement), and Boudiaf's Party of the Socialist Revolution. Henceforth, the FLN
would be the only legal party. Ben Bella then maneuvered
to gain FLN control over the UGTA (General Union of Algerian Workers), which he managed to do by packing that union's
congress early in 1963. He pushed a constitution on the Algerian Assembly which created a Presidential Republic with
a one party (the FLN) system. This constitution was adopted
by a national referendum followed by elections. In September
of 1963 Ben Bella was elected to a five-year term as President. Meanwhile, he had gained considerable popular support
by nationalizing the lands and other properties which had
been left vacant by fleeing European settlers, by engaging in
a number of programs that were often more show than sub-
stance, and by beginning to define "Algerian Socialism."

Opposition remained, however. In 1963, Ben Bella
had to fight off an armed rebellion based in Kabylia and led
by a prison companion, Ait Ahmed, and Mohammed Ou el
Hadj, a wilaya commander. Ferhat Abbas, disappointed because he had no power, resigned as president of the National
Assembly. He protested against Ben Bella's personal power.
In the same year, there was a border war between Algeria
and Morocco in the Saharan south. In 1964, a first FLN
Congress was finally called and the Charter of Algiers which
defined "Algerian Socialism" and the relations between state,
party, and army were adopted. Ait Ahmed did not like the
new arrangements and continued his Kabylia-based rebellion.
Another revolt began in the southeast, this one led by a wilaya
commander, Colonel Chabaani. Although both Ait Ahmed and
Chabaani were captured, and although the latter was executed,
Ben Bella did not feel secure. By mid-1964, he had eliminated practically all the "historic leaders" from public life
and he began to move against the supporters of Boumedienne,
his erstwhile ally. First, he ordered all prefects to report
directly to the presidency and thus bypass the Ministry of
the Interior. Ahmed Medeghri, the Minister of the Interior
and one of Boumedienne's staunchest supporters, resigned in
protest (July 1964). Next, Ben Bella attempted to dismiss
Bouteflika, the Minister of Foreign Affairs and another Boumedienne ally. Boumedienne retaliated by striking first in
a coup d'etat dubbed the "historical rectification" of June 1965.

The Boumedienne Regime

A new body christened the Council of the Revolution assumed
political authority and, with Ben Bella in prison, Boumedienne
emerged as Algeria's leader. He was President of the Council
which moved quickly to create a new government (July 10,
1965). Boumedienne became Prime Minister and Minister of
Defense. He also retained his position as President of the
Council of the Revolution. In the cabinet were several men
who had served under Ben Bella, for example, Medeghri and
Bouteflika. But the new ministers of state were generally
technocrats, and there were also a few military men. Soldiers dominated in the Council of the Revolution which frequently met with the cabinet which, in turn, was essentially
composed of civilians. Another change was the creation of
a five-man party secretariat under the leadership of Cherif
Belkacem: this new institution was charged with the task of
smoothing relations between the party (FLN) and the government. Just as important, Boumedienne dismissed a number
of European advisors, men of communist, trotskyite, and
maoist convictions, who had surrounded Ben Bella. These
consultants, Boumedienne felt, had no roots in Algeria; they
neither understood nor valued Algeria's Arabic and Islamic
culture. "Algeria," Boumedienne declared in a June 30,
1965, speech, "wants to be Algeria, and that is all."

        To achieve this objective Boumedienne and his col-
leagues in the Council of the Revolution and in the government began to create new political institutions and to redirect
the economy. Both the national structures and the economy
then in place, they felt, were ill-adapted to the needs of
Algerian development because of 130 years of colonialism,
eight years of war and three years of poor leadership. Just
as important, Boumedienne directed the seizure of the national
wealth which, all too often, was still controlled by foreign
interests.

        Institutional and political changes began at the lowest
levels of the administrative organization. There were communal elections in February 1967, elections to the wilaya
assemblies in May 1969, and the reorganization of the FLN
as a radical avant-garde party thereafter. This elite party,
with close and continuing links to the government, should
however be in constant contact with the masses that it should
lead. To this end, existing mass organizations such as the
UGTA (General Union of Algerian Workers) were encouraged
to grow and to be more active while new mass institutions

were created to represent the social and economic interests
of groups not well represented in older organizations. Thus,
the UNPA (National Union of Algerian Peasants) was founded
to represent agricultural laborers and the UNJA (National
Union of Algerian Youth) was organized in 1975, although it
did not have a constituent congress until 1978.

By far the most important tasks perceived and tackled
by the Boumedienne government were, however, in the realm
of economic planning and development. The Algerian government engaged in policies that mixed socialism and state cap-
italism; the primary purpose was to increase productivity and
to exclude foreign ownership of the means of production and
of the national resources. These goals were implemented in
Four Year Plans, the second of which was for the years
1970-1973, during which the government expected a capital
outlay of $5.4 billion. In the first stage of development,
the Boumedienne government chose to concentrate on capital-
intensive export industry, which did not immediately alleviate
chronic unemployment or better the lives of most Algerians.
But the idea was that this would lead to economic independence more quickly than any other development plan. Capital-intensive export industry was also expected to create investment capital quickly, capital that could then be reinvested.
This was important because Algeria, although welcoming foreign investment, expected to finance eighty percent of her
own development. Nevertheless, Algeria's foreign debt stood
at twelve billion dollars (US) by 1979. Few leaders were
worried, however, as Algeria was exporting fifty million tons
of oil a year and expected increased oil prices to pay the
debt. In addition to oil (which was expected to flow at the
rate of fifty million tons a year for about fifteen years) Algeria will also export 3,500 billion cubic feet of natural gas
each year. This also produces a considerable income.

President Bendjedid and Algeria's Future

Late in December 1978, Boumedienne died after a long illness. Rabah Bitat, the president of the National Assembly,
became interim president of the Republic. An FLN party
congress elected Chadli Bendjedid Secretary General of the
FLN and sole candidate for the presidency of Algeria. He
was elected on February 7, 1979. The smoothness with
which the transition of power occurred bore witness to the
effectiveness of the institutional changes engineered by Boumedienne. The publication of the 1979 budget also shows

that Bendjedid intends to implement the development plans
instituted under Boumedienne.   For the present, it is clear
that Algeria will continue to be "Algeria, and that is all."
President Bendjedid is a leader formed in Boumedienne's
mold.   Under Bendjedid, Algeria will be a socialist and Islamic country intent on controlling her own resources and
on becoming an industrial state that will be economically independent or at least non-dependent.   With this in mind, Algeria will trade with any and all countries.   The United
States has long since replaced France as Algeria's chief trading partner, although France remains as an important cus-
tomer and supplier.   Other important trading partners are
the German Federal Republic, Italy, and the USSR.

In international politics, Algeria will continue to be
basically non-aligned and a strong supporter of what the Algerian government sees as struggles of national liberation.
Thus Algeria will support south African struggles against
white minority rule and the Palestinian people's fight to have
a homeland.   Because of the Rhodesian issue, for example,
Algeria broke relations with Great Britain.   U. S.-Algerian
diplomatic relations were broken for several years after the
June 6, 1967, Arab-Israeli war.   Yet trade between the U. S.
and Algeria grew even while the two countries had no exchange of ambassadors.   While diplomatic relations have been
normalized, hard political issues still divide the U. S. and
Algeria.   Algeria's support for the liberation movement in
Western Sahara and the United States' reluctant support of
Morocco on the same issue, for example, could lead to diplomatic confrontation.   Expectations are, however, that even
in such an event, it will be business as usual.   Algeria is
now the source of about nine percent of the United States
foreign oil imports.   In spite of radical politics, Algeria will
continue to enjoy a good international credit rating and should
become one of the first Third World nations to achieve viable
development and a standard of life for its citizens comparable
to that of advanced industrial states.

ALGERIAN EXPORTS AND IMPORTS
(1961-1963)

[In millions of Algerian New Francs: $1 US = 4.9 AF]

Country	1961	1962	1963
EXPORTS			
France	2,930.2	3,246.3	2,816.8
Federal Republic of Germany	263.1	311.6	297.4
United States	1.3	26.0	4.1
United Kingdom	126.6	133.3	103.1
Italy	40.6	133.9	107.8
Morocco	20.7	14.1	16.2
IMPORTS			
France	4,376.1	2,778.3	2,736.9
Federal Republic of Germany	60.3	27.4	56.8
United States	206.4	245.0	218.5
United Kingdom	41.2	24.1	34.4
Italy	46.9	46.9	63.7
Morocco	103.5	80.1	55.8

ALGERIAN EXPORTS AND IMPORTS WITH
PRINCIPAL TRADING PARTNERS--1977

Country	Exports	Imports
USA	3092.94	632.696
Federal Republic of Germany	875.59	1059.48
France	757.62	1763.32
Italy	255.51	709.05
Other Countries	988.10	3152.91
Total	5907.01	7319.46

Figures are in millions of U.S. dollars.

Source: Embassy of the Democratic and Popular Republic of
         Algeria: Survey of the Algerian Economy (May
         1979).

ALGERIAN OPERATING BUDGET
(1964)

Figures are given in millions of francs. Equivalent value in 1964 was: $1 US = 4.9 AF. Currency was later changed to Algerian dinars (AD) with 1 AD equal to 1 AF (Algerian franc).

Presidency		40. 9
Ministry of National Defense		493. 8
Vice Presidency		0. 2
Ministry of State		0. 2
Ministry of Justice		47. 6
Ministry of Interior		264. 8
Ministry of National Economy		346. 5
Common expenses	255. 9	
Finances	69. 5	
Industry and energy	12. 5	
Commerce	4. 0	
Planning and economic studies	3. 3	
Professional Training Commission	1. 3	
Ministry of Agriculture		91. 2
Ministry of National Guidance		622. 1
Education	548. 9	
Youth and sports	55. 9	
Information	17. 3	
Ministry of Social Affairs		528. 5
Public health and population	184. 6	
Labor and social affairs	139. 3	
Veterans and war victims	204. 6	
Ministry of Foreign Affairs		47. 1
Ministry of Reconstruction, Public Works and Transports		114. 0
Ministry of Habous (Religious Affairs)		14. 7
Ministry of Tourism		20. 6
Total		$2,632. 2

Source: Adapted from Algeria, Journal Officiel, 3d year, No. 10, 1964.

ALGERIAN BUDGET
(1979)

[in millions of U. S. dollars]

Presidency of the Republic	25. 202
National Defense	602. 330
Foreign Affairs	71. 388
Agriculture and the Agrarian Revolution	140. 234
Interior	318. 165
Water Resources, Land Development and Environmental Protection	50. 780
Transportation	43. 620
Public Works	93. 251
Finance	118. 503
Light Industries	8. 678
Veterans	171. 464
Religious Affairs	32. 354
Public Health	318. 573
Education	1,099. 979
Justice	49. 641
Higher Education and Scientific Research	298. 997
Work and Vocational Training	81. 575
Housing and Construction	26. 907
Commerce	13. 809
Information and Culture	70. 210
Tourism	7. 364
Youth and Sports	63. 627
Heavy Industry	3. 514
Energy and Petrochemical Industries	3. 657
Planning	12. 474
Town Responsibilities	1,632. 800
Total	5,358. 887

Source: Embassy of the Democratic and Popular Republic of Algeria, Survey of the Algeria Economy (May 1979).

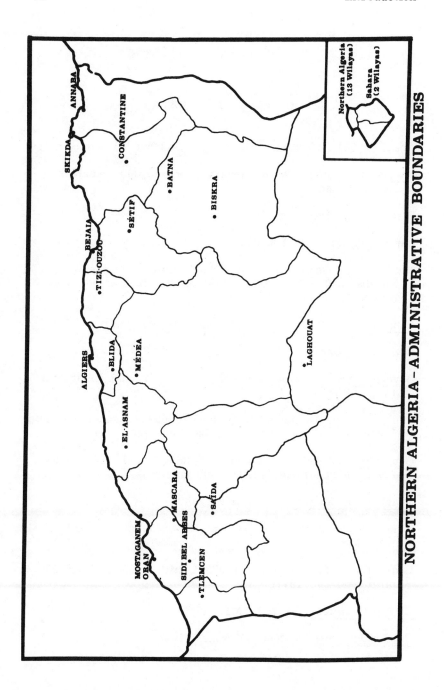

NORTHERN ALGERIA – ADMINISTRATIVE BOUNDARIES

Northern Algeria
(13 Wilayas)

Sahara
(2 Wilayas)

ALGERIA: BASIC DATA

Area: 2,381,741 square kilometers (952,696.40 square miles)

Population: 18,785,000 in January 1979 (960,000 Algerians living abroad)

Birth Rate: 3.2% per year

Capital: Algiers (2,500,000)

Major Urban Centers: Oran (6000,000); Constantine (500,000); Annaba (300,000); Skikda; Mostaganem; Bejaia; Sidi Bel Abbes; Setif; Blida; Tlemcen.

Language: Arabic (French is also still commonly used)

Religion: Islam

Government: Republic; Political Party--National Liberation Front (FLN)

Administrative Division: 31 Wilaya (regions), subdivided into 160 Daira (districts) and 704 Baladiyat (communes).

Currency: Algerian dinar (AD): 0.26 US $ (1 US$: 3.88 AD in March 1979). 1AD: 100 centimes

Weights and Measures: Metric System

Time: 6 hours ahead of EST in Winter; 5 hours ahead of EST in Summer

Gross Domestic Product: 80,573.1 million dinars ($20,938.4 million--IMF, 1977)

GDP per capita: $1,205 (IMF, 1977)

Oil Production: 57,2000,000 tons (1978)

Natural Gas Production: 11.1 billion cubic meters (1978)

Oil and Gas Revenues: $6.2 billion (1978)

Mineral Production: (1977)
      Iron Ore: 3,200,000 tons
      Phosphates: 1,100,000 tons
      Salt: 142,000 tons
      Marble: 85,000 square meters finished slabs (102,000
        square yards)

Agricultural Production: Wheat, barley, oranges, tangerines,
   lemons, grapes, dates, wine, etc.

1979 Budget: $9.58 billion (25% or $2.40 billion for education and training)

Gross Fixed Investment: $8.5 billion, or 51% of GDP (1978)

Planned Investment during 2nd 4-Year Plan (1974-77): $27.5
   billion

        Allocations: $12 billion for industry
                 $4.2 billion for agriculture
                 $3.8 billion for infrastructure
                 $3.6 billion for social service
                 $2.4 billion for education

1977 GDP growth: 7.8%

1977 Imports: $6.1 billion   Exports: $7.1 billion

1978 Exports to US: $3.4 billion (oil, natural gas)

1978 Imports from the US: $374 million (capital goods, grains)

WORKING HOURS
(Government and State Companies)

Winter		Summer	
Sat-Wed:	8 A.M.-12	Sat-Wed:	8 A.M.-12
	14:30-18:00 P.M.		15:00-18:30
Thurs :	8 A.M.-12	Thurs :	8 A.M.-12

Algerian offices are closed Thursday afternoons and Fridays.

During Ramadan (month of fasting) : 9 A. M. to 4:00 P. M.

Source: Embassy of the Democratic and Popular Republic of
Algeria: Survey of the Algerian Economy. May
1979, special issue entitled Directory of Algerian
Economic Agencies and State Corporations.

ABBREVIATIONS AND ACRONYMS

AARDES   Association Algérienne pour la Recherche Dé-
              mographique Economique et Sociale. Algerian
              Association for Demographic, Economic and So-
              cial Research.

ACTA   Association Générale des Travailleurs Algériens.
              A labour union created in 1962 to represent Al-
              gerian workers in France. It is affiliated with
              the UGTA.

ALN   Armée de Libération Nationale. Created by the
              CRUA in 1954, it was the revolutionary army of
              Algeria until independence was achieved in 1962.

AML   Amis du Manifeste et de la Liberté. In 1944-
              1945, this party, founded by Ferhat Abbas, tried
              to unite various groups interested in promoting
              legal, economic, social, and political reforms
              in favor of Algerians.

ANP   Armée Nationale Populaire. The post-independence
              Algerian national army.

APS   Algérie Presse Service. The news agency of
              the Algerian government.

BNASS   Bureau National d'Animation du Secteur Socialiste.
              The bureaucracy created to oversee self-manage-
              ment enterprises throughout Algeria after inde-
              pendence.

CAPCS   Coopératives Agricoles Polyvalentes Communales
              de Service. General Agriculture Service Cooper-
              atives.

CCAA   Conseil Communal d'Animation d'Autogestion.

A council in which the army, government and presidents of management committees are represented. Created to decentralize control of self-management enterprises.

CCE Comité de Coordination et d'Exécution. The first executive body of the FLN. It was created in 1956 at the Soummam Congress.

CCI Centre de Coordination Interservice. French military coordinating organization.

CCRA Coopératives de Commercialisation de la Réforme Agraire. Organ in charge of distributing and selling what was produced by self-management farms.

CCSA Caisse Centrale des Sociétés Agricoles. A government bank created to extend credit and loans for the socialist agricultural sector.

CFTC Confédération Française des Travailleurs Chrétiens. This was a French labor organization which was allied with the PCF and supported nationalists of Algeria during the period 1954-1962.

CGT Confédération Générale du Travail. Communist dominated French labor union.

CNDR Comité National pour la Défense de la Révolution. An opposition--essentially anti Ben Bella--coalition of which the FFS and PRS were members (1964).

CNRA Conseil National de la Révolution Algérienne. Legislative body of the FLN and ultimate authority within that party from the 1956 Soummam Congress to 1962.

CNS Compagnie Nationale de Sécurité. An Algerian security force created since independence.

COFEL Coopératives de Fruits et de Légumes. Fruit and vegetables cooperatives.

CRUA Comité Révolutionnaire d'Unité et d'Action. A

group of nine to thirty men (depending on interpretation) who started the War of National Liberation.   The CRUA was replaced by the FLN after
the beginning of hostilities.

DOP   Dispositif Opérationnel de Protection.   French
             counterinsurgency operational security organiza-
             tion.

DPU   Dispositif de Protection Urbaine.   Same as DOP,
             but specifically for urban areas.

FEMA   Fédération des Elus Musulmans d'Algérie.
             Founded by Dr. Mohammad Salah Bendjelloul in
             early 1920's, this federation was a party of es-
             sentially middle class Algerian elites.

FEMP   Fédération des Etudiants Militants du Parti.   A
             student organization sponsored by the FLN in
             1968.

FFFLN   Fédération de France du Front de Libération
             Nationale.   The branch of the FLN founded dur-
             ing the war to organize Algerian workers in
             France and to combat the influence of Messali
             Hadj.   AGTA replaced this organization in 1962.

FFS   Front des Forces Socialistes.   An opposition
             party, primarily composed of Kabyles and created
             by Ait Ahmed in 1963.

FLN   Front de Libération Nationale.   Algeria's only
             legal party, it was founded in 1954 when it re-
             placed the CRUA.

FNTT   Fédération Nationale des Travailleurs de la
             Terre.   A farm workers union created by Ben
             Bella in 1964 to supervise peasants' work on
             farms owned by the state.

FTEC   Fédération des Travailleurs de l'Enseignement et
             de la Culture.   Independent Algeria's teachers
             union.

GPRA   Gouvernement Provisoire de la République Al-
             gérienne.   Provisional government founded in
             1958 by the CNRA.   It operated in exile until
             independence was achieved in 1962.

ICTFU   International Confederation of Free Trade Unions.
             Organization of non-communist trade unions.

JFLN   Jeunesse du Front de Libération Nationale.   The
             FLN's youth organization created in 1963.

MDRA   Mouvement Démocratique de la Révolution Algér-
             ienne.   An opposition group founded in 1967 by
             Belkacem Krim.

MNA   Mouvement National Algérien.   The party created
             by Messali Hadj in 1955 to counter the FLN.

MTLD   Mouvement Pour le Triomphe des Libértés Dé-
             mocratiques.   Party that replaced the PPA after
             World War II.   It continued the nationalist work
             of earlier parties dominated by Messali Hadj.

OAP   Algerian Fisheries Board.

OAS   Organisation de l'Armée Secrète.   A European
             terrorist organization formed in 1961 to combat
             imminent independence for Algeria.

OAU   Organization of African Unity.

OCAM   Organisation Commune Africaine et Malgache.
             A grouping of moderate French-speaking states
             of Africa.

OCRA   Organisation Clandestine de la Révolution Algér-
             ienne.   An organization founded by Mohamed Le-
             bjaoui in 1966 to oppose the government.

ONAT   Office National Algérien du Tourisme.   Algerian
             National Office for Tourisme.

ONRA   Office National de la Réforme Agraire.   Office
             for the government in charge of socialist agri-
             cultural sector created in 1963.

OPA   Organisation Politique et Administrative.   Politi
             cal and Administrative Organization of the ALN
             during the Revolution.

ORP   Organisation de la Résistance Populaire.   Clan-
             destine opposition party formed to call for the

liberation of Ben Bella, Harbi, Zahouan and
Bachir Hadj Ali after the Boumedienne coup of
June 1965.

OS   Organisation Spéciale.   Clandestine group formed
          by impatient young "hawks" in Messali Hadj's
          MTLD. Operating from 1947 to 1950, when dis-
          banded by the French police, the OS had as mem-
          bers many of the persons who were to start the
          War of National Liberation in 1954.

PAGS   Parti d'Avant Garde Socialiste.   An opposition
          party that replaced ORP.

PCA   Parti Communiste Algérien.   The Algerian Com-
          muniste Party which became autonomous of its
          French parent organization in 1936 and which
          was outlawed in 1962 by independent Algeria.

PCF   Parti Communiste Français.   The Communist
          Party of France which helped create the PPA
          and the ENA.

PPA   Parti du Peuple Algérien.   Founded in 1937, it
          was the most vocal of the nationalist parties.
          It replaced the ENA and was in turn replaced
          by the MTLD.

PRS   Parti de la Révolution Socialiste.   Founded by
          Mohammed Boudiaf immediately after independence,
          it was a clandestine opposition party.

RADP   République Algérienne Démocratique et Populaire.
          Official Name of Algeria.

RFMA   Rassemblement Franco-Musulman Algérien.   A
          party founded by Dr. Bendjelloul in 1938 to push
          for demands for equality of Algerians with Euro-
          peans in Algeria.

SAP   Sociétés Agricoles de Prévoyance.   Organization
          in charge of provisioning self-management farms.
          Part of ONRA.

SAR   Section d'Amélioration Rurale.   French organiza-
          tion for rural improvement.

SAS	Sections Administratives Spécialisées. French specialized counterinsurgency organization.
SAU	Sections Administratives Urbaines. Same type of organization as the SAS for urban areas.
SMA	Scouts Musulmans Algériens. Algerian Boy Scout Organization first associated with Ben Badis and the Association of Reformed Ulama, but integrated into the JFLN since independence.
UDMA	Union Démocratique du Manifeste Algérien. Ferhat Abbas' integationist party founded in 1946 to seek Algerian autonomy within the French system.
UDRS	Union pour la Defénse de la Révolution Socialiste. An opposition party founded in 1963 by Mohamed Boudiaf, Mohand ou el-Hadj, Belkacem Krim and others.
UGEMA	Union Générale des Etudiants Musulmans Algériens. The FLN's student organization during the war of national liberation.
UGTA	Union Générale des Travailleurs Algériens. FLN affiliated labor union created in 1956 to unify Algerian working classes in support of the national liberation effort.
UNCAC	Union Nationale des Coopératives Agricoles de Commercialisation. Organization that replaced the CCRA and that manages the commercialization of goods produced by self-management farms.
UNEA	Union Nationale des Etudiants Algériens. A continuation of the UGEMA--a student union--in the post independence period.
UNFA	Union Nationale des Femmes Algériennes. Algeria's FLN affiliated women's union.
UPA	Union Populaire Algérienne. A party formed in 1938 by Ferhat Abbas. It was integrationist in purpose.
USTA	Union Syndicale des Travailleurs Algériens. The

MNA. affiliated labor union founded in 1956 to compete with FLN supported groups.

ZAA   Zone Autonome d'Alger.   Autonomous military region of Algiers, particularly during the Battle of Algiers.

GLOSSARY OF ARABIC, FRENCH, AND TURKISH TERMS
OFTEN FOUND IN LITERATURE ON ALGERIA

(French terms identified with an "F")

adjudant (F) :   company sergeant-major.

agha: captain general of the Turkish militia.   See bachaga.

aghalik: jurisdiction of an agha under Turks.

alfa: Esparto grass used in paper manufacturing.

ancien combattant (F):   ex-serviceman, veteran.

arrondissement (F):   administrative subdivision of departments.

arsch: property that may be inherited but cannot be alienated.
    Tribal land and a form of property based on labor invested
    in the land.

aspirant (F):   officer candidate.

autogestion (F):   self-management; certain farms and industrial
    plants that were, after 1962, run by the workers.   It
    was supposed to be a key element of Algerian social-
    ism.

azel: public domain during the Turkish period.

baccalauréat (F):   secondary school leaving--university entrance
    examination.

bachaga: Algerian "governors," highest rank in the caidat
    system of "native" administration in the French system.

baladiyat: commune.   A subdivision of a daira.

baraka: special power, usually from divine source, that may radiate to others; marabouts are supposed to possess baraka.

barbouze (F): undercover French government agents.

bay'ah: oath of allegiance to a new ruler.

Beni-Oui-Oui: derogatory term used to describe Algerian administrators or political persons who collaborated with France.

Bey: Turkish title of the Dey of Algiers' three principal vassals, the governors of Oran, Constantine and Titteri. Title of Tunisian ruler.

bicot (F): abusive name used to refer to Algerians.

bidonville (F): shantytown.

bled: back-country, outback.

bleu (F): double agent.

bleuite (F): state of being affected by double-agent.

bordj: fort.

burnous: loose woolen cloak woven into one piece.

cachabia: heavy, usually woolen winter garment worn by Algerian men.

cadi: judge.

caid: administrator.

caidat: French system of "native" administration.

casbah (or Kasbah): citadel, old Algerian quarters of cities.

chechia: woolen caps worn by many traditional Algerian men.

cheikh: chief.

chott: see shat. marsh, swampy area.

chouhada: martyr in the revolutionary war.

çoff: political party (informal), federation.

colon (F) : European settler.

comité de gestion (F): management committee. See auto-
    gestion.

commune de plein exercise (F): communes of colonial Al-
    geria with large European proportion of inhabitants
    that were given same administration as metropolitan
    communes.

commune mixte (F): communes in which European minority
    were governed by European administrators who con-
    trolled Algerians through caids.

dai'rah: circle (of authority), district. A subdivision of a
    wilaya.

department (F): largest administrative subdivision. See
    wilaya.

Dey: Turkish title of ruler of Algiers before the French
    conquest (1830).

dinar: Algerian unit of currency. In 1979 $1. 00 U. S. was
    equal to $3. 88 A. D.

Divan: The council of state during the Turkish rule of Al-
    giers.

djebel: mountain.

djemaa: see jama'ah.

djoundi: ALN soldier.

douar: village.

duwwar: clan.

élite (F): elite, usually political or educational.

erg: sand dune area (in Sahara).

évolué (F): educated Algerian who had been influenced by
the French.

failek: ALN battalion.

faoudj: ALN section.

fatma: maid, Algerian domestic servant.

fatwah: Islamic legal opinion.

fellagha: outlaw, Algerian guerilla.

fellah: peasant, small farmer.

fida'iyin: combattants of the faith, urban terrorists.

figuier (F): fig tree. Also an abusive name for Algerians.

firman: official decree issued by Turkish Dey.

fraction (F): part of a tribe or of a village.

garde-champêtre (F): rural policeman.

gégène (F): magneto and a tool used for torture.

gourbi: shack, small house of poor peasant.

groupe (F): squad.

habous: pious donation of land for a foundation devoted to
religious, charitable or cultural purpose.

hadith: Qu'ranic commentary.

hadj (hodjadj): one who has made a pilgrimage to Mecca.

haik: sheet-like garment, in white or black, worn by Algerian women when they go out in public.

harki: Algerian soldier in French auxiliary forces.

hubs: see habous.

imam: Islamic prayer leader

jama'ah: village assembly, assembly of elders.

jihad: holy war.

kasma: party council of the FLN at the commune level.

katiba: ALN company.

khalifa: deputy.

khammes: share cropper. tenant farmers who get 1/5 of the harvest for their labor and tools.

képis bleus (F): blue caps; term used to refer to SAS officers and men.

ksour: fortified village, fort.

lycée (F) : secondary school leading to baccalauréat and to universities.

Maghrib: Arab Northwest Africa. Present-day Tunisia, Algeria and Morocco.

maghzen: tribes allied to the ruler; also French native auxiliary troops in the SAS.

maquis (F): dense underbrush; term was used by the French to describe nationalist sanctuaries. Maquisards were the guerillas themselves.

marabout: holy man; usually leader of (or descendant of) a sufi (mystic) order in Islam.

mechta: village, area.

melk: freehold form of private property that is, however, difficult to alienate.

militant (F): active member of the FLN.

mintaka: a region, a subdivision of a wilaya.

moqaddem: leader of a religious brotherhood.

moudjahid (moudjahiddine): combattant, ALN soldier; guerilla.
It is a word derived from the Arabic for fighter in
a holy war.

mousseblin: militiaman, ALN guerilla.

mufti: islamic jurist.

odjak: Turkish military corps.

oued: river or dry-river bed.

pasha: governor of an Ottoman province.   Title of dey of
Algiers.

pied noir (F): black foot, derogatory term to refer to European settlers in Algeria.

préfet (F): prefect, administrator of a department.

qadi: see cadi.

qaid: see caid.

quadrillage (F): system of static control.

quartier (F): sector.

Qur'anic: of or pertaining to the Qur'an.

rais: leader or chief.

rattissage (F): raking over, a pacification operation.

ratonnade (F): rat hunt, looking for "Arabs" to kill.

r'ya (or raya): tribes at least partially subdued by the Turks.

razzia: foray, coup.

saff: see çoff.

section (F):   platoon.

sergent-chef (F):   lowest-ranked sergeant.

sharia: Islamic law.

sharif: a descendant of Muhammad through his daughter
        Fatima.

shat: Marsh, swampy area, also chott.

shaykh: see cheikh.

sirocco: hot wind from the Sahara.

soff: see çoff.

souk: covered market (traditional).

sous-préfet: administrator of an arrondissement.

taleb: teacher (Qu'ranic).

ulama: learned person, religious leader well versed in
        Qur'anic studies; usually refers to organization and
        people around Ben Badis.

ultras (F):   diehard European settlers who resisted all change.

umma: the community of Muslims, of all those who practice
        Islam.

wadi: see oued.

wali: chief administrator at the district level (Turkish).

wilaya: today these are administrative provinces; during the
        War of National Liberation, they were war zones.

youm el ilm: day of learning.

zawia (also zawiyah): religious center, usually a school is
    attached.

CHRONOLOGY: SELECTED EVENTS

1519 Turks begin to rule in Algeria.

1578 Maurice Sauron, first French consul accredited in Algiers.

1601 Spanish bombardment of Algiers.

1617 First French bombardment of Algiers.

1620 First English bombardment of Algiers.

1682 First Anglo-Algerian Treaty.

1740 Algerian intervention in and invasion of Tunisia. Algerian forces were not beaten back until 1756.

1791 Death of Muhammad Dey (July 12) and ascension of Baba Hassan.

1792 Spanish evacuation of Oran. Algero-Spanish treaty signed.

1796 United States Senate ratifies a treaty with Algiers.

1798 Mustafa becomes Dey on May 14.

1799 Algiers and Tunis break off relations with France. Peace reestablished in 1800.

1801 Another break, then peace, between Algiers and France.

1803 Darqawah, and Tijaniyah orders revolt against Turks.

1805 Ahmed becomes Dey after assassination of Mustafa (August 30). Famine. Massacres of Jews.

1807   Algero-Tunisian conflict.

1808   Execution of Ahmad Dey who is replaced by Ali
            al-Rassal (November 7).

1809   Ali-al-Rassal is strangled and Hajj Ali becomes
            Dey (February 7).

1813   Bey of Constantine attacks Le Kef.   Tunisians emerge
            victorious.   Oran revolts against the Dey of Algiers.

1814-   Kabyle revolt against government in Algiers.
1815

1815   Hajj Ali is strangled and Muhammad Khaznadji be-
            comes Dey (March 22).   Khaznadji is strangled and
            replaced by Dey Umar Agha (April 7).   The United
            States and the government of Algiers signs a treaty
            (July 7).

1816   Naval attack on Algiers under command of Lord
            Exmouth.   On October 8, Umar Agha is strangled
            and Ali Khodja takes over as Dey.

1821   Algero-Tunisian peace treaty.

1824   Renewed Kabyle revolt.

1827   Dey hits French consul with a fly swatter (April
            30).   The French begin a naval blockade (June 15).

1830   French Troops capture Algiers (July 5).

1831   Abd al-Qadir is elected Commander of the Faith-
            ful on November 22.   Three days later he entered
            Mascara.

1833   Abd al-Qadir entered Tlemcen in July.   French
            react and occupy Arzew and Mostaganem.

1834   Desmichels-Abd al-Qadir Treaty signed (February
            26).

1837   Tafna Treaty between Bugeaud and Abd al-Qadir.

1844   Battle of Lalla Maghniya between French and Mor-
            occan forces.   On September 10, Morocco signs a

treaty with France and promises not to aid Abd
al-Qadir (Treaty of Tangiers).

1845   Beginning of Bu Maza insurrection in Oran province.

1847   Bu Maza surrenders to the French (April 13).   Abd
            al-Qadir surrenders (December 21).

1848-   Despite safe conduct to go to the East, Abd al-
1852   Qadir is held in French prison.

1859   End of the French conquest of Kabylia.

1864   Revolt of the Ouled Sidi Cheikh of southern Oran
            province.

1870-   Kabyle Rebellion under leadership of Mohamed el-
1871   Mokrani and others.

1905   Hundreds of families from Tlemcen emigrate rather
            than to have their sons subjected to the French
            military draft.

1910   Young Algerians begin to demand rights for Alger-
            ians.

1915   Clemenceau reform bill creates an Algerian elector-
            ate.

1926   Founding in France of the ENA (North African
            Star) which would soon become Messali Hadj's
            party.

1931   Founding of the Association of Reformist ULAMA
            by Cheikh Abd el Hamid Ben Badis.

1934   Founding of the Federation of Elected Muslims.

1935   PCA (Algerian Communist Party) separated from
            PCF (French Communist Party).

1945   The May or Setif Rebellion and the French repres-
            sion which cost thousands of Algerian lives.

1948   Beginning of systematic tampering with elections
            by the French Colonial administration.

1954   Outbreak of rebellion throughout Algeria. Beginning of the War of National Liberation. (Nov. 1)

1962   Signing of Evian Agreements. Cease-fire. (Mar. 18)
Provisional Executive takes over in Algeria. (Apr. 7)
Referendum on Algerian independence 8,156,511 voted yes, 794,154 voted no. (Apr. 8)
Self-determination vote. 91% participated, 90% of them voted for independence. (Jul. 1)
Election of an Algerian Assembly with constituent powers. (Sep. 20)
Proclamation of a Democratic and Popular Republic. Ferhat Abbas is to be president and Ben Bella is to be in charge of the government. (Sep. 25)
Ben Bella becomes president of the Council of Ministers (159 for, 1 against, 19 abstentions). (Sep. 29)
PCA outlawed. Only legal party is the FLN. (Nov. 29)

1963   Creation of a Political Bureau. (Jul. 22)
Adoption of the Algerian Constitution by the Assembly in a vote of 139 to 23 with 8 abstentions. (Aug. 28)
Constitution approved by referendum. (Sep. 8)
Ben Bella elected President of the Republic. (Sep. 15)

1964   First Congress of the FLN. (April)

1965   Coup d'état leads to arrest of Ben Bella. National Revolutionary Council under Boumedienne takes over. (Jun. 19)

1965-
1968   Anglo-Algerian diplomatic relations broken over Rhodesian issue.

1966   First population count of independent Algeria puts population at 12,093,203 inhabitants. Population growth is estimated at 3% (Apr. 4-17)

1967   Algerian U.S. relations broken over Palestinian issue. Exchange of ambassadors was not resumed until mid-1970's.
Attempted coup against Boumedienne government. (Dec. 14)

1967-
1969   First Three Year Plan for Economic Development.

1968   Attempt on Boumedienne's life.   He was slightly
            wounded.   (Apr. 26)

1970   Beginning of First Four Year Plan.   (Jan. 1)

1971   Knowledge of Arabic obligatory for all persons of
            Algerian nationality in the administration or in public
            corporations.   (Jan. 20)

1971   Population estimated at 14,200,000.   Population
            growth estimated at 3.5 percent.   (December)

1973   Boumedienne international stature reinforced when
            he called for a new economic world order in which
            industrialized nations would share more equitably
            with the Third World.

1974-   Second Four Year Plan.   Socialism reinforced.
1979   Capital-intensive export industries stressed.

1978   Boumedienne died in late December after a long
            illness.

1979   Election of Chaldi Bendjedid as president of the
            Republic.   (Feb. 7)

1979   Beginning of Third Four Year Plan for economic
            development.

THE DICTIONARY

ABA, NOUREDDINE (-). Algerian poet who writes in French and is published in Paris. His latest collection appeared in 1978 and was entitled <u>Gazelle après minuit</u>--Chants d'amour et de guerre de la Révolution Algérienne.

ABBAS (alias) see BOUDJENANE, AHMED

ABBAS, FERHAT (October 24, [or August 24] 1899-). First premier of the Provisional Government of the Republic of the Algeria. Abbas was born into a family that had been identified with French rule. His father, a <u>caid</u> at Chahna, had been awarded the silver braid and rosette of the Legion of Honor. In 1909 Abbas entered the <u>lycée</u> at Philippeville. Following three years in the French army medical service, he entered pharmacy school at the University of Algiers. In 1933 he joined with others to form the Algerian Peoples Union, in support of full French citizenship for Algerian Muslims. He served as a volunteer at the beginning of World War Two but made a sharp break from his earlier views on assimilation after General Giraud refused his appeal to enlist Muslims on an equal basis. In 1943 he issued a manifesto proposing a free Algerian state within a French union and subsequently established the Democratic Union for the Algerian Manifesto. In 1946 he was elected to the French Constituent Assembly and became editor of the journal <u>Egalité</u>, which changed its name in 1948 to <u>La République algérienne</u>. He served as a member of the Muslim college of the Algerian Assembly from 1947 to 1955. During the first eighteen months of the Algerian War, Abbas acted as intermediary between the FLN and the French, but in April 1956 he joined with other moderates in asserting that the FLN was the only representative force for the liberation of North Africa. In 1957 Abbas served at the United Nations as FLN delegate, and he attended the North African Conference at Tunis in 1958. When the Provisional Government of the Republic of

51

Algeria was established in Cairo on September 19, 1958, Abbas was appointed first premier. In January 1961, he participated in an African conference to establish an African Charter, but shortly thereafter, in August, he and other moderates were ousted from the GPRA. In fall 1962 the Ben Bella government was established with Abbas being elected president of the Assembly. Abbas sought to establish a parliamentary form of government with multi-party system. Shortly after the Algerian Constitution was adopted, Abbas resigned as president and charged Ben Bella with distorting the Tripoli Program. Following an attempt to undermine Ben Bella in July 1964, Abbas was placed under arrest. In June 1965 he was released from confinement in the Algerian Sahara. Following the coup d'état of Boumedienne, Abbas was one of several notables who declined to serve as civilian head of the regime. Along with several others, he issued a series of manifestos in March 1976, condemning the lack of democratic institutions in Algeria and the strife among Maghribi nations. Shortly thereafter, he was placed under house arrest.

Ferhat Abbas is the author of several books among which were Le Jeune Algérien (1931) and La Nuit Coloniale (1962).

ABD AL-QADIR ben MUHYI al-DIN al-HASANI (May 26, 1807-1883). Head of Algerian resistance to the French incursions in Algeria (1832-47). He was acclaimed Commander of the Believers in Oran province in 1832. He concluded a peace treaty with the French in 1834, whereby they recognized his rule over the interior of Oran; however, the conflict was renewed in 1835. He concluded a second treaty with the French in 1837, again recognizing his rule over much of Algeria, but this agreement broke into open conflict in 1839. Abd al-Qadir fled to Morocco in 1843, but he was forced to leave that country the following year. He surrendered to French forces in 1847; despite promises to the contrary he was imprisoned from 1848 to 1852. He went to Brusa in 1853 and finally settled in Damascus in 1855, where he received the Grand Cross of the Legion of Honor for aid to Christians in Syria in 1860.

ABD AL-QADIR EL DJILANI (d. 1166). Middle Eastern religious leader who is considered the founder and patron saint of the Qadiriya, an Islamic brotherhood with numerous Algerian followers, particularly in Oran province.

ABD AL-RAHMAN, MULAY (1789-1859). Ruler of Alawi
dynasty in Morocco (1822-59); overpowered tribal revolts
(1824, 1828, 1831, 1848, 1849, 1853); aided Abd al-Qadir
against France (1833-44); acknowledged French control
over Algeria in Treaty of Tangier (1844) following military defeat.

ABDALWADIDES (BANU ABD AL-WAD). Name applied to a
portion of the Zanata tribe of Berbers. The name of
the dynasty of kings of the central Maghrib (1239-1554)
who took Tlemcen as capital. During that period, twenty-
seven monarchs from the family ruled. After the 12th
century Tlemcen assumed a significant cultural role in
the region because of its mosques, schools, and palaces.

ABDELGHANI, MOHAMED BEN AHMED (-   ). In
1959, his duties involved getting troops across the Morice
line into Wilaya V (Oran province). He was promoted to
the rank of captain in the ALN, stayed with the army
when it became the ANP and was given command of Military Region One (Blida) in May 1963. Since then he has
directed the Sidi-Bel-Abbes armored battalion and been
transferred to command the Fourth Military Region
(Ouargla). He became Minister of the Interior in 1975.
In 1979, he was appointed Prime Minister by President
Bendjedid. He is also a member of the Political Bureau
of the FLN.

ABDELHAMID, SID ALI (-   ). A PPA activist who
was a member of the MTLD central committee in 1952.
He did not like the OS and made speeches against it in
party meetings. He spent most of the revolutionary years
(1954-1962) in French prisons and he has stayed out of
politics since independence.

SI ABDELKADER EL-MALI (alias)   see   BOUTEFLIKA

ABDEL-KADER, HADJ ALI (-   ). Originally from
Kabylia, Hadj Ali Abdel-Kader apparently helped found
the ENA; but he quickly lost influence in this political
group which was taken in hand by Messali Hadj. Before
1926, Abdel-Kader was active organizing laborers from
French colonies for the French Communist Party.

ABDELMALEK, RAMDANE (-1954). Second in command
to Larbi ben M'hidi in western Wilaya (Oran) in 1954. He
was killed on the first day of the Algerian revolution.

SI ABDERRAHMANE (alias) see BENSALEM, ABDERRAH-
MANE

ABDESSELAM, BELAID (1928-   ). An instructor in the
FLN school at Oujda (Morocco) during the War of National Liberation, he was an advisor in Ben Khedda's
cabinet in 1961. He headed the Bureau of Economic Affairs of the FLN in 1962 and became director of the Algerian Office of Hydrocarbons in 1964. In 1965 he became Minister of Industry and Energy.

ADDUII, MUIIAMMAD (b. 1849 in Egypt; d. July 11, 1905).
Egyptian thinker and reformer whose political and religious ideas were felt among Algerian Muslim elites
near the end of the nineteenth century and after. He
was an Islamic scholar and jurist who wanted to adapt
Islam to a modern world that had been deeply changed
by European power and technology. In general terms,
he argued for modernization in Islamic law, administration, and education while also insisting that Islamic values
and culture should not be diminished.
        Put into Algerian terms, Abduh's program led
his followers to attack maraboutic brotherhoods for being
dangerous local misinterpretations of Islam, and also
the Young Algerians for not understanding that they need
not become Frenchmen to be cultured men.
        Abduh visited Algiers in September 1903, and
gave a series of talks. His writings had preceded him
and he had a following among Algerian elites who were
well-read in Arabic. Among his disciples were Abd al-
Halim Ibn Smaya, a professor at the Madrasah in Algiers, Muhammad al Sa'id al Zawawi, a Kabyle who published a short book in 1904 that clearly argued Abduh's
precepts about maraboutic brotherhoods and zawiyahs,
and Ibn al-Mansur al Sanhagi who founded an Arabic language reformist Muslim weekly, Du-1-Faqar, which was
entirely devoted to the spread of Abduh's ideas.
        Eventually, Ibn Badis and the Association of Re-
formist Ulama picked up Abduh's ideas and work and
really created institutions that could convince Algerians
that they could choose to be Algerians, Arabs and Muslims, that they need not be assimilated into French culture.

ABID, SAID (-   ). Abid and Zbiri were put in charge
of repressing the insurrection of Ait Ahmed and Mohand
Ou el-Hadj in Kabylia during the latter part of 1963, a

task they did not like.   Both were members of the small
group of officers who arrested Ben Bella on June 19,
1965.

ABUCAYA, SIMON (fl. 1790's).   Employee of the Bacri firm,
who maintained an office in Paris and styled himself
"General Agent of the Dey of Algiers."

ABU HAMIDI AL-WALAHASI, MUHAMMAD (1803-1847).   Theologian and marabout of the Walhasah tribe.   He served
as khalifa of Abd al-Qafir in Gharb from 1834.

ABU HAMMU MUSA I (-July 22, 1318).   Fourth king of
the Abdalwadid dynasty (1308-1318).   Abu Hammu repaired
the previous devastation that had been wrought on Tlemcen during the siege of the Marinides (1299-1307).   His
reign was distinguished by a replenishing of the treasury
of the dynasty and restocking of the foodstores.   Abu
Hammu Musa I extended the Abdalwadid authority over
the Tudjin and the Maghrawa tribes of the Chelifian plain.
He was assassinated by his son Abu Tashfin.

ABU HAMMU MUSA II (1324-November 21, 1389).   He was
born in Spain where his family had been exiled by Abu
Tashfin I.   After the defeat of the Abdalwadides by the
Marinides at the plain of Angad (1352), he fled to Tunis
with his uncle, Abu Thabit.   With the support of the
governor of Tunis and some Ifrikiyan chiefs, Abu Hammu
Musa marched on Tlemcen, where he arrived at the
time of the death of the Marinid prince.   He entered
the capital and was proclaimed king in 1359.   Though
forced to surrender Tlemcen three times to the Marinides, he returned in 1372.   During his reign he put down
several revolts within his subject states.   He wrote a
treatise on political ethics in 1379, built a new school
at Tlemcen, and installed the renowned teacher Sherif
Abu Abd Allah there.

ABU TASHFIN I (1293-1337).   Fifth king of the Abdalwadid
dynasty.   He seized power following the assassination of
his father, Abu Hammu Musa I.   Abu Tashfin began his
reign by exiling all pretenders to the throne.   His reign
was greatly influenced by his Catalonian adviser Hilal.
During the reign, he built Madrasa Tashfiniya.   His aid
to the dissidents of the Hafsid empire united the Hafsids
and the Marinides.   In 1332, the king of Fez attacked
his domain and laid seige to Tlemcen three years later.
Abu Tashfin died in the fall of the city.

ABU TASHFIN II (1351-1393). King of Tlemcen (1389-93). He was raised in Fez during the exile of his father, Abu Hammu II, and he returned to Tlemcen with him in 1359. Abu was involved in numerous efforts to wrest control from his father. With the support of the Marinide army, he finally defeated and killed him in 1389. Abu remained on the throne as a vassal of the Marinides.

ABU ZAIYAN I (-1308). Third king of the Zaiyanide dynasty (1304-08). He was proclaimed king during the siege of Tlemcen by the Marinide Abu Yakub (1299-1307). He negotiated with Abu Yakub's successor, Abu Thabit, for the release of Mansura and Tlemcen territory. Following his establishment as king, he severely persecuted the eastern tribes that had aided the Marinides. Before he was able to begin the rebuilding of Tlemcen, he became ill and died.

ABU ZAKARIYYA AL-DJANAWUNI, YAHYA EN AL-KHAYR (fl. c. 1125). Ibadi scholar. He studied under shaykh Abu al-Rabi Sulayman ben Abi Harun at the mosque of Ibnayn. He was famous because of his wide knowledge, especially his writings on religious jurisprudence.

ACH ACHAG. Algerian daily in Arabic published during the colonial period.

ACHOUR, AHMED BEN (-). Author of several "slice of life" novels written in Arabic and including, in rough translation of the titles, The Two Men and the Bear (1930), The Poor Among Us (1950), and Modern Marriage (1952).

ACHOUR, MOULOUD (1944-). Born in Kabylia, he writes short stories and novels in a clear style reminiscent of that of Mouloud Feraoun. His best known books are Le Survivant et autres nouvelles (1971) and Héliotropes (1973).

ADJOINTS INDIGENES. Muslim-born administrative assistants to the mayors of the communes de plein exercise. They served as a façade of native participation in the government of the municipalities. In the communes mixtes, they were appointed by the governor-general upon nomination by a prefect.

ADJOUL ADJOUL, BEN ABDELHAFID (1922-). A rebel chief in the Aurès region after the outbreak of revolution,

he was the son of a landed bourgeois who had attended
the Ben Badis Institute in Constantine in 1937, and who
had joined the PPA in 1951. In 1956, he surrendered
to the French and apparently encouraged his men to do
the same.

AL-AFGANI, GAMAL AL-DIN (-   ). Muslim reform
leader who, along with Muhammad Abduh preached in a
manner that led followers to the kind of orthodoxy represented by the Salafiyya movement. The influence of
these two religious and political leaders was felt among
Islamic elites in Algeria after 1900.

AGA (Agha). In Turkey, title of a military officer at the
court of the Sultan; in Algeria, superior to the caid and
subordinate of the bachaga. During the Regency in Algiers, title bestowed on head of the janissaries; from
1659 to 1671, the agas held complete power.

AGHABASI. Administrative post during the Regency.

AGHALIK. The jurisdiction of an agha; a geographical subdivision of the beylik.

AHMAD BEN AMAR (-   ). Khalifa of Abd al-Kadir
in Medjana (1839-?).

AHMAD BEN SALIM (-   ). Khalifa of Abd al-Qadir
in Hamza (1837-39); marabout; excellent cavalry commander; surrendered to French (1847); moved to Orient.

AHMAD BEN TAHIR (-1833). Qadi of Arzew. He taught
Abd al-Qadir from about 1815 to 1820. From 1831 to
1833, he collaborated with the French, but he was captured by the Algerians, and tortured and executed by
them at Mascara.

AHMAD BEY (1785-1850). Bey of Constantine Province
(1826-37). He served as khalifa of the bey from 1817
to 1818. Ahmad took part in the defense of Algiers in
1830 and upset French efforts in 1836 to occupy Constantine. The following year he was overpowered by the
French and fled to the south from which he conducted
periodic raids on the French. He surrendered in 1848
and died in Algiers two years later.

AISSAT, IDIR (-1959). Idir Aissat's political career
involved him first in the PPA, then in the MTLD and in

the CGT. He was a founder of the UGTA and, by February 1956, this organization made him Secretary General.
Arrested by the French authorities in May 1956, he was
apparently tortured, then moved from prison to prison
until he died in July 1959. French authorities announced
that he had committed suicide, but no investigation into
the exact cause of his death was ever permitted.

AIT AHMED, HOCINE (1921-   ). Hocine Ait Ahmed was
born to a well-to-do Kabyle family, his father having
served the French colonial regime as a caid. Nevertheless, Ait Ahmed apparently joined the PPA when he was
still in secondary school. In 1947, he helped create and
became the first director of a secret para-military organization, the OS. In 1950, he was replaced at the
head of the OS by Ben Bella, ostensibly because Ait Ahmed had proved himself to be too much of a Berberist.
He left Algeria in 1951 after French courts had condemned
him in absentia for various crimes against the state.
He took refuge in Cairo, traveling widely as a spokesman of the MTLD. As one of the first partisans of
armed revolution against the French colonial regime, he
continued to travel widely to defend FLN positions as a
member of that party's external delegation. The Soummam Congress of 20 August 1956 elected him to the
CNRA. Captured by the French authorities in the air-
plane kidnapping of 22 October 1956, he was to spend
the rest of the War of National Liberation in prison.
After independence, he opposed the Ben Bella group
which, with the backing of the general staff of the ALN,
seized power in Algiers. He refused membership in the
Political Bureau of the FLN, but was elected a deputy
in the first National Assembly of independent Algeria.
In 1962 he helped in drawing up the Tripoli Program
and, in 1963, he drafted decrees of workers' self-
management. Still opposed to Ben Bella, he formed an
insurrection from bases in Kabylia. Captured by the
government when his own military ally, Colonel Mohand
Ou el Hadj made peace with Ben Bella because of the
border conflict with Morocco, Ait Ahmed was condemned
to death. He nevertheless made his peace with Ben
Bella shortly before the latter was overthrown by Boume
dienne in June 1965. Kept in prison by the Boumedienne
regime, Ait Ahmed escaped from El Harrach and has
lived in exile since. An excellent theoretician, Ait Ahmed
is the author of a political book entitled **La Guerre et
l'après-guerre**.

AIT AL HOCINE, MOHAND (-   ). Although named to
the FLN's Central Committee in April 1964, Ait al Hocine was an important opposition leader just two years
later when he directed the OCRA, an anti-Boumedienne
and moderately pro-Ben Bella organization. OCRA operated from outside Algeria and demanded by whatever
means possible, a return to "legality and constitutional
practices." In the Central Committee, he was in charge
of finances. He also directed the pro-Ben Bella amicale
in France.

AIT DJAFER, ISMAIL (1929-   ). A native of Algiers, Ait
Djafer published a collection of poems entitled Complainte
des mendiants arabes de la Casbah et de la petite Yas-
mina tuée par son père, in 1953. It was an attack, in
French, on a system which did not grant justice to colonized Algerians. Some of the poems were re-edited by
Les Temp modernes, a French revue, in 1954.

AIX-LA-CHAPELLE, CONGRESS OF. Meeting of European
powers which sought to outlaw maritime piracy; eventually
led to 1819 flotilla under joint command of English Admiral Fremantle and French Admiral Jurien de La Gra-
vière, which demanded that Algiers subscribe to its provisions.

AKBI, ABDELGHANI (-   ). Minister of Commerce
(1979).

AKKACHE, AHMED (1928-   ). He was born in Algiers in
a family of dispossessed Kabyle peasants. A member of
the UJDA secretariat in 1946, Ahmed Akkache joined the
PCA's Central Committee in 1947, then the Political
Bureau in 1949. In 1951 he became senior editor of
Liberté. Finally he was promoted to party secretary in
1952.

AL-ALAWI, ABU AL-ABBAS AHMAD B. MUSTAFA (1869-
1934). Sufi born in Algeria of a famous family. Due
to lack of family income, he never attended school and
took upon himself the profession of cobbler at an early
age. Became follower of Muhammad al-Buzidi, who made
him a mukaddam in 1894. Succeeded al-Buzidi as shaykh
in 1909; declared independence of his zawiya from the
mother-zawiya in Morocco (1914) based on his practice
of the khalwa (or spiritual retreat). Because of his pre-
eminent position in Sufism, he became literary target of

reformist Salafiyya group. Started weekly newspaper in
Algiers to defend his conservative views, al Balagh al-
Djaza'iri. Opposed wearing of Western dress and other
tendencies toward westernization which brought him into
disharmony with French authorities. Published many
works in Arabic on Sufism.

AL-ALI, ARAR MOHAMMED (-   ). Author of the
second novel in Arabic published by SNED (National Publication and Distribution Company) and which appeared
in 1972. The title of this novel may be translated as
What the Wind Cannot Erase. He has since published
another novel the title of which might be The Ambitious
One if translated to English. Al-Ali's themes deal with
the end of the colonial period, the war of national liberation and other related topics.

AL-AZHIRI, CHEIKH (-   ). An ex-member of the
Ulama Association who, in the late 1930's, directed a
PCA front organization in Oran province which was supposed to substitute itself for the Algerian Muslim Congress (CMA).

ALGER REPUBLICAIN. Leading French language Communist
newspaper of colonial Algeria. The paper's consistency
in presenting and defending Muslim interests assured it
of a faithful readership that always reached many more
people than might be assumed for a paper that printed
25,000 copies each day. Even moderates of the UDMA
and political competitors in the MTLD liked Alger Républicain. The best known editors and contributors were
Henri Alleg, Roualem Khalfa and Isaac Nahori.

ALGERIAN MUSLIM REFORMIST MOVEMENT see Association des Oulema Reformistes Algériens

ALGERIAN SAHARA. Vast region south of the Saharan Atlas
with an area of over 804,000 square miles. The most
significant physical characteristic is the lack of rainfall,
generally less than four inches per year; however, the
area varies extremely. Usually the relative humidity
is in the range of 4 to 5 percent. Topographically the
area consists mostly of plains and plateaus with scattered
mountains. The surface consists of sand dunes (or ergs),
plains of stones (or regs), tables of denuded rocks (or
hammadas), and basins. Due to the scarcity of arable
land, there is severe overpopulation in the oases. Land

use patterns vary greatly from nomadic grazing to intensive irrigation farming. About two-thirds of the population are oasis dwellers, and one-third are nomads. The
most extensive developments in this region have been a
result of the growth of the petroleum industry which has
been a source of economic development in the region.

L'ALGERIE LIBRE. French language newspaper representing
the views of the MTLD.

AL HADDAD, AMZIAN BEN MUHAMMAD (1790-   ). Grand
master of the Rahmaniya Order. On April 8, 1871, he
proclaimed a jihad against the French in Algeria. By
July he had been forced to surrender to General Saussier.
Afterward he was taken to Bougie.

AL-HAFNAOUI, ABOULQASIM (1852-1942). Author, in 1907,
of a two volume biographical dictionary of famous Algerians from the 4th century of the hegira to his own days.
This dictionary is in Arabic.

ALI ABU TALIB (1779?-   ). Paternal uncle of Abd al-
Qadir; constantly involved in intrigues to supplant his
nephew.

ALI BEN SULAYMAN, MULAY (1815-   ). Cousin of the
sultan of Morocco, he was involved in a Moroccan in-
cursion of Oran province from November 1830 to March
1831.

AL JAZAIR. Arabic language newspaper of the MTLD. It
was published in only half as many copies as this party's
French language paper, L'Algérie Libre.

ALLIED INVASION OF ALGERIA (November 8, 1942--Opera-
tion Torch). Based upon the faulty assumption that the
French in North Africa would not resist because of American friendship and support of the Vichy authorities in
North Africa, a force of 107,000 Anglo-Americans, commanded by General Dwight D. Eisenhower, invaded Oran
in western Algeria and Algiers. A third arm invaded
Morocco. Algiers capitulated first that evening when
French General Alphonse Juin surrendered the city to a
joint US-British force of 32,000, commanded by General
Charles Ryder. French forces at Oran, however, re-
sisted for two days before surrendering to General Lloyd
Fredendall's 31,000-man force.

        The invasion also caught Admiral François Darlan
in Algiers. As the most important Vichyite in North
Africa and Commander-in-Chief of the French navy, he
was persuaded to order a cease-fire for all of North
Africa on November 10th, and undertook to govern it
in the Marshal's name on the 13th. The Americans had
planned for its candidate, General Henri Giraud, to as-
sume this leadership position but Giraud proved unable
to command respect or support. (On December 24,
1942, Darlan was assassinated and was replaced by Giraud on President Roosevelt's orders.)
        The Algiers landing force (recommissioned as the
British First Army, commanded by General Kenneth
Anderson), then moved on to occupy Bougie on November
11th, took Bone with airborne troops on the 12th, and
crossed over into Tunisia on the 15th. In southern Algeria, an American parachute unit occupied Tebessa the
same day and crossed over into Tunisia on the 16th.
        French resistance to the invasion held up the in-
vasion force's advance into Tunisia and permitted the
Germans to occupy the protectorate instead, thereby preventing a quick end to the North African phase of the
war. Despite French resistance, the Americans continued to support and work through the Vichy French hierarchy and administration in order to preserve order behind the lines.

ALLOUACHE, MERZAK (20th c.). Algerian filmmaker whose
    The Adventures of a Hero won a golden Tanit (Plate) at
    the Seventh Carthage (Tunisian) Film Festival in Novem-
    ber 1978. His film was also screened at the 1979 Can-
    nes Film Festival.

ALMOHADS (AL-MUWAHHIDUN). Name derived from belief
    in the unity of God; Berber dynasty which reigned in
    North Africa from 1147-1269; founder of doctrine was
    Muhammad ibn Tumart, who took title of Mahdi and en-
    tered struggle against Almoravid dynasty, the dynasty
    founded by Abd al-Mumin, who conquered Morocco in
    1147 and took title of Caliph. The Almohad empire be-
    gan to disintegrate in 1228; dynasty ended with the tak-
    ing of Marrakech (1269) by the Marinides.

ALMORAVIDS (AL-MURABITUN). A brotherhood of warrior-
    monks and Saharan Berbers; in the eleventh century under
    the spiritual direction of Abdallah ibn Yasin, undertook
    conquest of Morocco and founded dynasty under Yusuf

ibn Tachfin; their dynasty was crushed by the Almohads,
who took the capital, Marrakech, in 1147.

AMARA, LASKRI (-   ). Colonel condemned to death
in 1959 for his participation in the 1958 ALN Plot of the
Colonels.

AMFREVILLE, FRANÇOIS DAVY, MARQUIS D' (1628-1692).
French naval officer. He entered the service in 1645,
rising to the rank of ensign in 1665 and ship's captain
the following year. As squadron commander, he took
part with Duquesne in the bombardment of Algiers (June
26-27, August 20-September 4, 1683). On orders of
Louis XIV, he returned to Algiers in 1684 in search of
French slaves.

AMIR (also AMIR AL-MU'MININ). Commander of the believers; title of a caliph implying authority of religious
origin.

AMIROUCHE. Best remembered as leader of the Kabylia
region who seems to have gone berserk and prosecuted
and ordered killed a large number of people serving under his orders. He was himself killed in an accident
that was never fully explained.

AMIS DU MANIFESTE ET DE LA LIBERTE (AML). This
was a political organization formed by Ferhat Abbas in
March 1944. With the support of the Association of
Reformist Ulama and of liberal as well as radical Algerian politicians. The AML protested that de Gaulle's
wartime set of reforms did not provide Algerians with
enough freedom; the colonial administration still ruled
with too heavy a hand, as the elections of 1948 were to
prove. The AML was dissolved in 1945 as part of the
French reaction to the Sétif uprising. Even before dis-
solution, this organization had not managed to integrate
the various factions that supposedly supported it. Still,
it briefly enjoyed a wider support than any other party
before the FLN.

AMROUCHE, JEAN (1906-1962). An Algerian who wrote
extensively in French, Jean Amrouche may represent
better than anyone else the plight of North Africans
caught between two civilizations, that of their African
ancestors and that of the colonizing world of France.
Amrouche's parents were Kabyles who had converted to

Christianity. The quality of Jean Amrouche's literary
production clearly demonstrates how well he assimilated
French culture. His subject was always the same, Algeria. He tried, throughout his life, to explain Algeria
and the soul of Algeria to the rest of the world. He
published two excellent collections of poems, Cendres in
1934 and Etoile secrète in 1937. In 1939 he published
a translation of Algerian songs he had collected, the
Chants berbères de Kabylie. In 1943 he published a
beautiful and long essay which he entitled L'Eternel Jugurtha and which may well be the best attempt to explain
the Algerian soul.

AMROUCHE, MARIE-LOUISE (1913-   ). An Algerian author
who wrote in French, she has published under the name
of Marguerite Taos-Amrouche. Although born in Tunis,
her parents were Kabyles who had emigrated to Tunisia.
She is the sister of Jean Amrouche, thus a child of an
Algerian couple that had converted to Christianity. Educated in France, she settled there permanently in 1945.
She is the author of two novels Jacinthe noire which first
appeared in 1947 and was re-edited in 1972, and of La
rue des tambourins published in 1960. She also edited
a collection of Kabyle poems and tales entitled Le grain
magique which appeared in 1966.

ANNABA (Bône). A major port city of Algeria. Orginally
a Phoenician settlement known as Hippona, it was successively occupied by the Carthaginians, the Numidians,
and the Romans, who renamed it Hippo Regius. Augustine served there as Christian bishop from 395 to 430.
Taken by the Vandals in 430, it was recaptured by the
Byzantines. The Arabs occupied it toward the end of
the seventh century. As a pirate port, it was attacked
by the Pisans and Genoese in 1034. The Sicilian King
Roger II captured it in 1153 and established the Hammadids there. The Almohads took the city in 1160. The
Hafsids annexed it to their realm during the thirteenth
century. At its request the city was taken over by Khair
el-Din, who established a Turkish garrison which remained there until 1830.

AOUCHICHE, ABDELMADJID (-   ). Minister of Urban
Development, Housing and Construction (1979).

APULEIUS (2nd c. A.D.). Born at Madaure (present day
M'Daourouch), he was the author of a truculent and fan-
ciful Latin novel entitled The Golden Ass.

ARAB PRESS. In Algeria, the Arab press--with newspapers
such as al-Islāh, al-Farūq, Du-l-Faqar, al Basaïr,
al Shihab, and others--appeared after World War One.
Not as demanding as the press of Young Algerian tendencies, the Arab press was characterized by a concern for
community, not so much with changes in the relationship
between Europeans and Algerians or with demands for
political reforms. In general, the Arab language press
was, in the colonial period, of Islamic reformist lean-
ings, thus it attacked the cults of saints, the veneration
of marabouts, and social evils such as gambling, drink-
ing intoxicants, or being too much influenced by western
civilization.

ARAB TAXES. Special levies paid only by Algerians, not by
European settlers. It was a part of the indigénat and
was abolished in 1918.

AL-ARIBI, SIDI (-1834). First khalifa of Abd al-Qadir
(1832-33). He was chief of the Aulad Sidi al-Aribi clan
which controlled the Chélif. Al-Aribi was involved in an
uprising against the Emir in 1833 and in 1834 joined the
revolt of Mustafa ben Ismail. He was captured and imprisoned by Abd al-Qadir at Mascara and later died in
prison.

ARMEE DE LA LIBERATION NATIONALE (ALN). National
Liberation Army (from the French "l'Armée de libération
nationale"). Members of the CRUA organized the ALN
as the military arm of the revolutionary movement which
started the War of National Liberation in November 1954.
After independence, the ALN became the ANP or the Popular National Army.

ARMEE NATIONALE POPULAIRE (ANP). Popular National
Army (from the French "Armée nationale populaire").
Name of the Algerian army after independence was
achieved. Until 1962, this army was known as the ALN.

ARRASH, SIDI AL- (-   ). Marabout of Oran province,
admired by Abd al-Qadir and influential in his election
as Emir of Algeria.

ARSLAN, CHEKIB (1869-1946). An Egyptian who is often
called the father of pan-Arabism, Arslan happened to
be in Geneva in 1936 when Messali Hadj arrived there
while fleeing the French authorities. Arslan apparently

encouraged Messali Hadj to give more emphasis to the
Islamic character of the ENA and to move away from
the communist ideology that had led to the founding of
that organization. Messali Hadj followed this advice and
the ENA became markedly pan-Arabic.

ARUDJ, IBN YAKUB ABU YUSUF (-1518).   Turkish corsair and a founder of the Algerian regency.   Brought
up as a pirate in the Greek archipelago, he was captured
and forced to serve a term on the galleys of the Knights
of Saint John.   Afterward he returned to his piratical
cruises along the coast of Spain.   By 1510, he had attracted an armed force of over a thousand men and about
a dozen ships.   The sultan of Tunis allied himself with
Arudj and offered him the governorship of Djerba, which
became his headquarters.   From that focal point he set
about establishing alliances with local rulers.   At the
request of the shaikh of Algiers, Salim al-Tumi, Arudj
undertook an attack on Algiers to free it from the Spaniards.   When unrest began to spread against the Turkish
force, Arudj had the shaikh strangled in his bath and
himself proclaimed sultan by his forces.   A Spanish expedition to recapture Algiers failed in 1516.   At the request of townspeople from Tlemcen, Arudj left Algiers
to seize that town from the control of Abu Hammu, an
ally of the Spanish in Oran.   He placed his brother,
Khair al-Din, in his stead at Algiers and proceeded to
Tlemcen.   Instead of restoring the pretender Abu Zaiyan
to the throne, he took control of it for himself and had
the Zayanid princes put to death.   A Spanish force from
Oran besieged the town for six months in 1518.   He attempted to flee to the sea but was pursued by Spanish
cavalry and was slain at the ford of the Salado River.

ASABIYA.   Arabic word which might be translated as "clan-
nishness" or "esprit de corps."   Ibn Khaldun thought asabiya the highest form of allegiance and explained the
workings of North African dynasties in terms of asabiya.

ASBONNE, ABDALLAH D' (fl. 1830's).   French official.   A
Mamluk of Syrian birth, he was taken to France by Napoleon's army.   There he became a cavalry officer in
the Imperial Guard.   He served as a translator in the
French expedition against Algiers (1830).   From 1834
to 1835 he served as French consul at Mascara, but he
returned to Oran prior to the French defeat at Macta.

EL-ASNAM.   City of the interior, about half way between
Algiers and Oran and which the French called Orleans-
ville.

AS-SALAM.   An Algerian cultural review founded by Si
Hamza Boubakeur.   The first issue of As-Salam appeared
in September 1946.   In 1948, this revue became Salam
Ifrikiya which ceased publication in May of 1950.

ASSEMBLÉE ALGÉRIENNE (ALGERIAN ASSEMBLY).   Formed
in 1947-1948 to give institutional life to the Algerian
Statute, this body was composed of 120 delegates, half
of whom were Algerians.   The Algerian Assembly was a
kind of colonial legislature created to give Algeria more
autonomy.   The French were still very much in control,
however, as the Governor General could exercise the
veto.   Another way to control Algerians was through electoral manipulation.   The 1948 elections, for example,
were notoriously manipulated.   As a result, many Algerians became more radical.

ASSIMILATION POLICY.   In theory, the French government
in Algeria wished to make Frenchmen of Algerian subjects.   This objective was to be reached through contact
and education.   In fact, the policy foundered on the Algerians' fervent allegiance to Islam.   While the policy
was in effect, Algerians who acquired the accoutrements
of French civilization, including language, dress, education and if not religion, at least the willingness to abandon a personal status based in part on Islamic law,
could petition for French citizenship.   In fact, the process was so complicated that relatively few Algerians
ever became French citizens.   More Algerians might
have been assimilated if the procedures had not involved
giving up a personal status defined in Islamic law and
if the policy had not been applied by colonial officials
who were often against the policy and thus made the workings of the law next to impossible.

ASSOCIATION GENERAL DES TRAVAILLEURS ALGERIENS
(AGTA).   General Association of Algerian Workers (from
the French "Association Générale des Travailleurs Algériens").   A union founded in 1962 to help protect the
interests of some 800,000 Algerian workers who had
migrated to France in their search for work.   The AGTA
was affiliated to the UGTA.

ASSOCIATION DES OULEMA REFORMISTES ALGERIENS
(ASSOCIATION OF ALGERIAN REFORMIST ULAMAS).
Founded in 1931 by Abd al Hamid Ben Badis, it was
most effective in the Constantine region but quickly spread
to the colonial provinces of Algiers and Oran as well.
It was not a political party, but a religious group whose
cultural and educational program fostered the growth of
an Algerian national spirit.

By 1936, the Ulama organization had 130 schools
in Constantine department alone. In Ulama schools,
pupils learned in Arabic. There was no French content
and, indeed, many of the Ulama teachers did not know
French. In their schools and in the Algerian boy scout
movement which they also directed, the Ulama taught
young Algerians in a spirit best exemplified by their slo-
gan: "Islam is my religion; Arabic is my language; Algeria is my fatherland."

In the mid-1930's, the Ulama joined the FEM
(Fédération des Elus Musulmans) ENA (Etoile Nord-Africaine) and PCA (Parti Communiste Algérien) in the Muslim Congress, an attempt to unify all Algerian opposition
to the colonial regime.

Most Ulama leaders joined the FLN after the outbreak of the war of national liberation in 1954. They
continue to have some influence in independent Algeria
since that socialist regime does define itself, in part at
least, as an Islamic government. The ministry of religious foundations (habous), for example, has generally
been held by members of the reformist Ulama group.

ASSOCIATION OF ALGERIAN SUNNITE ULAMA. Anti-
Reformist organization formed in Algiers on September
15, 1932 in opposition to the Association of Algerian
Muslim Ulama. In opposition to the journal Sihab, they
established an Arabic newspaper named al-Ihlas ("Sincerity") in December 1932.

ASSOCIATION POLICY. When the assimilation policy proved
unworkable, French officials tried to justify French control of Algeria through recourse to the theory of association. Algerians, it was thought, would become civilized,
would be brought into the modern social and economic
world, through association with the superior civilization
of France. In practice, the association policy kept Algerians in a second class situation in their homeland itself.

ATERIAN. A prehistoric civilization, named for a major archeological site, Bir el-Ater, located 100 kilometers south of Tebessa. Arriving in the area at the time of the last ice age, the Aterian civilization extended from the Nile to the Atlantic down to the edges of the Sahara.

ATFIYECH, CHEIKH (1818-1914). Learned Ibadite scholar from the Mzab who published a 10 volume commentary on the Qu'ran (in Arabic).

AUGUSTINE [in Latin: Aurelius Augustinus] (354-430). Bishop of Hippo (modern Annaba) (394-430). Born in Tagaste, he was educated in Madauros and Carthage. He went to Rome in 383. Augustine was baptized by Ambrose in 387, and, after a short stay in Rome, he returned to Tagaste the following year. There he founded a monastery where he remained until 391 when he became a priest at Hippo. He succeeded Valerius as bishop of Hippo in 395, and he continued to reside there until his death during the siege of the city by the Vandals. He devoted much of his energies as bishop to healing the Donatist schism within the Christian Church. He is venerated in the Catholic Church as a saint.

AURES MOUNTAINS. Great massif of Southeastern Algeria and the Saharan Atlas. It contains Jebel Chélia, the highest peak in Algeria (7,638 feet). The Aurès is populated by the Chaouia, a Berber people. Located in the northern part of the massif, the Chaouia are sedentary and combine agriculture with semi-nomadic herding. Because of their ruggedness, the Aurès have continuously been the site of revolts against authority, against the Romans, the Arabs, the Turks, and the French in 1850, 1859, 1916, and 1955.

AWLAD SIDI SHAIKH. The most important tribe on Oran province who, before the conquest of Algiers by France in 1830, were virtually autonomous and only nominal subjects of the Dey of Algiers.

AZZEDINE, COMMANDANT. One of a handful of ALN officers in the General Staff before independence who were partisans of the GPRA, hence opponents of Boumedienne and his followers.

AL-AZZUZ, HASAN BEN (fl. 1835). Marabout of Tolga.

He served as khalifa of Abd al-Qadir in Ziban and East Sahara from 1837 to 1838.

AL BALAG AL DJAZ'IRI ("The Algerian Statement"). Weekly review published by Shaykh al-Alawi and his followers in Algiers. It opposed westernization and reflected the conservative Sufi beliefs of its publisher. Also defended the Sufi order from Salafiyya attacks.

BARBAROSSA see KHAYR AL-DIN

BARBARY WARS. The American name given to a series of conflicts fought from 1801 to 1805 and in 1815 between the United States and the states of the Maghrib. In 1812 the dey of Algiers sought increased tribute for the passage of American commerce through the Mediterranean. Upon the conclusion of the American War of 1812 (1812-1815), American Commodores Bainbridge and Decatur led a naval force against the Algerian fleet, capturing its flagship. Decatur then moved into the harbor of Algiers, threatening to bombard the port. In June 1815, the dey signed a treaty no longer requiring tribute of the United States, returning confiscated American property, releasing Christian hostages, and paying an indemnity for a captured brig.

AL-BARKANI, MUHAMMAD BEN A'ISA (-1847). Al-Barkani originally supported the French in 1830 and was named Quaid of Sharshal by General Clauzel. He shifted his allegiance to Abd al-Qadir in 1834. He served as khalifa of the Emir beginning in 1835, though temporarily replaced in 1837 by the Emir's brother Mustafa. He died in Fez.

AL-BASSAIR ("Clairvoyance"). Religious journal published daily in Arabic in Algiers from 1936 to 1939 and later from 1947 to 1956. It was a publication of the Association of Algerian Reformist Ulama.

BATTLE OF ALGIERS. A bombing and terrorism campaign authorized by the CCE of the FLN in 1957. In reaction, the French imposed strict repressive measures on the city as a whole and eventually dismantled the revolutionary apparatus in that city.

BEJAIA. Post-independence name of Bougie, an ancient city
and port of the Kabylia region, and now one of Algeria's
pipeline terminals for Saharan oil.

BELAID, ABDESSLAM (-   ). The son of a well-to-do
Kabyle landowner, Belaid joined the PPA while he was
still in high school (lycée). He was arrested for political activities detrimental to the state during "the events"
of May 1945. Released from prison, he became a member of the Central Committee of the PPA-MTLD and also
a founder of the UGEMA. He was in France when the
War of National Liberation broke, and he did not join the
FLN until after May 1955. Then he brought the UGEMA
with him. He was an assistant to Mehri, al Madani, and
Ben Khedda in various GPRA cabinets. Although he sided
with the GPRA against Ben Bella in the summer of 1962,
he was made first president of SONATRACH in June of 1965;
he became Minister for Industry and Energy later that year.

BELARBI, SIDI AHMED (-   ). Belarbi better known
as Boualem, his pseudonym, was a leader and organizer
of railroad workers who was sent to Moscow to study at
the KUTV in the period from 1931 to 1933. He was later
pushed out of leadership position within the PCA, apparently because of incompetence and because he was suspected of being a police spy.

BELHADJ, MOKRANE see OU EL-HADJ, MOHAND

BELHOUCHET, ABDELLAH (1924-   ). Born near Sedrata,
Belhouchet had attained the rank of sergeant in the French
Army before he joined the ALN. He fought in eastern
Algeria (Wilaya I and II) before crossing over into Tunisia. There he was involved in a 1958 coup against the
GPRA, arrested by the Tunisian authorities at the request of the ALN and imprisoned until the fall of 1960.
Freed, he joined an underground being organized along
the Mali border by Bouteflika, eventually becoming commander of this region. Belhouchet supported the Tlemcen group in the summer of 1962 and was appointed to
direct the commando section of the Military Academy at
Cherchell. He fought in the ANP in the Moroccan border
war, then was appointed commander of the Fifth Military
Region (Constantine). He replaced Abid Said at the head of
the First Military Region (Algiers) after the latter's suicide
in December, 1967. In 1978, he was a member of Boumedienne's Council of the Revolution.

BELKAIM, KADDOUR (-1940?). An Algerian member of
the PCA who became party secretary during the Blum
Popular Front era (mid 1930's). Arrested and put in
prison by the Vichy government, he died a prisoner.

BEN ALLA, HADJ (-   ). An officer in the ALN during the War of National Liberation and a companion of
Larbi ben M'Hidi until the latter's arrest in 1956, Ben
Alla became a member of the Political Bureau and of
the FLN's Central Committee after independence. In
1963 he was his party's director in charge of national
organizations. He also served as President of the National Assembly in 1964.

BEN ALI, CHERIF (-1897). Kabyle marabout and a
leader in the Kabyle insurrection of 1870 who also played
a double agent role and thus helped the French. In 1873,
he was condemned only to 5 years in prison, but this
sentence was suspended and he lost neither property nor
position.

BEN ARRASH, MAULUD (fl. 1830's). Prior to 1830 he
served as agha of the Sharq for Hasan Bey. He remained
in that post under Abd al-Qadir. He undertook a diplomatic mission to Paris in 1838.

BEN BADIS, ABDEL HAMID (1889-1940). Born in Constantine into a traditional family, he was educated in his native city, in Tunis and in the Middle East. He founded
two journals after he returned to Algeria, Al-Muntaqid
and Ash-Shihab. In 1931, he helped create the Algerian
Association of Reformist Ulama which was to have a
great deal of influence in shaping Algeria's Arabic Renaissance (Nahd'a). His motto, which became that of the
Algerian Muslim Boy Scouts' Movement was "Islam is
my religion, Arabic my language, Algeria my fatherland."

BEN BELLA, AHMED (b. December 25, 1916 at Marnia).
Probably the best known member of the small groups of
men who, as members of the CRUA planned and launched
the Algerian War of Independence.
        The youngest child in a family of five boys and
several girls, he outlived all of his brothers. His father
was apparently severe, particularly in his insistence on
the proper observance of the Islamic religion and of native customs. In spite of his father, Ahmed Ben Bella
was not well versed in Arabic. But he did manage to

finish French primary school by the time he was thirteen
years old. He was drafted into the 14th regiment of
Algerian Sharpshooters before the outbreak of World War
II and served with distinction in the Italian campaign,
even earning a Military Cross for valor. Back in Algeria in 1945, he witnessed the terrible repression of
the Setif uprising and quickly joined the illegal PPA.
He was later a member of the OS, participated in an attack on the main post office in Oran (April 4, 1949), was
captured when the French police discovered the OS, and
was imprisoned from 1950 to 1952 when he escaped.
        After his escape, Ben Bella fled to Cairo where
he engaged in various activities that eventually led to
the Algerian revolutionary breakout of 1954. Until his
capture by the French aboard a Moroccan plane (en route
to Tunis but diverted by the French to Algiers), he directed the collection of funds and materiel for the Algerian freedom fighters who had remained inside Algeria.
He was a prisoner in France until 1962.
        With independence, Ben Bella emerged as First
Prime Minister (1962-63), then was elected President of
the Algerian Republic (1963-65). He was overthrown by
the military coup of 1965 that established Houari Boumedienne as the chief of the Algerian state.
        While in power, Ben Bella helped restore order
in Algeria, steered his country toward a socialist economy, pushed for agrarian reforms, and spent considerable sums on education. In foreign policy, he supported
wars of national liberation throughout the world and, generally, allied Algeria with other Arab nations and the
Third World.
        His fate after his arrest during the coup of 1965
is not known, although various pro-Ben Bella and anti-
Boumedienne organizations were created (e. g. , OCRA
and PRS). He was freed in 1979 by President Bendjedid.

BEN BOULAID, MOSTEFA (1917-1956). First commander of
    the Aurès wilaya during the War of National Liberation,
    Ben Boulaid was born in Arris in 1917. His family were
    impoverished peasants. He himself was a milner who
    acquired enough capital to buy a bus line that served the
    Arris-Batna region. His political activity quickly led
    him into difficulties with the French authorities, and he
    lost his license to operate the bus line in 1951. By
    then, he had already been an active nationalist as a mem-
    ber of the PPA and the OS. He ran for the Algerian As-
    sembly in 1948, won a majority of the votes, but was

denied his seat by the colonial authorities. Ben Boulaid
was a founding member of the CRUA, one of the historic
leaders. Through intermediaries who were members of
the Central Committee of the MTLD, Salah Maïza and
Hamoud El-Hachemi, he tried to convince Messali Hadj
to join in the armed rebellion. This effort failed. Meanwhile, he sold much of what he owned to help finance the
revolution in the Aurès, a wilaya he could keep together
only with great difficulty. The French authorities managed
to arrest him in February 1955, but he escaped on November 4 of the same year. He died March 27, 1956
while trying to operate a field radio that had been booby-
trapped by the French army's special services.

BEN CHERIF, CAID (early 20th c.). A "Young Algerian" who,
in 1920, published Ahmed Ben Mostapha, goumier. Although perhaps lacking in literary polish, this book offers
evidence of criticism of the French system by colonized
Algerians who wrote in French.

BEN ISMA'IL, MUSTAFA (1769-1843). Influential chief in
Oran province. He was the agha of the Dawair and the
Zmalah until 1830. He allied himself with the Moroccans
from 1830 to 1831, then allied himself with Abd al-Qadir.
He rebelled against the Emir in 1834 and was defeated.
From 1836 to 1843, he served under the French as agha
of the Dawair and the Zmalah. He was appointed a brigadier general in the French army in 1837. Mustafa was
ambushed and killed in 1843.

BEN KERIOU, ABDALLAH (-1921). Inhabitant of Laghouat well known as a poet of what might be called Algeria's oral tradition.

BEN KHEDDA, BEN YOUSSEF (1922-   ). Born in 1922
at Blida, Ben Khedda became a pharmacist who joined
the PPA during World War II. He was Secretary General of the MTLD in 1954 when that party split into two
competing groups, the Messalists and the Centralists.
From 1960 to 1962, he was President of the GPRA. He
had already served as Minister for Social Affairs and as
a member of the CNRA and CCE. After independence
Ben Khedda competed with Ben Bella for control of the
State, and lost. He retired to private life until 1976
when he publicly criticized the socialist options of the
Boumedienne regime.

BEN KHEDDA, BRAHIM (-   ).   Brother of the more
    famous Ben Youssef Ben Khedda of the MTLD and FLN.
    Brahim Ben Khedda was regional secretary at Blida of
    the PCA and a member of that party's national Central
    Committee in the late 1940's and in the 1950's.

BEN KHEIR, MOHAMMED (-1889).   Celebrated popular
    poet, a practitioner of Algeria's oral tradition, who cele-
    brated the resistance of the Ouled Sidi Cheikh people of
    western Algeria.

BEN MADJOUB, MOHAMED OMAR (-   ).   In 1964,
    he was a Deputy in the National Assembly who had pre-
    viously served in various capacities in the FLN and ALN.
    In 1964, he was also a member of the FLN's Political
    Bureau and Central Committee.   He was one of the or-
    ganizers of the 1964 party congress.

BEN M'HIDI, LARBI (1923-1957).   A founding member of the
    CRUA, Ben M'Hidi was the first commander of the Oran
    wilaya.   He was born in Ain M'Lila in Constantine prov-
    ince into a family of relatively well-to-do farmers.   He
    became nationalist activist early on, was in the PPA and
    in the OS.   The French arrested him a first time in
    May of 1945.   On August 20, 1956, he gave command of
    Oran province to Boussouf.   He, himself, had been elected
    to the Committee for Coordination and Execution of the
    FLN by the Soummam Congress.   As a member of the
    CCE, M'Hidi was a partisan of the theses advanced by
    Ramdane Abane and Belkacem Krim, hence, in opposition
    to Ben Bella.   He believed interior leaders should con-
    trol the Revolution.   During the Battle of Algiers, he
    directed armed nationalist groups.   He was captured by
    Colonel Bigeard's men, who apparently tortured him in
    an attempt to get intelligence.   But he died (in 1957)
    without ever revealing any information.

BEN MOUSSA, SHEIK MOHAMMED (-   ).   Keeper of
    the Sidi Bou Medienne Mosque near Tlemcen.

BEN OTHMAN, SI HAMDAN (19th c.).   Advisor to Bey Hus-
    sein.   Author of several texts that give an Algeria-
    Turkish point of view about the French expedition of
    1830.

BEN SAHLA, MOHAMMED (end of 19th c.).   Practitioner of
    the oral tradition of Algeria who lived in Tlemcen.

BEN SAID, ABU ABD ALLAH MUHAMMAD see KADDURA
AL DJAZAIRI

BEN SALIM, AHMAD (fl. 1830's). Khalifa of Abd al-Qadir
in Hamza (1837-39). The Emir's last active khalifa,
Ahmad surrendered to the French in 1847 and left the
country.

BEN YAHIA, MOHAMMED SEDIK (1932-   ). Born in Djidjelli in lower Kabylia, he was the son of a mother who
spoke only Arabic but who encouraged her son to get as
much modern (i.e., French) education as possible. He
eventually earned a license (equiv. M. A.) in Law in
1953. With Ahmed Taleb and Lamine Khene, he helped
organize the UGEMA (Union Générale des Etudiants Musulmans Algériens) a pro-FLN student union. Between
1954 and 1956, he defended victims of repression in
Algiers. Then he escaped to Cairo shortly before the
French authorities were to arrest him.
        He was a member of the CNRA (Algeria National
Revolutionary Committee) in 1956, and represented this
group in Djakarta. He served under Ahmed Francis
when the latter was Finance Minister for the GPRA (Provisional Government of the Algerian Revolution), then as
cabinet director under Ferhat Abbas. He was a representative at the Melun and Evian talks and on Ben Youssef Ben Khedda's staff during the life of the third GPRA.
In 1963, Ben Yahia became his country's ambassador to
Moscow. He was to have moved to London shortly before Algeria broke relations with England in 1966. Later
that year, he became Boumedienne's Minister of Information, then the Minister of Higher Education and Scientific
Research when Bachir Boumaza went into opposition and
exile (July 1971). He replaced Bouteflika as Foreign
Minister in January 1979.

BEN YAHYA, BELKACEM (-   ). Director of El Moudjahid.

BENABDELMALEK, RAMDANE (-1 November 1954). He
was the only OS leader to attend the MTLD Congress of
April 1953. At first he sided with Messali Hadj, but
under the influence of Boudiaf, he switched to the argu-
ments in favor of immediate armed insurrection brought
forth by the CRUA. He was Ben M'Itidi's second in command for the Oran region when the War of National Liberation broke out and he was killed by French troops near

Cassaigne on the first day of the war.   He was originally
from Constantine.

BENACHENHOU, MOURAD (-   ).   Secretary-General
of the Algerian Finance Ministry in 1979.

BENAMARA, OMAR (-   ).   Algerian singer who won
two lyrical singing competitions in Paris on March 10
and 25, 1979.   He had previously been the director of
the Algiers polyphonic choir.

BENAOUDA, AMAR BEN MOSTEFA (-   ).   Originally
from Annaba, Benaouda was an early member of the PPA
and of the OS.   He was arrested by the French colonial
authorities in 1950, but escaped from prison in 1951.
An outlaw, he moved about Algeria, but particularly in
Kabylia until the outbreak of the War of National Liberation in 1954.   He declared himself in favor of armed
revolution and, at the Soummam Congress of August 1956,
he was named a member of the CNRA.   One of his first
duties with the CNRA was to go from Algeria to Tunis
to argue the supremacy of the interior delegation of the
FLN.   Later he served as a member of the Military
Organization Committee for the eastern war zone, then
as a member of the Algerian negotiating team for talks
with France.   Since independence, Benaouda has been
military attache at Cairo, Paris and Tunis, and, since
1975, ambassador to Libya.

BENCHENEB, MOHAMMED (1869-1929).   Translator into
French of numerous Arabic texts (chronicles, philosophical, poetic, and philological books) and author of books of
his own such as Traité de prosodie arab (1906) and Pro-
verbes arabes d'Algérie et du Maghreb (3 vols. , 1905-
1907).   Among the Arabic authors he translated or about
whose works he published critical editions were Ibn
Maryam, Al Ghorbrini, Az-Zadjadji and Aboul Arab Al-
Khochani.

BENCHENEB, SAADEDDINE (1907-1968).   Son of Mohammed
Bencheneb, he too published a great deal about Arabic
literature.   Some of his books were in Arabic, but most
in French.   His best known works are La Poésie arabe
moderne (1945) and Contes d'Alger (1946).   He was
awarded the Algerian Grand Literary Prize for these
two books.

BENCHRIF, AHMED (1927-   ).   A native of Djelfa, he was
a sergeant before World War II and had risen to the rank
of second lieutenant before he was arrested, in 1957,
for providing weapons to the ALN.   In July 1957, he
deserted the French army to join the ALN.   The next
year, he was appointed director of a nationalist military
school located in southern Tunisia.   He went underground
again in 1959 and became commander of Wilaya IV with
the rank of major in 1960.   He was also a member of
the CNRA.   Captured in October 1960, he was condemned
to death.   The sentence was not carried out and he was
released from French prison after the signing of the
Evian agreements.   Promoted to colonel in the ALN, he
rejoined the nationalists in Wilaya VI.   After independence
in 1962, he was put in charge of the Algerian gendar-
merie.   He apparently was a key actor in the June 1965
coup and has considerable influence in the ANP.

BENCHICOU, MOHAMED (-   ).   Journalist working
for the French language El Moudjahid.

BENDJEDID, CHADLI (1929-   ).   Born in Bouteldja in the
Annaba region on April 14, 1929, he was the son of a small
landholder.   He received some schooling at Annaba.
        An early member of the FLN and ALN, he rose
to the rank of captain and was in charge of a zone by
the end of the War of National Liberation.   In February
1961, Boumedienne, who was Chief of Staff, appointed
Bendjedid to the Operational Command of the nationalists'
Northern Military Zone.
        He became a major and commander of Algeria's
5th military region at the end of 1962.   He was transferred to the Second Military Region (Oran) in June 1964.
In 1969 he was promoted to the rank of colonel.   He
had meanwhile become a member of the Council of the
Revolution and was active in the "Revolutionary Readjust-
ment" of June 19, 1965 which led to the replacement of
Ben Bella by Boumedienne as President of the Algerian
Republic.   On the whole, however, he was a professional
and loyal army officer who played only minor political
roles until after 1978.
        Chadli Dendjedid was elected President of the Alger-
ian Republic on February 7, 1979.   He is also Secretary
General of the FLN, Algeria's only legal political party.

BENHABYLES, CHERIF (early 20th c.).   An author who belonged to the "Young Algerians" movement of the 1920's.
He wrote a 1914 brochure entitled L'Algérie française

vue par un indigène which pointed out some of the faults
of the colonial system in Algeria.

BENHEDOUGA, ABDELHAMID (1929-   ). Born in Mansoura near Setif, Benhedouga is one of Algeria's leading
authors who always writes in Arabic although he knows
French well. In 1958, he published an essay entitled
Algeria Between Yesterday and Today (author's translation
of the Arabic title) and, at about the same time, he
joined the ALN-FLN underground as a propagandist. During the War of National Liberation and after, he published
several collections of short stories: The Seven Rays and
Algerian Shadows, both in 1960, and The Writer in 1974.
He is best known, however, for his novel, The Wind from
the South which was first published in 1971 by the SNED
(National Publishing and Distribution Company). This
book has already been translated into French, Dutch, and
Polish; German, Spanish and English translations are in
the works. Since 1971, he has also published The End
of Tomorrow. He is a frequent commentator on radio
and television who has also published poetry, in Arabic,
such as a volume entitled Empty Souls (1967).

BENI-OUI-OUI. Disparaging and uncomplimentary term given
to Algerians who associated with the French during the
colonial period.

BENNABI: MALEK (1905-1973). Algerian author who was
born in Constantine in 1905, was educated in French
schools there, in Algiers, and in Paris. He was a
writer and journalist who contributed most often to La
République Algérienne and wrote several books among
which are Vocation de l'Islam (1954) and L'Afro-asiatisme:
conclusion sur la Conférence de Bandoeng (1956).

BENSALEM, ABDERRAHMANE (1923-   ). Born in the
region along the Tunisian border, Bensalem was an officer in the French army who deserted to the ALN in
1956. He had had considerable military experience fighting in Italy during World War II and Indochina thereafter.
He had earned numerous citations for bravery. In November 1960, he crossed into Tunisia and, there, commanded various ALN troops. A strong partisan of the
General Staff against the GPRA during the civil war of
the summer of 1962, he was elected to the National Assembly and became a member of that body's Armed
Forces Committee. In 1964 he gained membership on

the General Staff of the ANP and on the Central Committee of the FLN, a position he still holds. He was a Boumedienne partisan.

BENTALEB, MOHAMMED (1931-   ). Born near Affreville, he was the son of a relatively well-off family. He received a certificat d'études before joining the French army. He served in Indo-China as a sergeant. Back in Algeria as a civilian, he joined the ALN and served under Si Larbi in the Miliana region until the end of the Revolution.

BENTAMI, DJILALI (-   ). A resident of Algiers and an ophthalmologist by profession, Bentami was a "Young Algerian" who led a delegation to Paris in 1919. In meetings with Poincaré and other French political leaders, he requested rights for Algerians. His group, for example, suggested that Algerian soldiers should be able to choose naturalization without being forced to renounce their personal rights as defined by Islamic law. Other demands included a call for an end of the indigénat and for sufficient and serious representation for Algerians at every level of government, including some elected representatives in Paris itself, either in the Chamber of Deputies or in some special body. These demands of the "Young Algerians" created quite a debate in the French press, and probably influenced the shape and content of the Jonnart law of 1919, although Bentami and his friends got considerably less than they wanted. Bentami was married to a French woman.

BENTOBBAL, LAKHDAR (1925-   ). Originally from Mila, where he was born in 1925, Bentobbal is presently president and director general of the national steel society. Condemned to death in 1950 for his participation in the activities of the PPA and of the OS, he went underground. He supported Boudiaf in the meeting of 22 in 1954. He was a representative at the Soummam Congress and was elected to the CNRA. He replaced Youssef Zighoud. He left Algeria in 1957, supported Krim and helped eliminate "centralists" who followed Ben Khedda. He was active in the GPRA as Minister of the Interior from 1958 to 1961, and a Minister of State in the Ben Khedda government of 1961.

BENTOUMI, AMAR (-   ). Minister of Justice in the first independent Algerian government and a radical politican in the National Assembly of the Algerian Republic.

81 Benzine, Abdelhamid

BENZINE, ABDELHAMID (-). Along with Amar Oussedik, he was an ex-MTLD member who joined the PCA
in the late 1940s and became an editor on the staff of
Alger Républicain.

BESSAOUD, MOHAMED (-). A member of the Tlemcen regional committee of the PCA, he had a brother
who was a leader of the local UDMA.

BEY. Governor of a beylik in the Regency of Algiers.

BEYLIK. One of four administrative subdivisions of the
Regency of Algiers.

BISKRA. An oasis and town of the Sahara. The present
city is built on the site of the Roman town of Vescera.
It was given its present name by the Aghalids, who conquered it in the eleventh century. By the thirteenth century, the city had become the leader of the southwest
Hafsid states and essentially an autonomous city, pros-
pering from the caravan trade between the Sahara and
the Tell. In 1402, the Hafsids reasserted full authority
over Biskra. Following the decline of the Hafsids, Biskra became a fief of the nomadic Dawawida. Under the
Turks, the city fell into decline. A French army under
the Duke of Aumale occupied it in 1844. The city is
capital of the Ziban, whose villages extend from the
southern edges of the Aurès to Shat Melrir.

BITAT, RABAH (b. December 19, 1925, in Ain Kerma).
A member of the CRUA and of the ALN, Bitat commanded
revolutionary forces within Algeria itself, first in northern
Constantine province, then around Algiers and in the capital itself. He was captured by the French police on
February 23, 1955, and spent the rest of the War of National Liberation in prison. He was named an honorary
member of the GPRA (1958-1962), and emerged from
the war to serve in various ministerial positions under
Ben Bella, then under Boumedienne.
    Drafted into the French army in 1939, he fought
for the "cause of liberty" only to return to Algeria just
in time to witness the horrible Sétif repression of 1945.
He joined the MTLD in 1948 and had attracted enough
official colonial attention by 1950 to have earned condem-
nation in absentia to five years exile from Algeria. But
he never left his native land, preferring to go underground
and to continue working for national liberation from within.

Of the nine "historic leaders" of the Algerian
revolution, four (Didouche, Ben Boulaid, Ben M'hidi, and
Boudiaf) are in opposition and exile, one (Ben Bella) was,
until 1979, under strict house arrest, and only one (Bitat)
is still an active political leader. He has served as
Minister of State for Transportation in Boumedienne's
government, a position he held until 1976. When Boumedienne died in 1978, Bitat served as interim head of state
until the election, early in 1979, of President Chadli
Bendjedid. He is President of the Algerian National Assembly.

BLUM-VIOLETTE PROPOSAL. Effort by the Popular Front
Government of French Socialist Premier Léon Blum in
1936 to satisfy the program of Algerian moderates. It
called for a certain number of educated Algerian Muslims to be allowed to become French citizens without
surrendering their Muslim personal status in matters
such as marriage, divorce, and inheritance. Due to
strident colon opposition, the proposal was never discus-
sed in the legislature. As a result, Dr. Bendielloul in
1937 called for the resignation of Muslim elected officials
if the proposal were not voted on. Many returned to
their posts upon being given assurances that the proposals
would be presented; however, the failure to keep that
promise led to disillusionment among many Algerian moderates.

BOU GDEMMA, SIDI (11th c.). Founder of Ghardaiah, the
most important of the M'Zab's seven cities that are the
center of the Khardjite sect in Algeria. Although set in
an inhospitable portion of the Sahara, Ghardaiah is presently surrounded by some 250,000 palm trees, all of which
have to be watered from wells that produce brackish
water.

BOU MEZRAG (-1906). Kabyle who was a leader in the
insurrection of 1870-71. Captured and condemned to
death in 1873, his sentence was commuted to exile and
he was sent to Noumea instead. He was allowed to return to Algeria in 1905, where he died within a year.

BOU QOBRIN, ABDERRAHMAN (-   ). Eighteenth century "holy man" who founded the Rahmaniya brotherhood
which had many followers in Kabylia.

BOUALEM, KHALFA (-   ). A leader in the Muslim

scouts movement who joined the PCA and collaborated
with Amar Oussedik as an editor of Alger Républicain.

BOUAZIZ, YAHIA (-   ).   Algerian historian whose
The Revolution of 1871:   Role of the El Mokrani and El
Haddad Families was published by the Algerian national
publishing and distribution company in 1979.

BOUBAKEUR, SI HAMZA (20th c.).   Founder, in 1946, and
editor of As Salam, an Algerian cultural revue that became Salam Ifrikiya in 1948 and ceased publication in
1950.

BOUBNIDER, SALAH (1925-   ).   Born in Oued Zenati near
Constantine, Boubnider was a café waiter until he joined
the FLN in 1954.   He rose within the ALN to the post
of military assistant to the commander of Wilaya II in
late 1959 and was promoted to the rank of colonel in
early 1962.   Since independence, he has been relieved
of his command by the Tlemcen goup, reinstated as com-
missar for political and administrative affairs, engaged
in anti-Ben Bella activities, arrested (and released) for
these subversive activities in the summer of 1963, and
appointed to represent Algeria at the United Arab Command in Cairo.   A strong Arabist, he has worked hard
to establish a special relationship between the Syrian
Baath party and the FLN.   His pseudonym is Saout el
Arab.

BOUCHAMA, RABI (-1959).   Algerian poet tortured to
death in 1959 by the French "Forces of Order."

BOUDA, AHMED (-   ).   A member of the PPA during
World War II, he was also a delegate in the Algerian
Assembly in 1948.   He was apparently a convinced opponent of Messali Hadj.   The French authorities arrested
him in November 1954 but released him again in April
1955.   Leaving Algeria soon after, he became the FLN's
representative in Libya.   He tried to mediate between
the GPRA and the Ben Bella Group during the summer
of 1962.   Failing, he gave up politics to become a teacher
in Algiers.

BOUDIAF, ABDELHAFID (-   ).   A cousin of Mohamed
Boudiaf who was active as a member of the PCA then
joined the ALN-FLN.

BOUDIAF, MOHAMED (b. June 23, 1919 at M'Sila). One of
the historic leaders who, along with Ben Bella, Aït Ahmed
and others worked in the OS and eventually in the CRUA,
two organizations whose members prepared and launched
the War of National Liberation.
Drafted into the French army in 1943, he tried
to organize nationalist cells among Algerian soldiers.
After the war he directed the PPA section in Bordj-bou
Arreridj, a small but strategically located city halfway
between Constantine and Algiers. In 1947, he created a
branch of the OS in the department of Constantine. In
1953-1954, he was a party organizer for the MTLD in
France. In late October 1954, Boudiaf was the key
liaison officer between the internal and the external members of the CRUA.
After independence, Boudiaf emerged as an opposition leader and was arrested by the Ben Bella government. Eventually released, he went into exile in France
where he led the PRS, an anti-Boumedienne organization.
He is one of the few "historic leaders" who have written
books. Boudiaf's book Où va l'Algérie? explains some
of his theoretical disagreements with the Ben Bella regime.

BOUDJENANE, AHMED (1929-1968). Born at Ouled Ali near
Tlemcen, Boudjenane was an activist MTLD member who
had gone into Moroccan exile as early as in 1948. While
in Morocco, he studied at the Karaouiyyin University
(Fes). He joined the FLN's Wilaya V, rising to the rank
of captain in command of the Wilaya's zone II. In 1961
he was demoted to lieutenant for refusing to cross the
Morice line. In the summer of 1962 civil war, he sided
with the Tlemcen group; he was appointed head of the
Second Military Region and was active in the Oran Federation of the FLN. In the spring of 1964, he became director of the Military Academy at Cherchell and he was
named to the General Staff. He died in an automobile
crash in January 1968.

BOUDJERA, RACHID (1941-   ). Born at Ain-Beida, he
has attracted attention particularly because of his use
of the French language. Two novels, written in a raging
and delirious style, according to most reviewers, are
La Répudiation published in 1969 and L'Insolation (1972).
He is generally liked by the establishment of independent
Algeria, even though he writes only in French.

BOUHADJAR, BENHADDOU (1927-   ).   Born near Oran,
Bouhadjar was a farm hand before the 1954 War of National Liberation.   He had been a member of the OS
and he was arrested in 1950 and not released until mid-
1953; the charge was terroristic activities.   He joined
the ALN in 1954 and became commander of Wilaya V in
1960, when he was also promoted to colonel.   During
the civil war of the summer of 1962, he supported Ben
Bella.   He was Ben Bella's chef de cabinet and head of
the Oran federation of the FLN.   He was promoted to
the FLN Central Committee in April 1964.   Since the
June 1965 coup, he has kept his party offices, but has
not had government positions.

BOUHALI (-   ).   The secretary of the PCA after World
War II, he had apparently been to Russia for training in
the KUTV.

BOUKADOUM, MESSAOUD (-   ).   The son of a well-
to-do landowner and bureaucrat, he did university work
in France.   He apparently joined the ENA in 1933, while
still a university student.   He was the GPRA's ambassador to Belgrade between 1960 and 1962 and was offered
the post of ambassador to Dakar after independence.   He
refused this diplomatic assignment taking, instead, a
position with SONATRACH at Skikda.

BOUKHAROUBA, MOHAMMED   see   BOUMEDIENNE

BOUKHORT, BEN ALI (-   ).   An Algerian communist
leader who was promoted to the party's regional secretariat during the mid 1930's in the communist effort to
arabize their Algerian branch.   Boukhort resigned from
the PCA in 1940 in protest against the Russian invasion
of Finland.   As did most of the Algerian communist
leaders promoted within the party in the mid 30's, Boukhort probably studied at the KUTV in Moscow.   Condemned to 20 years of forced labor for anti-French propaganda, he was arrested in 1946 and promptly joined the
UDMA when released, and served as secretary of the
Algiers section until 1950.

BOULHAROUF, TAYEB (-   ).   A native of Annaba,
he joined the PPA during World War II and became a
member of the central committee of the MTLD.   During
the War of National Liberation, he was an organizer with

the FCFLN in France, Switzerland, then Italy. He was
a participant in the Evian talks and has, since independence, been Algeria's ambassador in Rome and in Belgrade.

BOULKEROUA, MOUSSA (-   ). Boulkeroua's father
was a great landed proprietor. He himself went to Paris
for university studies and, while in France, he joined
the ENA. Back in Algeria, he helped organize the Skikda
section of the PPA in 1937. In 1948, he was elected to
the Algerian Assembly, but the colonial authorities annulled his election, arrested him and sent him to prison
for two years. An opponent of Messali Hadj, he quit
politics even before the outbreak of revolution. He was
nevertheless arrested in November 1954. Liberated, he
did not join in the war effort, and he now lives in France.

BOUMAZA, BACHIR (1927-   ). Originally from the region
north of Setif, he is the son of a small merchant. While
working in France, he joined the MTLD and eventually
became secretary to Messali Hadj, the president of that
political party. He joined the FLN and became leader
of the FFFLN soon after the outbreak of the War of
National Liberation. The French authorities arrested
him in December 1958, but he managed to escape in
October 1961. During the civil war of the summer of
1962, he sided with Ben Bella and the Tlemcen group.
By September of that year, he had become Minister for
Labor and Social Affairs in Ben Bella's first government.
He was promoted to Minister for Industry, a more important position, in 1963 and retained that porfolio until
the coup of June 1965. After that coup, he fled Algeria
(in October 1966), helped found the opposition group
known as OCRA, and was expelled from the Revolutionary
Council.

BOUMEDIENNE, HOUARI (b. Mohammed Boukharouba, 1925-
1978). Boumedienne is the war name of a man from
Guelma who joined in the nationalist camp in 1955 and
who, by the end of the War of National Liberation, was
in charge of the Algerian armies in Tunisia and Morocco.
At independence, he joined forces with Ben Bella, led
his troops into several pitched battles with freedom fighters who had spent the war years in Algeria, and then
gained power for the group of political and military elites
who were led by Ben Bella. A member of Ben Bella's

various governments, he eventually led a military coup
(June 1965) against his ally and replaced him as President of the Algerian Republic.

Weak at first because he lacked popular support,
Boumedienne instituted a collegial system of government.
When a military coup against his own leadership failed,
in December 1967, he seized his chance to assert complete control over Algeria.

Rather moderate in both domestic and foreign
affairs, Boumedienne has insisted on state control of all
industry while he also sought and guaranteed foreign in-
vestments. He has maintained close contacts with the
Communist countries while at the same time negotiating
important contracts with the United States, France, and
other Western nations. He died in December 1978 after
a long illness.

BOUMELIK, ABDELKADER (-1956). Nationalist executed
by the French after they had condemned him to death
and all appeals failed.

BOUMENDJEL, AHMAD (1908-   ). A lawyer in Algiers
who was a member of the Union Démocratique du Manifeste Algérien (UDMA), a liberal party led by Ferhat
Abbas. He joined the FLN after the outbreak of November 1, 1954, served as an advisor in the Provisional
Government (GPRA) and was a member of both the Melun
(June 1960) and Evian (May 1961) Conferences between
the French Government and the FLN. After independence,
he was a member of the National Revolutionary Committee, and Minister of Reconstruction, Work and Transport
(1962-1964). In 1964, he was eased out of office in Ben
Bella's attempt to gain uncontested power.

BOUSSAHA, MABROUKA (1944-   ). Born at Tiaret, she
represents the new wave of Algerian poets who write in
Arabic and who prefer to leave revolutionary themes behind while writing about love and the search for happiness.

BOUSSELHAM, ABDELKADER (-   ). Director of the
Political Affairs Section of the Algerian Ministry of Foreign Affairs (1979).

BOUSSOUF ABDELHAFID (1926-   ). A native of northern
Constantine province, he apparently joined the PPA when
still very young and became a leader in the OS. He was
daira chief at Skikda, then in Oran province. He sup-

ported Boudiaf at the time of the MTLD split and was
one of the 22 at the June 1954 meeting that prepared the
outbreak of November 1954. He began the war as Ben
M'Hidi's assistant, then became colonel in charge of
Wilaya V (Oran). He was elected to the CNRA (1956),
then to the CCE (1957), before becoming Minister for
General Liaison and Communications (1958). He supported Ferhat Abbas, then Ben Khedda for the presidency
of the Council of Ministers. In 1961, he was in charge
of supplies and armaments. He has not been active in
politics since the FLN crisis of 1962.

BOUTEFLIKA ABDELAZIZ (1937-   ). Bouteflika was born
in Oujda and received his primary education there. He
went on to school at Tlemcen. When the UGEMA called
a general strike in 1956, he quit school and joined the
nationalist underground in Wilaya V. He quickly became
the Wilaya's political officer, then joined the General
Staff of the ALN in 1960. Bouteflika's war name was
Si Abdelkader el-Mali. In 1962, he was a go-between
for the General Staff and Ben Bella, when the latter was
still in prison. He sided with Ben Bella and Boumedienne
in the Algerian civil war that followed the achievement
of independence. As a result, he became Minister for
Youth Sports and Tourism in September 1962, then Foreign Minister in 1963, a position he held until 1979. He is
a member of the FLN's political bureau. It was Ben Bella's
attempt to remove Bouteflika as Foreign Minister that pre-
cipitated the coup of June 1965 through which Boumedienne
took control of Algeria. Presently, he is a Minister
without portfolio and an Advisor to President Bendjedid.

BOYER, PIERRE (1772-1851). French military officer.
Boyer held the rank of lieutenant-general under Napoleon
in 1814. He entered the service of Muhammad Ali in
1824 but left it two years later. He rejoined the French
army and served as commander of a division in Algeria
in 1830. From 1831 to 1833, he was commandant of
the French army in Oran, where his cruelty was particularly noted.

BRAHMIA, BRAHIM (-   ). He became Secretary of
State for Forestry and Afforestation on March 8, 1979.

BRAZZAVILLE CONFERENCE. French senior colonial administrators, responding to a call by General de Gaulle,
met at Brazzaville in the French Congo in January 1944.

The purpose of the Conference was to decide on new policies with respect to French Africa. While the conference
yielded a decision to abolish the indigénat and a recom-
mendation for the administrative decentralization of French
Africa, it also rejected policies that might lead to self-
rule or independence. In general terms, it proposed
reforms in favor of natives in overseas territories. But
these were offered as a reward for the African contribution to the war effort, not as a "national" right.

BRERHI, ABDELHAK (-   ). Minister of Higher Education and Scientific Research (1979).

BROSSARD, MARQUIS DE (1784-1867). French military officer. He participated in the French expedition to Algiers in 1830 and was promoted to brigadier general in
1831. He served as commander of the French army in
Óran in 1837. He was found guilty of misappropriation
of funds in 1838 and sentenced to six months' imprisonment, but the decision was annulled in 1839. He was
acquitted by a council of war that same year and retired
from the service.

BUGEAUD, THOMAS ROBERT, born BUGEAUD DE LA PI-
CONNERIE (October 15, 1784-June 10, 1849). Born of
a noble family of Perigord, Bugeaud could not be admitted to the school for senior officers at Fontainebleau but
in 1804 did enter the ranks of the grenadiers of the guard,
which served as a training ground for junior officers.
He joined the Army of the Rhine and participated in the
German campaign of 1805. In 1808 he joined the Army
of Spain where he distinguished himself at the battles of
Saragossa (1809) and Lerida (1810). In 1811 he was promoted to major, and he became a colonel in 1814 before
his thirtieth birthday. Following his marriage in 1818,
he settled down to the life of a gentleman farmer. He
wrote a number of tracts promoting improved agricultural
techniques. This fame led to his election as deputy of
Dordogne (1931). As a result of the July Revolution, he
was able to return to the army as marshal de camp that
same year. At the time of the expedition to Algiers, he
opposed French occupation. In 1836, Bugeaud was sent
to Algeria to disengage Abd el Qadir from his siege of
the French camp at Tafna River. He dealt the emir a
solid defeat at its tributary, the Sikkak. Bugeaud was
later authorized to negotiate a treaty with Abd al Qadir.
The Treaty of Tafna, signed on May 30, 1837, abandoned

the major part of Algeria to the Emir in exchange for peace. By the time he was appointed gouverneur-général by the Soult-Guizot government in December 1840, he was reconciled to the concept of continuing French occupation. During his administration of Algeria, he maintained full control over the local French bureaucracy. He maintained a constant policy to overcome Abd el Qadir, and he eventually resigned his post in June 1847 partly because he could not obtain permission to pursue the emir into Morocco and because of inroads on his civil authority as a result of the Ordonnance of April 15, 1845. The final blow was rejection of his plan of military colonization. Upon his return to French politics, he was elected president of the Chamber of Deputies in January 1848. Called to command the defense of the regime on February 24, he could not stay the tide. After having his offer of services to the provisional government rejected, he returned to farming. He was elected deputy from Charente-Inférieure in 1848 and again in 1849. He died shortly after being named commander of the army of the Alps.

AL-BUKHARI, HAJJ (1804-   ). Aide to Abd al-Qadir. As Qaid of Mascara from 1832, he controlled the khalifa of that district.

BU-MAGLA (fl. 1850). Leader of the 1851 uprising in Little Kabylia against the French.

BU-MAZA ("The goat man") (fl. 1845). Religious chief and Mahdi of the Dahra and the Warsenis. He led those tribes in their rebellion against the French in 1845. He was finally forced to surrender in April, 1847.

BUREAUX ARABES. An institution during the French colonial period through which the French army maintained control over Muslim populations in those geographic areas not under French civil control. Created in 1841, the bureaux initially attracted young Arabic-speaking French officers, who were paternalistic toward native populations.

BURNOUS. A long, flowing cloak of wool, often symbolizing authority.

BU-ZIAN (fl. 1850). Leader of a revolt at the Zoatcha oasis, which broke out when the French attempted to increase taxes on palms.

CAISSE ALGERIENNE DE CREDIT AGRICOLE MUTUEL. Although this bank was supposed to help all agriculturalists in colonial Algeria, it was in fact heavily oriented toward Europeans for the simple reason that Algerians rarely held mortgageable land titles.

CALIPH (KHALIF). Supreme ruler in Islam, title of successors of the prophet Muhammed.

CANTONNEMENT. Policy favored by the bureaux arabes in the 1850's. It removed the semi-nomadic tribes from large areas of their former holdings and confined them to Arab-Berber reservations. The objective of this policy was to open Algerian lands to Europeanization. The policy was reversed by the senatus-consulte of April 22, 1863, whereby Napoleon III attempted to halt the transfer of Muslim property to Europeans. Unknowingly the reform merely placed the communal lands in private ownership.

CAPSIANS. An ancient people who occupied the area of Algeria as early as 6,000 B.C. They were the first Berber population and adopted neolithic culture.

CASBAH (Kasbah or Qasabah). The citadel or fortified seat of Turkish authority in the Regency of Algiers.

CAVAIGNAC, LOUIS-EUGENE (1802-57). Commandant of French garrison at Tlemcen (1836-37); governor-general of Algeria (1848); chief of the executive (1848).

CHAABANI, MOHAMED (-1964). Chaabani was a Wilaya commander during the War of National Liberation who, as an ANP commander after independence went into opposition to the Ben Bella regime. Although in opposition, he was named to the Political Bureau and Central Committee of the FLN in 1964. Still refusing to obey the central government, he was tried and executed for treason in September 1964.

CHAAMBA. A nomadic Arab group of the Sahara. Besides the Tuaregs, the Chaambas are the most important group of inhabitants in the Algerian Sahara.

CHABOU (alias) see MOULAY, ABDELKADER

CHAFII, ABDELMADJID (-   ). Arabic novelist who published My Friend Told Me in 1954.

CHAMOUQUAT, ISMAIL (-   ). Author of an arabic
    language novel entitled The Sun Shines for Everyone and
    published by SNED, the national publishing and distribu-
    tion company.

CHAOUIS.   Berber inhabitants of the Aurès mountains in
    Southern Constantine province.

CHARTER OF ALGIERS.   Promulgated at the April 1964
    FLN Congress, it was a policy program which attempted
    to define the direction of Algeria's future.   In general,
    this document defined more carefully the objectives of
    the FLN which were first put forth in the Tripoli Char-
    ter of June 1962.   Algeria, this Charter of Algiers an-
    nounced, would follow policies described as based on
    scientific socialism.   Although the FLN would follow
    Marxist principles, Algeria was not Communist; indeed,
    it was strongly attached to Islamic beliefs.   Nevertheless,
    scientific socialism meant ultimate ownership of the means
    of production by the public.   The state would plan all
    that had to do with the economy and would control social
    welfare.   Finally, the working classes would have a mo-
    nopoly of all economic and political power, although that
    monopoly would be controlled by the FLN.   There would
    be direct linkage between the party and the government.
    Thus, for example, it was the FLN which nominated
    Bendjedid for election as the third President of indepen-
    dent Algeria.   The FLN, a one-party system, has cre-
    ated a number of mass organizations (UGTA, UNFA,
    JFLN, UNEA, etc ...) through which it maintains chan-
    nels of communications with the Algerian population.
    But the party itself is an elitist "avant-garde" group
    which in 1964 only had 3 percent of the total population
    in its militant ranks.

CHERCHELL   see   SHARSHAL

CHERFA, MOHAMMED (1914?-1956).   The son of a bachagha
    of Djemaa Saharidji in Kabylia, he was a trained and
    practicing medical doctor.   He was killed by nationalists
    although he was about to be arrested by French authori-
    ties for having given medical assistance to nationalists.
    He had claimed he did so only because of threats.

CHIBANI, SAID (1925-   ).   A member of the Algerian Re-
    formist Ulama Association, he was elected a deputy of
    the first National Assembly after independence.

CHICHANI, BACHIR (-1955).   He was Ben Boulaid's as-
    sociate in the Aurès region after the outbreak of Novem-
    ber 1954.   After Ben Boulaid's arrest in 1955, he tried
    to take over leadership of the Wilaya.   But he was as-
    sassinated on orders of two of his colleagues, Laghrour
    and Adjoul-Adjoul.   As was true of most nationalist lead-
    ers, he had been active in the PPA and had risen in the
    ranks to chief of the Batna daira by 1952.

CHORFA.   Churafe--descendants of the prophet.

CHOUADRIA.   Along with Ouzegane, he was a candidate in
    the 1945 elections for a seat representing the second
    electorate in Constituant Assembly.   He garnered about
    135,000 votes, or 1/5th of the total cast.

CLEMENCEAU REFORMS OF 1919.   As a result of the sac-
    rifices of Algerians during World War I combined with
    a sense of impending serious discontent within Algeria,
    the French left voted in a series of limited reforms to
    the status of Algerian Muslims during the immediate
    postwar years.   In 1919, a law was passed allowing edu-
    cated Algerians to obtain French citizenship provided
    they would abandon personal status under the Muslim
    civil law.   Few Algerians were willing to make this con-
    cession.   Other efforts at reform ended the highly dis-
    criminatory taxes against Muslims, provided them with
    one-quarter of the seats in the Conceils Generaux, and
    allowed Algerian members of Conseils Municipaux to
    vote in mayoral elections.   The decree of March 20,
    1919, put this into effect.

CLUB OF NINE   see   HISTORICAL LEADERS.

COMITE DE COORDINATION ET D'EXECUTION (CCE).
    Executive body of the FLN created in 1956 at the Soum-
    mam Conference to manage the party's affairs between
    meetings of its legislative body, the CNRA.   It was the
    CCE which ordered the urban terrorism which led to
    the Battle of Algiers in 1957.

COMITE INTERMINISTERIEL DES AFFAIRES MUSULMANES
    (CIAM).   Interministerial Committee on Muslim Affairs,
    an organization created in 1919 to help coordinate poli-
    cies toward Muslim subjects.   Having been set up, the
    CIAM was generally ignored thereafter.

COMITE NATIONAL DE LA REVOLUTION ALGERIENNE
(CNRA). This was a body created by the Soummam conference and meant to serve as a parliament for the revolutionary organization. The FLN's ultimate authority
rested in the CNRA. Between meetings of the CNRA,
the CCE (Comité Central Executif) exercised supreme
authority.

COMITE NATIONAL POUR LA DEFENSE DE LA REVOLU-
TION (CNDR). Opposition groups formed in the summer
of 1964 by combining the PRS and FFS. A wave of ar-
rests followed the announcement of the organization of
the CNDR. Among those arrested by the Ben Bella regime were "Liberals" like Ferhat Abbas and Abderrahmane Farès and suspected pro-Khider sympathizers, including Commander Azzedine, and deputies, presumably
protected by parliamentary immunity, Boualem Oussedik,
Brahim Mezhoudi, and others. While Ben Bella survived
the challenge to his authority which the CNDR represented
in the summer of 1964, his position remained shaky.

COMMITTEE OF TWENTY-TWO. Presumably a group of
nationalists who met at the Clos Salambier near Algiers
in June or July 1954 to discuss armed revolution and
whether to organize before or after the outbreak of hostilities. Their leaders were the six internal members
of the club of nine (Boudiaf, Ben Boulaid, Mourad Didouche, Belkacem Krim, Rabah Bitat and Larbi Ben
M'Hidi). Scholars argue about whether the club of nine
or "historical leaders" were the original CRUA, or whether
the twenty-two were the original CRUA.

COMMUNE DE PLEIN EXERCICE. A form of municipal
government introduced into Algeria by the French in
1834 and modelled upon the French "commune," having
an elected mayor and council. In these municipalities,
Muslim Algerians were subjected to local justices of the
peace.

COMMUNES MIXTES. Municipal government under the French
occupation introduced as early as 1868 into those areas
that had formerly been under military occupation. These
were administered by appointed agents of the governor-
general and assisted by commissions. In 1881, the judicial authority formerly held by the justices of the peace
were transferred to appointed French officials who held
broad discretionary powers. These continued until 1928.

COMPANIE NATIONALE ALGERIENNE DE NAVIGATION
(CNAN). Algerian national shipping company which, in
1979, had 71 vessels of various categories. By 1980,
the CNAN was expected to have several additional ships
among which were four general carriers, four grain
ships and three additional tankers. Several tankers are
specifically designed to carry LNG (liquified natural gas).

CONGRES MUSULMAN ALGERIEN (CMA--ALGERIAN MUSLIM
CONGRESS). Short-lived organization created to coordinate the efforts of all Algerian institutions dedicated to
the pursuit of Algerian interest in colonial Algeria. This
congress was a coalition of the PCA, Ulama Association,
Messali Hadj's party and the parties generally reflective
of the opinions of Ferhat Abbas and Dr. Bendjelloul (1936-
1937).

CONSEIL D'ALGERIE. Reform assembly proposed by the
Clemenceau government to represent Muslim Algerians
in Paris.

CONSEIL SUPERIEUR DU GOUVERNEMENT. Assembly during the period of French control over Algeria, established
by a decree of August 23, 1898. It was composed of
high administrative officials and elected and appointed
persons. Of the sixty members, twenty-two were administrators, thirty-one were elected by the Délégations
financières or the conseils généraux, and seven were
appointees of the governor-general. It consisted of only
seven Algerian Muslims, four elected by the Muslim section of the Délégations and three appointed by the governor-
general.

CONSEILS GENERAUX. A parliamentary body at the departmental level of colonial Algeria. After 1855, Algeria
representatives were appointed to these councils, but
they were always in the minority.

CONSEILS MUNICIPAUX. Municipal councils in colonial Algeria. As early as in 1847, Algerians were represented
on these councils, although they were always in a minority and they were generally appointed by French authorities. In contrast, the European settlers on the councils
were elected and were guaranteed a majority of the seats.

CONSTANTINE (KUSTANTINA). A major city of Algeria
located 330 miles east of Algiers. Built on a rocky

plateau marked on the northeast, northwest, and southeast by deep ravines, the city is on a site that serves
as a natural bastion.   Roman writers mention the existence of a town named Cirta, evidently of Carthaginian
origin.   At the time of the Punic wars it was the capital
of Numidia.   The town was seized by the Romans during
the first century B. C.   Emperor Maxentius had Cirta
razed in 311 when it supported the usurper Alexander.
Constantine rebuilt it in 313, and it was renamed in his
honor.   Constantine was captured at the time of the Vandal invasion, but it was returned to the Emperor in 442
by Geiserich.   After the fall of Rome, Constantine became independent until the Byzantines captured it in 533.
It probably fell to Arab conquerors during the seventh
century.   The town was faithful to the Almohads until
the breakup of the Empire when it recognized the authority of the Hafsid Abu Zakariya.   During the fifteenth century the town was under the control of a few strong families.   Not until 1534 did the Turks secure firm control
of the city; and subsequent revolts to Turkish rule erupted
in 1567, 1572, and 1642.   As the beylik of the East
during the sixteenth century, Constantine witnessed a
strengthening of Turkish control.   During the eighteenth
century, it was the object of a major rebuilding program
by the Turkish rulers.   A period of disruption followed,
and seventeen beys ruled during the period from 1792
to 1826.   The last bey of Constantine, Ahmad, was formally deposed by decree of French General Clauzel in
1830; however, the French were unable to enforce it until the siege of 1837.   Due to its intransigence, the town
remained under French martial law until 1848.

CONSTANTINE PLAN.   French effort announced in 1958 as
a non-military means of gaining Algerian support.   As
originally proposed, it encompassed the expenditure of
a billion dollars per year for a period of ten years for
economic and social development.   While many of its
rural programs were failures, it did result in improved
roads, soil conservation programs, hydroelectric plants,
housing construction, and development of some industry.

CORIPPUS (-   ).   Latin poet who was active during
the Vandal period of Algerian history.

COUNCIL OF THE REVOLUTION.   An institution created
after the Boumedienne coup of June 1965 to replace the
National Assembly and the Political Bureau of the FLN.

This council was to function as the "supreme authority of
the Revolution" in an interim required until a new constitution could be elaborated and take effect.

COUP OF JUNE 19, 1965.   On June 19, 1965, a group led
by Boumedienne arrested Ben Bella and, in a bloodless
coup, took over power.   The purpose was to put an end
to Ben Bella's personal rule, to stop his policies which
aimed at exporting Algeria's socialist ideas abroad, and
to place priority instead on Algeria's need for economic
development.   Provoked by Ben Bella's attempts to bypass the Political Bureau, Boumedienne's new government
gave the impression of being one of collegial rule and
the executive government was theoretically the new Council of the Revolution.

CREMIEUX DECREE.   A law of October 24, 1870, whereby
the French government conferred French citizenship upon
many Algerian Jews.   By doing so, it reinforced the
isolation of the Muslims in Algeria.

CRISIS OF SUMMER 1962.   With the achievement of independence, the revolutionary unity of the FLN broke down and
was replaced by factional conflicts for control of the
government.   The struggle for power involved some pitched
battles between internal army units and the external army
coming in from Morocco.   A coalition between Ben Bella
and Boumedienne, commander in chief of these external
forces, finally gained the upper hand and Ben Bella became the President of the new nation.

DAHLA, SAAD (-   ).   Originally from Chellala in the
southern parts of Algiers province, he did his secondary
schooling in Blida.   He joined the PPA and was, for a
time, Messali Hadj's secretary.   Promoted to membership in the central committee of the MTLD, he opposed
his old boss.   Arrested by the French authorities in November 1954, he was liberated in April 1955 and quickly
joined the FLN.   He was elected to the CNRA and to
the CCE in August 1956, but lost his seat on the CCE
in 1957.   He rose gradually within the GPRA, becoming
Minister for Foreign Affairs in 1961.   He was one of the
chief negotiators at Evian and the Algerian ambassador
to Morocco after independence.   He has since taken on
the position of director of Berliet-Algérie.

DANSA, SIMON (fl. early 17th century). Sailor born in Fles-
singue, Holland. He arrived in Marseilles early in the
seventeenth century. Having begun a hearty Mediterranean trade, he moved to Algiers in 1606 and became a
corsair. In three years he captured over 40 Christian
vessels under the title "Captain Devil." For returning
a group of captured Spanish Jesuits to Henri IV, he was
acquitted of his crimes against France and returned to
Marseilles in 1609. The city of Marseilles paid him an
annual salary of 7,000 écus to convoy its ships to Malta.
After 1610, his whereabouts are unknown.

DAR-AL-SULTAN. The region of Algiers governed directly
by the Dey and his diwan.

DAR-EL-BEIDA. Formerly, Maison Blanche near Algiers,
Dar-el-Beida is Algeria's principal airport.

DARQAWA (or DARKAWI). An Islamic Order founded in
northern Morocco in the late eighteenth century by the
Idrisid sharif Mawlay al-Arbi al-Darkawi. The Order
promoted the practice of frequent prayers in its meeting
places. The membership is still concentrated in north
and eastern Morocco and western Algeria. The Order
has been involved occasionally in the politics of the region. Ibn al-Sharif led a rebellion against the Turks in
Oran province from 1803 to 1809. Members of the Order
accused Abd al-Qadir of collusion with the French for
his treaties of Desmichels (1834) and Tafna (1837). In
1864, it called for a jihad against the French. By the
end of the nineteenth century, the Order numbered about
14,500 members in Algeria.

DAWAIR. A group of families attached to a chief. Before
the French conquest, the term applies especially to four
groups attached to the Bey of Oran. Organized as militia,
they lived off the land put at their disposal by the Turks,
drawing spoils from revolting tribes. The tribe split
between Abd al-Qadir and the French during the early
1830's. The assassination of their leader Mustafa b.
Ismail, in 1843 brought to an end their greatest power.

DEBAGHINE, MOHAMMED LAMINE (1917-   ). Medical
doctor born in 1917 at Cherchell. He apparently joined
the PPA in 1939 and, although declaring himself against
the Nazis, he refused service in the French army during
World War II. He was a deputy in the French National

Assembly from 1946 to 1951, was kicked out of Messali
Hadj's party in 1949, and was asked, in 1954, to lead
the insurrection. He refused. When he was later appointed chief of the external delegation, Ben Bella and
Boudiaf both refused to recognize his authority. He
served on the CNRA (1956) and CCE (1957) but was eased
out of positions of authority in 1959. Since independence,
he has practiced medicine at El-Eulma.

DEBECHE, DJEMILA (20th Century). Although born in Setif,
Debeche usually resides in France where she works for
the ORTF, the official French radio and television organization. She is a thoroughly acculturated Algerian who
has written numerous articles on education and on the
social and professional situation faced by Algerian women.
Between 1945 and 1947, she edited L'Action, a literary
and artistic revue directed at women. She has also
published two novels, Leila, jeune fille d'Algérie (1947),
and Aziza (1955) both of which reflect her interest in
women's issues. All of her work is in French.

DECLARATION OF THE SIXTY-ONE. Shortly after the outbreak of the revolution, moderate (non-revolutionary)
Muslim elected officials met and passed a resolution
calling for Algerian autonomy which would allow Algerians to live their own lives. Among the supporters of
this declaration were Ferhat Abbas and Ahmed Francis,
both of whom would soon be forced to abandon the search
for moderate solutions and to join the revolutionaries.

DECREE OF MARCH 20, 1919   see   CLEMENCEAN REFORMS
OF 1919

DELAVIGNETTE REPORT OF 1955. Study made for the
French Economic Council in July 1955 by Robert Delavignette. The Report revealed the significantly unequal distribution of arable land in Algeria between settlers and
Algerian Muslims. Of 15 million acres of arable land,
25,000 Europeans controlled 6,875,000 acres; and 15,000
Muslims possessed 1,875,000 acres. 500,000 Muslim
owners held 6,250,000 acres. Additionally, the Report
demonstrated that the lands held by the settlers were the
most fertile. In terms of industrial conditions, the Report noted a distinct difference in the minimum hourly
industrial wage between Algeria and France.

DELEGATIONS FINANCIERES. French institution imposed on Algeria by decree of August 23, 1898. It consisted of an assembly which performed certain budgetary tasks under the control and direction of European settlers. It served as a settler-dominated check over the governor-generals. Representing interests rather than individuals, it was composed of three sections: twenty-four elected by landholding Europeans, twenty-four elected by Europeans in the cities, and twenty-one Muslims selected in various ways. Normally the three sections met separately and voted separately in a final plenary session. Sessions were not public until 1918, and even then, publication of the minutes was under the control of the governor-general.

DESMICHELS, LOUIS ALEXIS, BARON (1779-1845). French military figure. He commanded the French forces in Oran from 1833 to 1835, negotiating the so-called Desmichels Treaty with Abd al-Qadir in 1834. Desmichels was appointed inspector general of cavalry in 1835, was promoted to lieutenant general the following year and reappointed inspector general of cavalry in 1836.

DESMICHELS TREATY OF 1834. An agreement concluded on February 26, 1834 between the commander of the French forces in Oran, General Desmichels and the Amir Abd Al-Qadir. It recognized the amir's authority in the district of Oran (excluding the cities controlled by the French: Arzew, Mostaganem, and Oran). It also provided the amir with arms to subdue those tribes that rejected his authority over them. Although the treaty was accepted by the French government, it was violated by the French governor-general Marshal Clauzel. The treaty was superseded in 1837 by the Treaty of Tafna.

DEY. European title of the ruler of the Regency of Algiers. The Deys of Algiers were generally elected by fellow Janissary officers. There was a succession of some 30 deys between 1671 and 1830. Nominal vassals of the Ottoman empire, deys in fact exercised virtually absolute power in the regency and they were independent of their suzerains in Constantinople.

DIB, MOHAMMED (1920-   ). Born in Tlemcen, Dib now lives in Paris. A poet and novelist, he has published eight novels, two collections of short stories and two volumes of poems. Three of his novels, La Grande Maison (1952), L'Incendie (1954) and Le Métier à tisser

(1957) are particularly important as mirrors of what was
happening in Algeria just before and during the War of
National Liberation. All of Dib's work is in French and
tends to advocate revolution. His latest collection of
poetry, Feu Beau Feu was published by Seuil in Paris
and re-edited by SNED in 1979. His most recent novels
were La Danse du roi (1968), Dieu en Barbarie (1970)
and Le Maître de chasse (1973).

DIDOUCHE, MOURAD (1922-1955). One of the "historic
leaders," he was the first revolutionary commander in
Constantine region. He was a member of the PPA from
1945 on, a leader in the OS, and an early opponent of
Messali Hadj when the latter dragged his feet about armed
insurrection. Sought by the colonial police from 1950
on, he served as Boudiaf's associate in France where,
before the outbreak of the War of National Liberation,
Boudiaf and Didouche organized Algerian workers in
support of nationalist causes. He was killed in combat
while covering the retreat of an armed group which he
had personally directed (January 1955).

DINAR. The basic monetary unit of the Algerian government
since April 1964. At that time it replaced the French
franc at par value until the French devaluation of 1969
when it maintained its value. Since 1971, the dinar has
been valued at 180 milligrams of gold. The dinar is
further divided into one hundred centimes. Since January 1974, the Algerian government has allowed the value
of the dinar to "float."

DINET, ETIENNE (1861-1929). Although a Frenchman, since
he was born in Paris, he emigrated to southern Algeria
and wished to be an Algerian. He settled in Laghouat,
then in Bou Saada. In 1913, he converted to Islam and
took the name of Nasr-Eddine. With his Algerian friend
and mentor, Sliman Ben Ibrahim, he collaborated on a
number of novels among which were Tableaux de la vie
arabe published in 1904 and Khadra, danseuse des Ouled
Naïl in 1910. Dinet is considered a precursor of Algerian authors who wrote in French (as opposed to French
authors who wrote about Algeria).

DIWAN (also DIVAN). Council in Turkish Algeria that was
usually composed of five high functionaries of Turkish
origin who assisted the Dey in governing the country.

DJAFFAR, INAL (-   ). One of Ben Yahia's collaborators in the Ministry of Information (1966-1971).

EL DJAMAHIR. Post-Independence army newspaper.

DJEBAR, ASSIA (1936-   ). A native of Cherchell and an
Algerian who writes in French, Djebar is particularly
interesting because of her treatment of "women" and of
the "couple," difficult subjects in the Algerian context.
Her novels to date include: La Soif (1957), Les Impa-
tients (1958), Les Enfants du nouveau monde (1962) and
Les Alouettes Naïves (1967). The last two novels are
set in the war years (1954-1962).

EL-DJEZAIRI, EMIR SAID (-   ). Descendant of Abd
al Qadir who, on July 7, 1962 informed the GPRA by
telegram that he renounced all claims to the Algerian
throne but wished to move from Damascus to Algeria as
a simple citizen.

AL-DJILALI, MOHAMMED (-   ). According to Abdallah Rakibi, an Algerian literary critique, Al-Djilali was,
between 1925 and 1940, a pioneer in the production of
novels which he types as didactic tales. Al Djilali wrote
in Arabic.

DJILANI, EMBARKE (-   ). A school teacher from El-
Eulma who was a member of the PPA and of the central
committee of the MTLD. He was treasurer of the MTLD
when the French authorities arrested him in November
1954. Freed from colonial prisons in April 1955, he
joined the FLN and helped create the UGTA. He also
helped organize the FLN Congress of 1964.

AL-DJOUNEIDI, KHALIFA (-   ). Author of Broken
Nests (1972), a novel written in Arabic.

DONATISM. Prominent North African Christian sect that
broke with prevailing church in 312 over the election
of Caecilian as bishop of Carthage. Its believers claimed
that the validity of sacraments required that its ministers
be in a state of sinlessness. They also opposed state
interference in church matters. Their life's goal was
martyrdom following a life of penance. The movement
was named for Donatus, primate of Numidia, who led
opposition to Caecilian's election. In 321 Emperor Constantine granted toleration to the Donatists, but in 347

Emperor Constans exiled the group's leaders to Gaul.
In 412 and 414 strict laws denied them ecclesiastical
and civil rights, but they survived in North Africa until
the Arab invasions.

DOUDOU, ABOULAID (-   ). Author of the Algerian
novel written in Arabic and entitled The Hour Has Rung
(1968). Doudou has also written a play, The Earth
(1968), also in Arabic.

DRAIA, AHMED (1929-   ). A native of Souk Ahras, he
joined the ALN early in the War of National Liberation.
He spent two years in Tunisian prisons for his participation in an anti-GPRA conspiracy. When independence
was achieved, he had been liberated and sent to the area
bordering on Mali to help organize nationalist forces
there. He joined the CNS (Compagnie Nationale de Sécurité) in 1963, and was named director of the presidency's security force in March 1965, then commander
of the CNS. He was close to Boumedienne in spite of
efforts by Ben Bella to draw him away from Boumedienne.
In 1978, Draia was a member of the Council of the Revolution, and he is a member of the Political Bureau of
the FLN named in 1979.

DU-L-FAQAR. Name of one of the prophet Muhammad's
swords and of a mimeographed weekly newspaper edited
by Ibn al-Mansur al-Sanhagi. The first issue appeared
in Algiers on October 5, 1913, was hand written and
was completely devoted to the reformist ideas of Muhammad 'Abduh.

DURAND, JUDA (-1839). He grew up in France and
served as secretary and translator for Husayn Pasha
until 1830. As representative of Abd al-Qadir in Algiers
from 1834 to 1835, he performed various commercial
and diplomatic functions. He participated in the negotiations of the Tafna Treaty (1837).

EBERHARDT, ISABELLE (1877-1904). French author of
Russian birth who married an Algerian officer in the
Spahis (a native corp), Sliman Ehni. She converted to
Islam and idealized Arab culture and Muslim mysticism.
Among her works, all published posthumously, are Notes
de route (1908), Dans l'ombre chaude de l'Islam (1921),

Trimardeur (1922), Mes Journaliers (1923) and Contes
et paysages (1925). Along with Etienne Dinet, she is
considered a precursor of Algerian authors who wrote
in French.

EDITIONS LIBERTE. The press of the PCA.

EDUCATION IN ALGERIA. By 1978, there were 3,000,441
   pupils in primary schools, 678,310 in middle schools
   and 161,888 in secondary and technical schools. The
   Ministry of Education estimated that 89% of all six-year-
   olds were in first grade, and nearly 75% of all children
   of elementary school age were enrolled. (In contrast,
   only 15% of comparable Algerian children were in school
   in 1954, the last "normal" year in the French colonial
   period.) Also in 1978, there were 8,530 primary schools,
   865 middle schools, 162 secondary schools, 20 technical
   and 40 teachers' training institutes. These various institutions were staffed by 84,377 primary school teachers,
   21,900 middle school and 7,736 secondary school teachers.
   Of the 10,000 students who passed the baccalaureat (high
   school leaving--university entrance examination), 9,000
   enrolled in universities. The universities also enrolled
   another 7,650 students from other sources.
        As had been true since independence in 1962, Algeria
   continued, in 1978, to "Arabize" its educational system.
   As a result, 99% of primary school teachers, nearly
   80% of the middle school teachers and 45% of the secondary school teachers were Algerians. Also, practically
   the whole of the primary system was taught in Arabic.
   But success of the policy was less complete at the highest level: in 1978, fewer than 33% of all university students were studying in Arabic. Although this represented
   a rise from only 8% in 1970, little headway had been
   made between 1970 and 1978 with respect to "Arabization"
   in technical and in scientific courses.

EGALITE. Newspaper published in French and presenting
   the views and positions of Ferhat Abbas and his friends.

EHNI, SLIMAN (late 19th, early 20th c.). Algerian officer
   in the Spahis who married Isabelle Eberhardt.

ELECTIONS OF 1948. These were the first elections under
   the new Statute for Algeria which had been devised largely
   on lines set by de Gaulle at the Brazzaville Conference
   during World War II. While the new law was supposed

to reward "colonials" for their participation in the war
against Germany, the elections were so shamefully managed by the Governor General of Algeria that practically
no nationalists were elected. Therefore these elections
marked the end of a possible decolonization through
French constitutional means.

EMIR KHALED see KHALED, BEN HACHEMI

ENTENTE FRANCO-MUSULMANE. Anti-reformist Muslim
Algerian newspaper published in Constantine from 1935
to 1942. Its editor was Muhammed Salah Bendjelloul,
and a prominent contributor was Ferhat Abbas.

L'ESTAFETTE D'ALGER. First French newspaper published
in Algeria. It was printed by a French war correspon-
dent, J. Toussaint Merle, who brought a portable print-
ing press with him in the Expedition of 1830.

ETOILE NORD AFRICAINE (THE NORTH AFRICAN STAR):
ENA. Organization founded in 1925 by Messali Hadj to
defend "the material, moral, and social interests of
North African Muslims." From the beginning the ENA
demanded full independence of all North Africa (including Algeria, Tunisia, and Morocco). The organization
was quickly controlled by Algerians, and other nationali-
ties lost interest in it. The French government formally
dissolved the ENA in 1929, and many of its members
went underground. In 1933, the organization reappeared
and held a general assembly in France which passed
resolutions on the details of independence. In 1934, the
ENA was reorganized under the name of the National
Union of North African Muslims. Messali was again
imprisoned for a year, this time for "reestablishing a
dissolved organization." After being released he fled
to Switzerland. There--under the influence of Chekib
Arslan--he drew away from Communist influence and
became more closely identified with Pan-Arabism. Despite the initial favorable attitude of the Popular Front
Government in allowing him to return to France in 1936,
it dissolved the ENA in January 1937. This time the
organization was succeeded by the PPA (Parti du Peuple
Algérien), a clearly Algerian group.

EULDJ, ALI see KILIJ, ALI

EVIAN AGREEMENTS. FLN-French accords signed on

March 18, 1962 which established a cease-fire in the
War of National Liberation and which defined the conditions of French withdrawal from Algeria and of Algerian
independence.

EXMOUTH EXPEDITION. A naval force brought to Algiers
in August 1816 under the command of British Viscount
Exmouth. In May 1816, two hundred coral fisherman at
Bona under British and French protection were killed.
On August 27, British and Dutch ships bombarded Algiers.
According to the settlement, Dey Omar agreed to abide
by the terms of the Congress of Vienna and the Peace
of Paris, abolished the practice of imprisoning Christian
prisoners, returned ransom payments received during
the year, compensated the British consul for his imprisonment, and made a public apology to the consul. Due to
the disgrace, Omar was strangled by Janissaries in January 1817.

FACI, SAID (-   ). Author of a book written in French
and critical of French policies in Algeria, L'Algérie sous
l'égide de la France (1936).

FALAKI, REDA (1920-   ). Born in Algiers, his real
name is Hadj Hamou. He published one novel, Le Milieu
et la marge, in 1964.

FANON, FRANTZ (1925-1962). Born in Martinique, Frantz
Fanon was educated in Paris and a practicing psychiatrist
who joined the FLN in Algeria and became a leading
spokesman of the theory that mobilization of the people
against a common enemy (colonialism) ends divisions
among dominated peoples and elevates deeds of violence
which become a bond between the men engaged in a common struggle. He is the author of several books including:
A Dying Colonialism (1967), Toward the African Revolution (1970), The Wretched of the Earth (1968) and Black
Skin White Mask (1967). [All dates are those of English
editions.] All these books have been translated from
the French, the language in which Fanon wrote. During
the revolution, he was an editor and contributor of the
nationalist's organ El Moudjahid published underground in
Algiers, then in Rabat and Tunis. Fanon died of leukemia
in 1962.

FAQIH (-   ). Theologian and legal expert.

FAQIR (plural, fuqara). Member of a Sufi order.

FARES, ABDEL RAHMAN (1911-   ). Born in Algiers, he
    eventually graduated from the University of Algiers and
    became a Muslim notary public. He ran for public office
    and served on the Algiers Municipal Council and in the
    Algerian Assembly. He was speaker of the latter body
    (1953-56) and one of the leaders in gaining support for
    the "Declaration of the Sixty One" (1956). A moderate,
    he nevertheless served as an intermediary between the
    French and the FLN (1956-1961) until the French arrested
    him. In 1962, he was President of the Algerian Provi-
    sional Executive Council which facilitated the transition
    of power from colonial to independent Algeria. He es-
    tablished a private legal practice in Algiers in 1962 then
    was arrested for "political reasons" in 1964.

FARES, BEN M'HEL (-   ). Born near Boghari, he
    joined the PPA during World War II. He was a member
    of the MTLD's permanent delegation in France. He be-
    came director of APS, was deputy for Medea in the 1962
    Constituent Assembly, and has served as director for
    press and information in the Ministry for Foreign Affairs.

FARHAT BEN SAID (-1840). Having first led unsuccess-
    ful rebellions against the Turks in Constantine province
    (1820-21, 1822), he was reconciled with them. Farhat
    was dismissed by Ahmad Bey in 1830 and began hostili-
    ties against him which lasted until 1837, when he joined
    efforts with Abd al-Qadir. That same year he was ap-
    pointed first khalifa for the Emir in Ziban and the eastern
    Sahara. After the conquest of Constantine in 1837, he
    allied himself with the French, for which he was captured
    and imprisoned by Abd al-Qadir at Tagdempt.

AL FARUQ. Weekly arabic language journal that first ap-
    peared in Algiers in 1913. It was a reformist publica-
    tion dedicated to Islamic patriotic, educational, moral,
    economic and social reform.

FATWAH. Formal Islamic legal opinion.

FEDERATION DES ELUS MUSULMANS D'ALGERIE. Founded
    in Constantine by Dr. Bendjelloul during the 1920's, this
    party soon acquired branches in Oran and in Algiers

provinces. Its aim was to achieve assimilation for Algerians. Nevertheless, the members were critical of French colonial administration and made numerous demands for reforms that would benefit Algerians. The FEMA had two newspapers that expressed its views, L'Entente and La Voix indigène.

FEDERATION NATIONALE DES TRAVAILLEURS AGRICOLES (FNTA). National Federation of Agricultural Workers which claimed 350,000 members in 1978. It was organized for wage earners in the agricultural sector who were not well represented in the UNPA (National Union of Algerian Peasants) which represented farmers who live from their own production.

FERADJ, COLONEL (-   ). Killed in Wilaya V during fire fight with the French.

FERAOUN, MOULOUD (1913-1962). An Algerian born to the family of a poor Kabyle peasant, Feraoun nevertheless managed to progress through the French school system and to earn a degree at the Bouzareah Normal School (Teachers College). He became one of the most prolific Algerian authors to write in the French language. In all of his books, he tried to demonstrate that "Kabyles were men like other men," and to present to the world the soul of Kabyles. During his life (which was cut short by murders of the extremist settler organization, the OAS), he published three novels, a collection of essays about Kabylia, and a translation of the poems of a fellow Kabyle, Si Mohand. His novels are: Le Fils du pauvre (1950) La Terre et le sang (1953) and Les Chemins qui montent (1957). The essays published in 1954 are entitled Jours de Kabylie. The translation of the poems of Si Mohand appeared in 1960. Three posthumous works are Journal 1955-1962 (1962), Lettres à ses amis (1969) and an unfinished novel, L'Anniversaire (1972).

FERME EXPERIMENTAL D'AFRIQUE. A joint-stock company formed by Clauzel to control 1,000 hectares of land near Maison-Carré, leased at one franc per hectare.

FERROUKHI, MOSTEFA (-1960). A native of Miliana, he joined the PPA in 1942. He received his secondary schooling in the madrasah in Algiers. After World War II, he was a member of the central committee of the MTLD and, in April 1948, he became a delegate in the

Algerian Assembly. Along with most of the MTLD leaders,
he was arrested by the French authorities in November
1954, but released again in April 1955. He then moved
to France and to Tunis in 1957. He was an administrator in the Interior Ministry of the GPRA when named
Ambassador to China. He died in a plane crash near
Kiev while on his way to China.

FERRY REPORT. A report made by a commission of the
French Senate under the chairmanship of Jules Ferry in
1891. Following a trip to Algeria, the commission proposed greater equity of taxes on Muslims, slight increase
in Muslim representation on departmental and municipal
councils, and reforms of local government and courts as
they affected Algerian Muslims. It further recommended
the strengthening of the Governor-General's authority by
abolishing the rattachements. Response to the commission's report was delayed by Ferry's death in 1893, and
none of the immediate reforms proposed was implemented
until later.

FILALI, ABDALLAH (-1957). Born near Collo he lived
mostly in Constantine where he was a painter. He joined
the ENA and was a founding member of the PPA. Activity in this party earned him the attention of French
colonial authorities who arrested him in 1937 and condemned him to a five-year prison terms. Liberated, he
continued his nationalist activity under the name of Mansour. He was condemned to death for his role in the
May 1945 uprising. Avoiding the colonial authorities, he
was a leader of the MTLD Federation in France and,
after 1956, worked in the UGTA and in the MNA. He
was killed in 1957 by an FLN commando. After 1949,
he also used the name of Lekhfif.

FOREIGN DEBT. In 1979, Algeria's foreign debt stood at
$12 billion (US). Algerian leaders and foreign investors
seemed unconcerned, however, and expected this debt to
be managed without difficulty. This expectation was
based on the rising price of oil, and Algeria's exports
of 50 million tons a year expected to last at least 15
years. Income was also expected for even more impres-
sive natural gas resources.

FORGE. A journal devoted to Franco-Algerian and Franco-
Maghribi literature, it was founded in 1946 and ceased
to appear in 1947 after only six issues had appeared.

The editors, Julia, Roblès and Safir were Europeans and Algerians.

FOUDALA, BAHI (-   ). Novelist who writes in Arabic and published In the Heart of the Furnace in 1964.

FRANCIS, AHMED (1911-   ). Born in Algiers, Ahmed Francis was educated in French schools and became a Doctor of Medicine. A member of the UDMA, he joined the FLN during the War of National Liberation and served as Minister of Finance and Economic Affairs in the GPRA (1958-61) and after independence (1962-63). He was a member of the FLN Delegation at the Evian Conference.

FRANCO (SABIR). Informal language of Algiers during the Regency. A combination of Arabic, Spanish, Turkish, Italian, and Provençal.

FRONT DE LIBERATION NATIONALE (FLN). This is the only legal party in independent Algeria. It was founded by the CRUA (Comité Révolutionnaire d'Unité et d'Action) which launched the War of National Liberation. The primary aim in creating the FLN was to gather all nationalists into one organization that would direct the revolution and gain independence for Algeria. In a tract circulated soon after the November 1, 1954 outbreak, the FLN declared its aims to be the restoration of a sovereign Algerian state. All Algerian residents who opted for Algerian citizenship would be citizens with full rights. By 1956, all but a few MNA (Mouvement National Algérien) diehard supporters of Messali Hadj had joined the FLN. Among the members were former supporters of the MTLD, UDMA, Association of Reformist Algerian Ulama and many Communists.
    At the Soummam Congress of August 1956, the FLN declared itself the sole representative of the Algerian nation. It was the FLN that finally represented the nation at the Evian talks through which independence for Algeria was finally achieved in 1962.
    The FLN operates through a Comité de Coordination et d'Execution (CCE) which is an executive body and through the Conseil National de la Révolution Algérienne, a legislature. In 1958, the CCE created the GPRA (Gouvernement Provisoire de la Républic Algérienne) whose first president was Ferhat Abbas.
    The proclamation of independence which followed negotiations between France and the FLN at Evian was

immediately followed by a power struggle among party
leaders, a fight that was won by Ben Bella and Boumedienne. The FLN retained an important role in the Government of the Algerian state through this party's Political Bureau which was created in July 1962. In 1963 all
parties except the FLN were declared illegal.
 The FLN continues as the sole party of Algeria
with a role that is defined in the Constitution. It is
still dedicated to socialism, pan-Arabism and nonalign-
ment. In spite of various attempts to reorganize it and
to breathe life into it, the party remains torn by faction-
alism and has never achieved for itself the position en-
visioned by the Ben Bella government as well as by the
Boumedienne regime. The present leader of the FLN is
Muhammad Cherif Messadia.

FRONT DES FORCES SOCIALISTES (FFS). A clandestine
 opposition organization representing essentially Kabyle
 dissidents and led by Ait Ahmed and commander Mohand
 ou el Hadj. The FFS did manage to keep voting in the
 Kabylia region down in the September 8, 1963 constitutional referendum. But the opposition could not really
 stop Ben Bella's drive for the presidency of the Algerian
 Republic. He was in fact elected on September 15. The
 FFS became ineffective when Mohand ou el Hadj, faced
 with the conflict along the Algeria-Moroccan border, decided to join Ben Bella's regime. Ait Ahmed was captured and condemned to death. But his sentence was
 commuted to life imprisonment. In July 1966, he escaped from prison and went into exile in France where
 he continues to be an opposition leader.

FRONT POPULAIRE. French newspaper published in the
 early 1949s and bought by the Communist Party in 1946.
 Thereafter it was known as Alger Républicain, a newspaper with a circulation of 25,000 and with special interest in Muslim issues that insured it a good readership.

FRONTO (2nd c. A.D.). Born near Cirta (Constantine?), he
 was the preceptor of Marcus Aurelius. Fronto was the
 author of a Latin work entitled Discourses and Elegies.

FULGENCIUS, FABIUS (5-6th c.). Latin mythographer who
 was born in Tebessa.

FUNDUQ. A term of Greek origin orginally describing an

inn where persons and animals could be lodged. The
funduq (funduk) was composed of a courtyard enclosed on
all sides by buildings. During the Middle Ages, funduks
assumed national identities as waystations for merchants
involved in international trade. Later they became more
clearly identified as warehouses for merchant goods from
those nations.

GAETULIANS. An ancient nomadic people who inhabited the
    southern slopes of the Atlas range and the Saharan border-
    lands. As cavalry allies of Jugurtha, they first fought
    Rome 111-106 B.C. After a major defeat by a Roman
    army under the command of Lentulus Cossus in 6 A.D. ,
    they acknowledged Roman control. Afterward, they served
    as auxiliaries in the Roman army.

GAISERIC (also GENSERIC) (389-477). Vandal king of North
    Africa (428-77). He was the son of Godigisebus and a
    slave. After conquering territory in Lusitania, he led
    his army into Africa in 429. Aided by the Berbers and
    the Donatists, he conquered much of Numidia. In 435,
    he entered into the Treaty of Hippo Regius, establishing
    an alliance with the Roman Emperor of the West Valen-
    tinian III. A second treaty in 442 recognized his sover-
    eignty. In 455, when the usurper Maximus murdered
    Valentinian, Gaiseric marched on Rome and sacked it,
    returning to North Africa with Valentinian's widow Eudoxia.
    After an extended period of hostility with the Eastern
    Roman emperors, Gaiseric concluded a treaty of peace
    with that empire in 476 whereby the Vandal Kingdom re-
    ceived its formal recognition.

GARAVINI, CARLO (fl. 1835). Italian merchant. He left
    Modena for Algiers in 1827 to establish his business.
    In 1835 he was appointed consul in Algiers for the United
    States of America. Two years later he agreed to serve
    in a similar capacity for Abd al-Qadir. In 1838 the
    French government withdrew his exequator as U.S. consul.

GELIMER (fl. c. 525). Last Vandal king of North Africa
    (520-34). He rose to power over his brother Hilderic
    with the assistance of the army but refused to acknow-
    ledge Roman Emperor Justinian. Defeated by Justinian's
    armies at the battles of Decimum and Tricamarum in
    533, he fled to the protection of the Berbers. Eventually

captured by the Romans, he was taken to Constantinople.
Shortly afterwards, he received some domains in Galatia,
where he took up residence, still faithful to his Aryan
beliefs.

GHANIYA. Important family of Sanhadja Berbers who attempted
to restore Almoravid rule to the Maghrib during the
twelfth and thirteenth centuries. The name is derived
from an Almoravid princess married to the head of the
family, Ali b. Yusuf. Two of Ali's grandsons, Ali ibn
Ghaniya and Yahya, were involved in campaigns around
Bougie, Constantine, and Algiers. However, their efforts eventually failed under the weight of Almohad forces.

GHAZALI, AHMED ALI (-   ). Member of the Central
Committee (1979).

GHERROUDJ, ABDELKADER (-   ). A distant relative
of Messali Hadj who was a member of the central committee of the PCA in 1947 and after. He joined the
ALN after the outbreak of revolution and even became an
officer.

AL-GHUMARI, MUHAMMAD WALAD (-1835). Chief of
the Angad tribe of southwestern Oran province. Originally an ally of the Turks, he allied himself with Mustafa
ben Ismail. In 1835, he rebelled against the Emir, was
captured, and executed at Mascara.

AL-GOLEA. Saharan oasis visited for the first time by a
European in 1859. A permanent French garrison was stationed there in 1891. It remained the deepest French
station in the Sahara until 1900.

GOUDJIL, SALAH (-   ). Minister of Transportation
(1979).

GOUM. North African form of Arabic KAWM, a body of
armed horsemen. The goum of the Regency of Algiers
obtained their official position in the military from the
Turks. The goums served as an advance guard among
the makhzen tribes in enforcing Turkish rule. Shortly
after the French occupation of Algiers, they extended
the concept to all tribes. These forces served to maintain military security and protect caravans. Being maintained as auxiliary forces, they were segregated from
the regular troops and provided their own supplies.

GOUVERNEMENT GENERAL DES POSSESSIONS FRANÇAISES DANS LE NORD DE L'AFRIQUE. French administration of conquered portions of Algeria that was created on 22 July 1834. At the time, France controlled only Algiers, Oran, Bougie and Bone, and the immediate hinterlands of these cities.

GRINE, BELKACEM (-1954). A companion of Adjoul Adjoul, a rebel chief in the Aurès region during the War of National Liberation. Grine Belkacem was killed during the first month of revolution in 1954.

GROUPE D'ETUDES DES QUESTIONS INDIGENES. Organization formed in the French Chamber of Deputies in 1912 to obtain reforms in the status of Algerian Muslims. Formed under the leadership of Georges Leygues.

GUENDOUZ, NADIA (-   ). Algerian poet who writes in French.

GUENEZ, MAHMOUD (-   ). In 1964, Mahmoud Guenez was put in charge of creating a popular militia. This was an institution Ben Bella wanted as a counterweight to his cabinet colleague's ANP, which was Boumedienne's power base. Clearly, Ben Bella could not have become President of Algeria without Boumedienne's help. Just as clearly, he sought to diminish his ally's power as quickly as possible.

EL-HACHEMI, HAMOUD (-1954). Killed early in the War of National Liberation, El-Hachemi had been a member of the PPA, the OS and the FLN. He was an early partisan of armed rebellion and, along with Salah Maiza and Mostefa Ben Boulaid, he tried to reconcile the Centralists and the Messalists in the MTLD.

EL-HADDAD, CHEIKH (-1874?). A leader of the Kabyle insurrection of 1871 who was condemned to five years in prison in 1873. He died the next year while in an infirmary.

HADDAD, MALEK (1927-   ). Born in Constantine, he went through secondary school in his native city, then attended the University of Aix-en-Provence. After a career as a journalist and free lance writer, he pub-

lished a number of books including two collections of
poetry, Le Malheur en danger (1956) and Ecoute et je
t'appelle (1961) and four novels, La Dernière impression
(1958), Je t'offrirai une gazelle (1959), L'Elève et la
leçon (1960), and Le Quai aux Fleurs ne répond plus
(1961). All of Haddad's works are clearly marked by
the themes of fatherland, exile and commitment. It is
Haddad who once said: "The French language is my
exile." He has not written anything since 1962 when
Algeria achieved independence.

HADJ AHMED (1780-1850).   Last bey of Constantine.   He
was the son of an Algerian mother and a Turkish father.
In 1798, he was named caid El Aoussi. He first served
as caliph to his father the bey, then succeeded him as
bey in 1826. After the fall of the dey of Algiers in
1830, he assumed the title of pasha and only representative of the Sultan. He vied with a French force for the
occupation of Bône in 1832. A succession of French
officers attempted to subvert Ahmed's rule--Rovigo, Clauzel, Damrémont. Bugeaud, commander at Oran, finally
succeeded in negotiating a treaty with Abd-el Qadir at
Tafna. The emir considered Ahmed a Turk rather than
an Algerian and refused to ally his forces with him.
Ahmed refused to negotiate on Damrémont's terms: recognition of French sovereignty, acceptance of a French
garrison at Constantine, and a two million franc per
year indemnity. Damrémont and his successor Valée
undertook a siege of Constantine in October 1837, which
ultimately prevailed. Ahmed finally surrendered in 1848.
After an unpopular period of incarceration, he was granted
a pension and allowed to live out his days with his family.

HADJ ALI, BACIIIR (1923-   ).   Kabyle communist who, in
1945, was a member of the central committee for the
Algiers region of the PCA while he also served on that
party's amnesty committee. In 1946, he was an editor
with Liberté. The next year (1948), he became senior
editor of this party newspaper, he gained a seat on the
Political Bureau of the PCA and served as interim secretary as a replacement for Amar Ouzegane. In 1949,
Bachir Hadj Ali became secretary of the PCA. In 1961,
he published an excellent collection of poems written in
French, entitled Chants pour le onze décembre.

HADJ HAMOU, MOHAMED (-   ).   Hadj Hamou was
Minister for Information in Ben Bella's first cabinet.

An unknown, he was apparently a boyhood friend of Ben Bella's who was included in the government to help counter the influence of Boumedienne and of his entourage.

HADJ OULD OMAR, BENALAH (-   ). An ex-sergeant in the French Army who even earned some military decorations. In 1954, he abandoned his duties as an employee at the Oran city hall to join the ALN. He was apparently Larbi Ben M'Hidi's associate when captured in November 1956.

HADJERES, SADEK (1928-   ). As soon as he joined the PCA in 1950, he was put in charge of communist students. He was promoted to the Central Committee in 1952, founded and directed an intellectual review entitled Progrès in 1953, and was made a member of the Political Bureau in 1954. He was born in Kabylia.

HAJJ. Pilgrimage to Mecca; title of one who has performed such a pilgrimage.

HAMADI, SMAIL (-   ). Secretary General of the Government of President Bendjedid (1979).

HAMIDA, REIS (-1815). Last great corsair captain of the Regency period. Son of a simple tailor, he advanced from cabin boy to reis before gaining command of the corsair fleet. His most famous exploits were aboard the Portekiza, a Portuguese frigate he captured in 1802. Until 1809, the vessel gained renown throughout the Mediterranean. After that period he sailed it boldly into the Atlantic. Hamida's vessel was alone when attacked by a United States squadron in 1815 off the coast of Cape de Gata, and he was killed in the ensuing battle.

HAMMAD, BEN BULUKKIN (11th century). Berber leader, founder of Hammadid dynasty. His father was the Zirid governor of the Maghrib under Fatimid Caliph al-Mu'izz. Upon the death of his father, his brother bestowed upon him the governorship of Ashir. He continued the war against the Zenata, raising the siege of Ashir in 1005. When his suzerain attempted to deprive him of the governorship of Tidjis and Constantine, he rebelled and declared himself a vassal of the Abbasids. The war continued until 1018. The peace treaty led to the division of the Zirid realm--Hammad retained Mila, Tobna, the Zab, Ashir, and lands of the central Maghrib.

HAMMADID. Berber dynasty of the central Maghrib (1014-
1152). Founded by Hammad ben Bulukkin, the dynasty
reached its golden age at the beginning of the twelfth
century under the rule of al-Nasir ben Alennas and al-
Mansur. After becoming suzerain of Algiers, Milyana,
Nigaus, Hamza, and Constantine, al-Nasir attempted to
extend his empire eastward. After his defeat at Sbeitla
in 1064, he regained the offensive and extended his control to the Zab and as far as Wargla. During his reign,
he expanded commercial opportunities for Italian traders
at Bougie and indirectly corresponded with Pope Gregory
VII. His successor, al-Mansur moved the capital to
Bougie. In 1136 the Genoese plundered Bougie. Following this, the Berber tribes rose, and the Almohads invaded central Maghrib. Yahya, the last Hammadid, surrendered to the Almohads in 1152 and died at Salé (1163).

HAMMOUD, RAMDAN (1906-1925). Young Arab poet of Algeria who fought traditionalism and who wrote on the
Turkish revolution and the beginning of Algerian nationalism.

HAMOU, HADJ ABDELKADER (early 20th c.). An Algerian
who wrote in French and used his ability to agitate for
reforms in favor of Algeria. He was the author of Zohra,
la femme du mineur a novel published in 1925, and collaborator with Robert Randau in the 1933 book entitled
Les Compagnons du jardin, which presented a political
dialogue.

IBN AL-HAMRI, MUHAMMAD (-   ). Prosperous merchant of Tlemcen; qaid of Tlemcen (1830); proclaimed
himself pasha in opposition to Abd al-Qadir; fled to Morocco after occupation of Tlemcen by the amir (1833);
reconciled and served as Abd al-Qadir's qaid (1834-37).

HARATIN. Former serfs of the Tuaregs in the Sahara.

HARBI, MOHAMED (-   ). Director of Révolution
Africaine.

HASAN AGHA (-1549). Khalifa of Khair al-Din in Algiers. Born in Sardinia, Hasan was taken prisoner by
Khair al-Din and placed among his eunuchs. When Khair
al-Din was recalled by Turkey (1536), he placed Hasan
in control. Much of Hasan's reign is unknown, but during his administration, Algiers was saved from the attack

by Charles V (1541). In later years, Hasan retired from
public life in disgrace.

HASAN BABA (-1683). As corsair-captain, he took part
in the revolt of 1671 that replaced power of aghas with
deys. When his father-in-law, Hadjdj Muhammad Triki,
fled to Tripoli upon learning of the approaching French
fleet, Hasan Baba seized power (1682). He successfully
repulsed the initial attack by Duquesne's fleet from August 26 to September 12. When Duquesne returned in
1683 to renew the bombardment, Hasan Baba agreed to
negotiate and turned over hostages, among them his rival
Hadjdj Husayn ("Mezzomorto"). When the latter gained
his release he returned to the other captains and led
them to murder Hasan.

HASAN BEY (fl. 1820's). Bey of Oran (1817-31). Prior to
becoming bey, he had served as an army cook and merchant. As bey, he kept Abd al-Qadir and his father under house arrest at Oran from 1824 to 1826. He did
not actively oppose the French occupation of Oran and
quietly moved to Algiers in 1831. From there that same
year he traveled to Alexandria, Egypt, and from there
to Mecca.

HASAN PASHA (HASSAN IBN KHAYR AL-DIN) (-1572).
Beylerbey of Algiers (1546-1551, 1557-1561, 1562-1567).
Son of Khayr al-Din. Organized two campaigns to take
Tlemcen from the influence of the Spanish (1544; 1546).
Upon the death of his father in Istanbul, he was named
beylerbey. Involved in war with Moroccans as a result
of the Saadid Muhammad al-Shaykh's seizure of Tlemcen
(1550). As a result of intrigues, recalled to Turkey in
1551, but sent back in 1557. Returned to defeat the
Moroccans at Tlemcen (1557) and humiliated the Spanish
in battle on August 26, 1558. In an effort to gain Turkish control over Kabylia, attempted to enroll Kabyles
against the Moroccans. He was seized by Janissaries
and returned to Istanbul in chains (1561). Returning to
Algiers the following year, he took part in the Ottoman
siege of Malta (1565). After recall in 1567, took part
in the Battle of Lepanto. On December 2, 1571, he was
again ordered to Algiers, but ill health probably pre-
vented his going.

HASAN VENEZIANO (fl. 16th c.). Corsair-captain. Controlled the ta'ifa of the corsairs from 1582 to 1588, during which time he was actual ruler of Algiers.

HASSANI, MOUSSA (-   ). An officer of Boumedienne's
    General Staff who was appointed to direct the PTT (Poste-
    Télégraph-Téléphone) in Ben Bella's first cabinet.

HASSI MESSAOUD. Algeria's biggest oil field which is com-
    posed of more than 300 wells and which produced about
    three-fifths of Algeria's local revenue in 1972.

HASSI R'MEL. Saharan gas field which produced 140 billion
    cubic feet in 1970, 490 billion cubic feet in 1975 and
    which is expected to produce 9800 million cubic feet of
    dry gas per day by the end of 1980. By 1980, this field
    is also expected to produce 55,000 metric tons of conden-
    sate--as gas derivative used in the petrochemical indus-
    try and a product which fetches a higher price per ton
    than oil--each day. Pipelines are to evacuate all this
    production in three directions: One set of lines will go
    to Arzew in the west, another in Skikda to the north,
    and a third will join a transmediterranean pipeline which
    will carry some 402.5 billion cubic feet per year for
    25 years to Italy. This eastern line will also deliver
    gas in Tunisia.

HILDERIC (463?-533). Vandal king of North Africa (523-
    30). Hilderic spent much of his youth in Constantinople.
    Upon his accession to the throne, he extended religious
    freedom to those Christians that his predecessors had
    persecuted. He also attempted a reconciliation with
    Roman Emperor Justinian. Hilderic was deposed by the
    Vandal army in May 530, and executed by Gelimer, his
    successor.

HIPPO REGIUS see ANNABA

HISTORICAL LEADERS. Name applied to the nine nationalists
    most closely associated with the outbreak of the War of
    National Liberation in November 1954. The group was
    divided into three external members--Ben Bella, Ait
    Ahmed, and Mohammed Khider--who were to supply the
    internal members taking positions of political and mili-
    tary leadership in Algeria itself--Boudiaf, Ben Boulaid,
    Mourad Didouche, Belkacem Krim, Rabah Bitat and Harbi
    Ben M'Hidi.
        There is some argument among scholars about
    the historical leaders or the club of nine, and their im-
    portance in launching the Revolution. Another interpre-
    tation is that the honor should go to the Committee of

twenty-two, that the core of the CRUA was not the club of nine, but the twenty-two.

HISTORICAL RECTIFICATION. This is the name given to the coup d'état which elevated Boumedienne to supreme power and sent Ben Bella to prison. The idea is that Ben Bella had turned the regime into a system typified by a personality cult and away from the revolutionary course of "Algerian Socialism."

HOFFMAN, SLIMANE (-   ). Party official in the FLN and occasional representative of President Bendjedid abroad (1979).

HOGGAR. High mountains of the southern Algerian Sahara.

HOUHOU, REDA (1911-   ). Born near Biskra, he was the son of a pious and traditional family. He joined the Reformist Ulama Association after WWII. In 1956, he was taken hostage by the French authorities in Constantine after the assassination of the police chief.
    Houhou is a novelist and short-story writer who expressed himself in Arabic and whose best known works are With Hakim's Ass (1953), The Inspiring Woman (1954), and Human Types (1955). Earlier, in 1947, he had published a short novel entitled The Beauty from Mecca. He was generally critical of his own society during the colonial period and a sharp observer of the world he lived in.

HUBS (Fr. HABOUS). Inviolable property, the profits of which are committed to religious purposes.

HUNERIC (-484). Vandal king of North Africa (477-84). He was the eldest son of Gaiseric. Sent to the court of the Roman emperor of the West as a hostage, he was married to the daughter of Emperor Valentinian III in 455. During his reign, he led the defense against marauding Berbers and suppressed a revolt in the Aurès.

AL-HUSAYN BEN AL-HUSAYN (-1838). Last dey of Algiers (1010-1030). Born in Izmir, Husayn was serving as tribute collector at the time of the death of dey Ali Khodja. Despite local rebellions during his reign, he was able to establish internal calm by the late 1820's. Yet his troubles largely resulted from his encounters with European governments in which he refused to com-

promise the honor of the Regency.   His expulsion of the
British consul led to the bombardment of Algiers by a
British fleet in June 1824.   The affair of the fly-swatter
with French consul Deval in April 1827 led to a blockade
of the Algerian coast by the French.   As a result of
other conflicts, the expedition of a French armed force
against Algiers was undertaken in 1830.   The dey capitulated on July 5 and left the continent for Italy.   He
eventually settled in Alexandria where he died.

HUSAYN PASHA, HADJIDJI (known as "MEZZOMORTO")
(-1701).   Algerian corsair and dey.   He is supposed
to have been born in Majorca, but he first appears as
a famous corsair as early as 1674.   At the time of the
French bombardment of Algiers (1683) he served as a
hostage from the dey of Algiers to the French.   Upon
his return to Algiers, he led a rebellion against dey
Baba Hasan, had him executed, and succeeded him as
dey.   In 1684 he negotiated a peace with the French.
Hostilities were soon renewed, and the French again
bombarded Algiers in 1688.   This time Husayn responded
by conducting a series of raids along the French coasts
and marauding French shipping.   In 1689, he was appointed Grand Admiral of the Ottoman fleet, but internal
strife caused him to flee Algiers to Tunis before receiving the appointment.   A distinguished period of service in reforming and strenghtening the Turkish fleet
followed.

IBADISM.   An early movement of dissent in North African
Islam.   It is thought to have been an offshoot of the
Kharijite movement.

AL-IBADIYYA (also ABADIYYA, IBADA).   A major Kharidji
sect of southern Algeria (Wargla and Mzab), named for
Abd Allah ben Ibad (or Abad) al-Murri al-Tamimi.   A
shaykh from Basra, Salama ben Said, was the first to
preach Ibadi doctrines in the Maghrib, at Kairawan.
This led to the establishment of a large Ibadi community
in Tripolitania during the succeeding twenty years.   The
Ibadi tribes of Nafusa and Hawwara conquered all of
Tripolitania and occupied al-Kairawan in 758.   Eventually
the Ibadi state extended from Barka to the land of the
Ketama under the imamate of Abu al-Khattab.   However,
this rule was ended by an Abbasid army from Egypt in

the battle of Tawargha (761). The remaining Ibadi forces
fled to Tagdempt where Abd al-Rahman ben Rustam, a
former Ibadi governor of Kairawan, established the new
Ibadi capital. Under this imam's two successors, Ibadism
reached its zenith. By the end of the eighth century, the
imamate of Tagdempt reached from Tlemcen to Tripoli.
The Ibadi state survived until 909 when it was finally
crushed by the armies of Abu Abd Allah al-Shii, who
founded a Fatamid kingdom.

IBN AL-HAJJ A'ISA (-   ). Khalifa of Abd al-Qadir
in West Sahara; dismissed (1839).

IBN BADIS, ABD AL-HAMID B. AL-MUSTAFA B. MAKKI
(1889-April 16, 1940) see BEN BADIS

IBN GHANIYA, ALI (-   ). Ruler of a short-lived Almoravid state in the late twelfth century based on the
Zirid triad of Algiers, Midiyah, and Miliana.

IBN KHALDUN, WALI AL-DIN ABD AL-RAHMAN B. MU-
HAMMAD B. MUHAMMAD B. ALI BAKR MUHAMMAD
B. AL-HASAN (1332-1406). Arabic historian and philos-
opher born at Tunis. The Maranid invasion provided
him with a number of theological and literary instructors
during his early years. In 1349, an attack of Black
Death took his parents, which had a traumatic effect on
his life. Shortly thereafter he left for Fez, where he
became a court functionary. Following an attack on the
area by the amir of Constantine, Ibn Khaldun began a
series of circuitous moves around the area. He returned
to Fez in 1354 as part of the sultan's secretariat. For
his court intrigues, he was imprisoned (1357-1358). With
the death of the sultan, Ibn Khaldun became court poet
of his successor. From 1362 until 1368 he was at the
courts at Granada and Bougie. Moving to Biskra, he
withdrew from politics and attempted to become a man
of letters. Again the effort failed. He moved to Tlemcen in 1375 but shortly thereafter went into refuge in a
fortress near Frenda. There he stayed for four years
and did much reflecting over his ideas. He returned to
Tunis in 1378 to begin a new career as teacher and
scholar. As a result of a conspiracy against him, he
fled to Cairo in 1382. At Cairo he continued his career
as teacher and scholar until his death. He is best known
for two works, his Ibar, or "Universal History," and
his Mukaddima, or "Introduction" to his thought.

IBN NUNA, MUHAMMAD (fl. 1830's).   Prosperous merchant
   of Tlemcen.   He served as qaid of Tlemcen in 1830.
   Proclaiming himself pasha in opposition to Abd al-Qadir
   in 1832, he was forced to flee to Morocco in 1833 when
   the Emir occupied the city.   The following year he submitted to the Emir, who appointed him qaid, a post in
   which he served until 1837.

IBN SMAYA, ABD AL-HALIN (-   ).   A teacher at the
   Algiers madrasah who, in the early years of the 20th
   century helped spread the reformist ideas of the great
   Egyptian thinker, Muhammad 'Abduh.

IBN TACHIFIN, ALI IBN YUSUF (1084-1143).   Son of founder
   of the Almoravid empire; he succeeded his father in
   1106.   His reign was beginning of Almohad movement;
   his troops won many victories in Spain.

IBRAHIM, SLIMAN BEN (d. 1953).   Collaborator and companion of Etienne Dinet, a Frenchman who converted to
   Islam.   With Dinet, Ibrahim published several Algerian
   novels in French among which were Tableaux de la vie
   arabe (1904) and Khadra, danseuse des Ouled Nail (1910).

AL-IBRAHIMI, BACHIR (1889-1965).   Born at Bejaïa in Kabylia, he became a leading companion of Ben Badis and a
   well known orator in the Association of Reformist Algerian Ulama.   He achieved a great reputation as an
   Arabic and Islamic scholar while contributing numerous
   articles to his association's various journals.

IFREN.   Important Berber tribe during the first three hundred years of the Hidjira.   They were the most powerful
   of the Zenata tribes at the time of the Arab conquest,
   and they played a significant role in the Berber revolts
   of the ninth century.   The Ifren continued to control
   Tlemcen until the conquest by the Almoravids, who sys-
   tematically massacred the remnants of the tribe.

AL IHLAS.   "Sincerity," an Arabic newspaper of the anti-
   reformist Association of Algerian Sunnite Ulama   (1932-
   9).

IKDAM, L'.   Small French language newspaper formed in
   1919 when two earlier papers, L'Islam and Le Rachidi
   combined forces.   It was a newspaper that fought, mildly
   at least, for Algerian rights and demands.

IKHWAN (singular, AKH). Members of a Sufi order.

IMALAYEN, FATIMA-ZOHRA see DJEBAR, ASSIA

IMPOTS ARABES. Following a Turkish model, this was a
   direct French tax on the Algerian population. Colonial
   settlers did not pay this tax, and it was not abolished
   until 1919.

INDIGENAT, L'. Civil status of Algerians who had not become naturalized Frenchmen. The indigénat was expressed as a collection of special laws that applied only to
   Muslims in Algeria, not to French citizens in the colony.
   After World War I--and because many Algerians had
   served the French loyally against Germany and even
   against Turkey--Algerians demanded more equal treatment. Perhaps they were also influenced by Woodrow
   Wilson's Fourteen Points. In any case, the indigénat
   was often the focus of demands for change, one of the
   institutions that politically aware Algerians wanted to see
   destroyed. According to the code, for example, Algerians could not move about without an official travel per-
   mit. Non-naturalized Algerians also paid special taxes.
   See ASSIMILATION POLICY.

INDUSTRIALIZATION, LIGHT INDUSTRY. According to Algerian sources, there were only 181 factories in the light
   industry category in Algeria before 1972. These factories employed some 30,000 workers. In 1976, a Ministry
   of Light Industry was created with functions that had
   earlier been the province of the Ministry of Industry and
   Energy. The objective of the new ministry was to de-
   velop light industry as a source for added employment
   and to further coordinate national development.

INTERMINISTERIAL COMMITTEE OF WAR. The first GPRA
   was reorganized at the Tripoli meeting of January 1961.
   The government remained that appointed in September
   1958 with the following changes: Krim became Foreign
   Minister and Krim, Boussouf and Bentobbal constituted
   the Interministerial Committee of War which was in
   charge of coordinating anything that had to do with the
   pursuit of military effort in Algeria and of getting supplies to the internal leaders. This committee was eliminated at the August 1961 Tripoli meeting.

IRATEN. A tribe of Great Kabylia. Throughout the Turkish

period, they continued to be independent until subdued
by the French in 1857.   They revolted unsuccessfully in
1871.

AL-ISLAH (meaning "THE REFORMATION").   Reformist Muslim Algerian journal published in Biskra from 1927 to
1930 and again in 1940.   Its director was Tayyib Uqbi
(Tayeb El Oqbi).   Though poorly funded and appearing
erratically, it encouraged successor journals and generally reflected the opinion of the Algerian Reformist
Ulama.

ISLAM.   State religion of Algeria since the National Charter
of 1976.   By the middle of the seventh century, the first
waves of Arab penetration of the area of Algeria began.
Within a century Islamization was nearly complete.
Throughout the period of French occupation, Islamic religious leaders provided a source of anti-French turbu-
lence.   The fact that devout Muslims could not become
French citizens added to the hostility.   Today almost the
entire population is Islamic.

ISLAM, L'.   Small French language newspaper or newsletter
representing Algerian interests and tolerated by the
French authorities even during World War I because it
supported the French war effort.   In 1919, L'Islam joined
forces with a similar publication, Le Rachidi, and became L'Ikdam.   Because of the fairly liberal attitude
of the French government after the war, L'Ikdam became
a more effective voice for Algerian demands.

ISSAD, HASSAN (-   ).   Along with Hadj Ali Abdelkader,
he was a founder of the ENA which was quickly taken
over by Messali Hadj.   Issad had also been active in
leading laborers in various organizations created by the
PCF and the CGTU.

LA JEUNE MEDITERRANNEE.   Short-lived periodical founded
in May 1937 as a house organ for the "Maison de la culture d'Alger," a Communist discussion group.   Albert
Camus edited La Jeune Méditerrannée shortly before
he resigned from the PCA.

JIHAD.   A holy war waged as a religious duty.

AL-JILALI, ABDERRAHMAN (1906-   ). Algerian historian
   who wrote in Arabic and tried to revive his countrymen's
   patriotism by recalling the great examples of the past.
   His most important work is the General History of Algeria published in 1954. He was a member of the Association of Reformist Algerian Ulama.

JIZYAH. A capitation tax levied by an Islamic state upon
   infidels.

JONNART, CELESTIN AUGUSTE CHARLES (December 27,
   1857-September 30, 1927). Educated at the Lycée de
   Saint-Omer, Jonnart served in the French chamber as
   a deputy from Pas-de-Calais (1889-1914). He was head
   of the Tirman cabinet and governor-general of Algeria
   from 1882 to 1885. He continued as head of the Algerian service to the Minister of the Interior from 1885 to
   1888. He served three terms as governor-general in
   residence (1900-01, 1903-11, 1918). During his second
   term, he encouraged the growth of French-Algerian cultural associations. In 1910, Jonnart was appointed President of the Suez Canal Company. He served in the
   French Senate from 1914 to 1927.

JONNART LAW 1919. This was a reform bill in favor of
   Muslims and intended as a reward for Algerian participation in World War I. It created an electorate of some
   421,000 Algerians who had not opted for French citizenship and who voted in a separate second electorate, the
   first being reserved for European settlers and those few
   Algerians who had become naturalized Frenchmen. Access to the second electoral group was granted to those
   Algerian men who, by virtue of economic position, education, or relatively long service in French institutions,
   had been most affected by the French presence in Algeria.
   Specifically, the second electorate included licensed merchants, school certificate holders, civil employees, landowners and veterans. They could elect their own representatives, but within severely limited bounds: not more
   than one-third of municipal councilmen in local councils
   or one-fourth on lesser councils could be elected by the
   second electorate. Also, there was no change in the
   makeup of that peculiar institution of colonial Algeria,
   the Délégation Financière. In the long run, this law
   was revolutionary because it created a large body of
   Algerians who could vote and who soon became politically
   aware. Then political parties were created to appeal to

these voters, FEMA (Fédération des Elus Musulmans)
and, eventually, the PPA (Parti de Peuple Algérien).

JOURBAL, TAYEB (-   ). Appointed by the CCE to
take control of Wilaya VI after the Soummam Congress
(August 1956).

JUGURTHA (?-104 B.C.). King of Numidia (118-106 B.C.).
He was the illegitimate son of Mastanabal and grandson
of King Massinissa. After his father's death, he was
raised by his uncle Micipsa with his cousin and principal rival, Adherbal. His uncle sent him to command a
Numidian force in Spain under Scipio Africanus Minor in
134 B.C. Upon his uncle's death in 118 B.C., succession controversies led to civil war. Jugurtha gained the
upper hand, and when Adherbal took refuge in the fortress
of Cirta in 112, Jugurtha laid siege and eventually massacred all of the inhabitants, including a number of Italian merchants, which provoked Roman hostility. After
the Roman senate sent an army to Numidia under consul
Bestia, a temporary peace was declared. Shortly thereafter the conflict resumed, and the Roman army suffered
a major defeat at Suthul. A conciliatory peace was concluded by the Romans in 109, which created a furor in
Rome. A new army was sent to Numidia under Quintus
Metellus (109-106). Jugurtha was finally defeated in a
pitched battle on the Muthul River in 106 B.C. He was
later captured in an ambush and sent as a prisoner to
Rome, where he soon died under mysterious circumstances.

KABYLES. Berber people inhabiting the mountainous regions
east of Algiers and west of Sétif from the Mediterranean
Sea to the southern slopes of the Djurdjura highlands.
There is also a large Kabyle population in Algiers. In
Kabylia itself, most are agriculturalists, although the
population pressure on the land has forced many Kabyles
into temporary migration to where jobs and incomes are
available, primarily Algiers and France.
    Generally, Kabyle villages are administered by a
jama'ah which is an assembly of adult males. In the
jama'ah, decisions are reached by consensus. Kabyles
rule themselves according to their own set of customary
laws which deal with property, persons, crimes, and
behavior. Although not "arabized," Kabyles are Muslims so they are also affected by Islamic Law.

Practically all Kabyle villages are divided into competing political groups known as soffs. But because the jama'ahs govern by concensus decisions rather than majority votes, and because the lesser soffs in one village are generally allied to the dominant soff in another nearby village, the potential for violence is generally slight.

Women do not have a direct voice in the public affairs of Kabyle society, which is patrilinear. But within the family circle they can achieve considerable power, particularly if they are blessed with sons. While men spend most of their time outside the home, at work, the jama'ah, cafe, etc., in the company of other men, women stay at home and in other women's preserves such as the baths or the fountains.

Women generally dress in loose and brightly colored cotton garments, wear heavy silver jewelry and cover their heads with silk scarfs. Men wear flowing robes, woolen burnoses and skull caps or chechias.

KABYLIA. Mountainous region of the Tell. The name seems to have arisen from the Arabic word for "tribe," which was used in early writings as a substitute for "Berbers." The term is sometimes used to identify the entire range of Algerian mountains from the coast to Tunisia. Kabylia is divided into several distinct areas, the most prominent of which is Great Kabylia, extending from the Mediterranean on the north to the valley of the Wad Sahel on the east, and the valley of the Wad Buduau on the west. Little is known of the history of Kabylia before the sixteenth century, except a persistent resistance to conquest. Ibn Khaldun notes that the authority of Bougie over the area was nominal. During the Turkish occupation Kabyle political and administrative institutions remained intact. The area was temporarily under French control from 1857 until 1871. Following the collapse of that rebellion, much of the land was sequestered for European colonization.

"KADDURA AL-DJAZAIRI" (ABU ABU ALLAH MUHAMMED BEN SAID) (fl. 17th century). Mufti. Kaddura was of Tunisian origin but moved to Algeria. He is reputed to have been the most learned mufti in the Algeria of his age. He died in Algiers on October 12, 1687.

KADIRIYA. Order of dervishes named after a twelfth-century figure, Abd al-Kadir al-Djilani, head of a school of

Hanbalite law at Baghdad. During the resistance to the
French conquest in the nineteenth century, Abd al-Qadir,
son of a chief of the order, used the religious organization as a base of support.

AL-KAHINA ("the woman soothsayer") (-698 or 702 A. D.).
Name traditionally given to a Berber leader of the Aurès
region. According to Arabic writers, she led the Jerawa
tribe of Jewish Berbers against the Arab invaders.   In
her defeat of Hasan ibn al Numan, she befriended the
prisoner Khalid ben Yazid and later adopted him.   Supposedly, Yazid betrayed her to her enemies, and she
died in combat.

KAID, AHMED (1927-   ).   Kaid, whose war name was
Major Slimane, was born near Tiaret, where he attended
primary school.   He was eventually enrolled in the French
military school at Hussein-Dey, then in the Normal School
in Algiers.   Although he joined the FLN after the start of
the War of National Liberation, his political activism to
that point had been in the moderate UDMA.   He rose to assistant chief of staff of the ALN during the war and also
served on the CNRA.   He sided with the Ben Bella-
Boumedienne group (also known as the Tlemcen group)
in the summer of 1962.   He was elected to the National
Assembly in 1962 and became Minister of Tourism in
1963.   After a public disagreement with Ben Bella, he
resigned from the government in late 1964, he kept his
seat on the Central Committee of the FLN.   After the
Boumedienne coup of June 1965, he served as spokesman
of the Revolutionary Council.   Thereafter, he served as
Minister for Finance until December 1967, at which time
he became head of the FLN.

KASDI, LT. COL MERBAH (-   ).   Member of the
Political Bureau (1979).

KASSIM, MOULOUD (-   ).   Member of the Central
Committee who frequently represented President Bendjedid
abroad.

KATEB, YACINE (1929-   ).   Born in Constantine, he was
expelled from school after the 1945 Setif uprising.   He
went to work as a reporter for Alger-Républicain.   His
most famous literary work is a novel, Nedjma, which
was first published in 1956.   Written in French, this
novel has been translated into several languages.   Kateb

has also published a collection of poems <u>Soliloques</u>, also
in French, which appeared in 1946, and some plays, <u>Le
Cercle des représailles</u> (1959) and <u>La Femme sauvage</u>
(1963).

KELLOU, MOHAMED (-   ). Chairman of the Foreign
Affairs Committee of the National Popular Assembly
(1979).

KESSOUS, MOHAMMED-AZIZ (1903-1965). "Young Algerian"
of the early 1900's and author of <u>La Verité sur le mal-
aise algérien</u> which was published in 1935. It was critical of the French system in Algeria.

KETAMA. One of the great Berber clans. At the time of
the introduction of Islam to the Maghrib, it occupied all
the land between the Aurès and the Mediterranean. The
empire of the Fatimids was established with the assistance of the clan. After the exit of al-Muizz, remaining
members of the clan fell under the control of local rulers.
Due to their identification with the Ismaili sect, they
became a constant object of harrassment. By the late
nineteenth century, they had practically disappeared.

KHADIR, IDRISS. Author of <u>Basic Elements of Philosophy</u>,
a secondary school textbook on the Philosophical systems
of the Western and Muslim Worlds published by SNED in
1979.

KHALDI, ABDELAZIZ (1917-1972). Author of <u>Le Problème
algérien devant la conscience démocratique</u> which was
published in 1946 and attempted to secure reform in favor
of Algerians from the French government of Algeria.

KHALED BEN EL-HACHEMI (also spelled KHALID) (February
20, 1875-January 1936?). "Emir Khaled" is sometimes
considered as "founder of the Algerian nationalist movement." The grandson of emir Abd al-Qadir, he was born
and grew up in Damascus, Syria. His father moved to
Algeria in 1892. Khaled began his French education at
Louis-le-Grand in 1892, then was admitted to St. Cyr
the following year. He began a career in the French
army and by 1908 had been promoted to the rank of captain, highest office an Algerian could attain. He resigned
from the army in 1910 but returned soon after, receiving
the rank of chevalier of the Legion of Honor in 1913.
He served in the army throughout the war. In 1918 he

reportedly led a group of Algerian soldiers that attempted
to meet with President Woodrow Wilson in an attempt to
have the Fourteen Points applied to Algerians. In the
years following World War I, Khaled broke with the Young
Algerian movement, as leader of the non-naturalized fac-
tion, over the issue of abandonment of Muslim custom.
He proposed instead the cessation of foreign immigration
to Algeria, the provision of French citizenship with Muslim status, abolition of the communes mixtes, compulsory
education in both Arabic and French, and equal representation (European/Algerian) in assemblies. On this platform he substantially won in the 1919 municipal elections
in Algiers. His efforts to raise interest in these issues
through his French language journal Ikdam led to his
abrupt departure (exile?) from Algeria in 1923. As war
heated up between French forces and Abd al-Krim, he
moved from Paris to Alexandria. There he was accused
in 1925 of conspiring against the French. As a result
of the charge, he challenged the French consul to a duel
whereupon the French ambassador demanded his extradi-
tion. He is assumed to have returned to Syria where he
reportedly died about January 1936. In 1924, he published a book entitled La Situation des musulmans en
Algérie.

KHALIFA BEN MAHMUD (-1835). Consul for Abd al-
Qadir in Arzew from 1834 to 1835. He was killed in
action at the Battles of Macta.

AL KHALIFA, MOHAMED LAID (1904-1979). Algerian poet
and educator. He received a traditional education, attended the Zitouna in Tunis, and taught in private schools
and in Arabic (not French) colonial schools, of his native
Algeria. In 1966, he was awarded the Union of Algerian
Writers' literary prize. A member of the Association
of Algerian Ulama, he was put under house arrest in
1954 at the outbreak of the War of National Liberation.

KHAMMAR, ABOULQASIM (1931-   ). Born at Biskra he
is a poet who uses free verse in Arabic. His most recent publication in 1967, was entitled Leaves.

KHAMMES. Term used to identify sharecropping labor in
which the worker received one-fifth of the crop (from
the Arabic khammes: "five").

KHAREDJITES. Separatist Islamic sect represented in

Algeria by the M'zabites who inhabit seven cities created
by their ancestors in the Sahara around Ghardaiah.

KHARFI S. (-   ). Author of a study of Algerian poetry
from 1830 on, and entitled "Poetry and National Resistance in Algeria," published in 1979 by SNED.

KHAROUBI, MOHAMED (-   ). Minister of Education
(1979).

AL-KHARRUBI, MUHAMMAD (fl. 1830's). Secretary for
Hasan Bey prior to 1830, he served Abd al-Qadir in the
same capacity from 1833 to 1839. He deserted the Emir
in 1844.

KHATIB, YOUCEF (1932-   ). Born in Orléansville (El
Asam) he was a member of the UGEMA and a second
year medical student when the student union called for
a general strike in 1956. He joined the ALN, served
as a doctor and rose to the position of head of medical
services in Wilaya IV. Promoted to the rank of major
in 1961, and to the rank of colonel in 1962, he took command of the Wilaya and fought against the troops representing Boumedienne and Ben Bella during the civil war
of 1962. Thereafter, he left the army to renew his
medical studies, was a deputy in the National Assembly,
and a member of the Political Bureau of the FLN until
the June coup of 1965 and of the party's Secretariat
thereafter until 1967.

AL KHATTAB, UMAR BEN (d. 661). Second Khalif or successor of the prophet Muhammad. Umar was the supreme ruler of the Muslim community during the early
years of the Arab conquest of the Maghrib. Because
the first victories in North Africa were so difficult,
Umar is said to have coined the phrase "African divides."

KHAYR AL-DIN (also spelled KHAIR AL-DIN, also known as
BARBAROSSA) (c. 1483 [1466?]-July 4, 1546). Most
famous Turkish corsair and beylerbey of Algiers. He
gained renown as a pirate under the command of his
brother Arudj. When his brother undertook an expedition
against Tlemcen, he appointed Khayr as governor of
Algiers. When word of the death of his brother arrived,
Khayr was chosen by his fellow corsairs to succeed.
Finding himself beset by uprisings, he paid homage to
the sultan of Constantinople, Sulim. The sultan placed

upon him the titles of pasha and beylerbey, sent him
2,000 men with artillery and delegated to him authority
to recruit volunteers. Upon the arrival of these forces,
Khayr immediately proceeded to put down a conspiracy
of Algerians, and turn back a Spanish force under Ugo de
Moncade. Unfortunately Khayr was defeated by a Tunisian army in Kabylia, forced to flee to Djidjelli and
abandon Algiers. From his base at Djidjelli, Khayr
began to regain territory. He seized Collo (1521), Bône
(1522), Constantine, and finally reoccupied Algiers in
1529. In 1534 he took revenge against the Tunisians by
plundering Tunis. At the direction of the sultan, Khayr
returned to Constantinople to undertake a naval campaign
against Charles V. He continued to serve the sultan
in the Mediterranean until 1544, when he retured to Constantinople. He is buried in the mosque at Büyük Dere.

KHAYRAH BEN ALI ABU TALIB (fl. 1830's). Only wife of
    Abd al-Qadir from 1823 until 1843.

KHEMISTI, MOHAMED (-1963). Khemisti was secretary
    to A. Fares, leader of the Provisional Executive in
    1962. He was a young student who was a native of Mag-
    hnia, where Ben Bella himself was born, and who helped
    facilitate the transfer of power from the Provisional Ex-
    ecutive to Ben Bella. He was named Foreign Minister
    in Ben Bella's first cabinet. Khemisti was assassinated
    on April 11, 1963.

KHIDER, MOHAMMED BEN YOUSSEF (1912-1967). The son
    of a poor family from Biskra, Khider was born in Al-
    giers and eventually became a bus driver/fare collector.
    He joined the North Africa Star (ENA) then the PPA.
    He campaigned and was elected deputy for Algiers in
    1946, but went into exile in Cairo after his car, with-
    out his knowledge, was used in the OS-organized 1950
    holdup of the Oran post office. A partisan of armed re-
    bellion, he tried to reconcile Messalists and Centralists
    when the MTLD split into two factions. The French
    authorities arrested him on October 20, 1956 and he spent
    the rest of the War of National Liberation in prison. He
    was elected to the CNRA even while in prison and, in
    1962, he supported Ben Bella and became Secretary Gen-
    eral of the FLN. Then he disagreed with Ben Bella
    about the role of the party and of the army in independent
    Algeria. Thereupon, he resigned, but kept some party
    funds which the Algerian state tried hard to recover.
    Finally, Khider was assassinated in Madrid in 1967.

KHOBSI, MOHAMED (-   ). A native of the Ghardaiah
region who served as Minister of Commerce in Ben
Bella's first cabinet. He was considered "reactionary"
by members of the Boumedienne clan and, more generally, a friend of Mohamed Khider.

KILIJ, ALI (c. 1500-1587). Beylerbey of Algiers (1568-
1587). Born in the Calabrian town of Licastelli. Originally a galley slave, he became an Islamic convert. He
served as lieutenant to corsair admiral Torghud Re'is
at battle of Djerba and on expedition to Malta (1565).
From 1565 to 1568, he served as viceroy of Tripoli,
after which he succeeded Salih Pasha to the same post
at Algiers. He extended Algerian control westward and
reached Tunis in 1957. In 1571, he commanded the left
wing of the Ottoman fleet at the Battle of Lepanto. In
recognition of his safe return to Istanbul with a part of
the fleet, he was given the title Pasha. He spent his
remaining years on maritime expeditions and rebuilding
the Turkish fleet. (Also known as Uluj Ali, Euldj Ali,
or Ochialy.)

KIOUANE, ABDERRAHMANE (-   ). A lawyer and
PPA activist, he attained a variety of leadership positions
within the MTLD. Although he worked for Jacques Che-
vallier, the mayor of Algiers when the War of National
Liberation broke out, he was arrested in November
1954 and released in March 1955. After his release,
he was a partisan of internal autonomy, not of independence. This position caused him to be attacked in various FLN tracts. He was slow to join the FLN but was
nevertheless appointed GPRA ambassador to China in
1961. He has not played an important role since independence.

KOULOUGLIS. Term of the regency period used for sons
of the ocak by Maghribi women.

KREA, HENRI (1933-   ). The son of a mixed marriage
(his mother was Algerian, his father European), he was
born in Algiers. Krea is a pseudonym. He published
one novel, Djamal, in 1961, and some plays including
Le Séisme (1958) and Théatre Algérien (1963). But he
has been even more active in poetry. He has lived in
France since Algeria became independent. His best
collection of essays, in terms of Algerian content, may
by La Révolution et la poésie sont une seule et même chose
(1957).

KRIM, BELKACEM (1922-1970). Belkacem Krim was born
near Dra-el-Mizan and began his adult life as an employee of the Mirabeau mixed commune. In 1945 he
joined the PPA as well as the OS. From 1947 on, following the assassination of a forest ranger, he was always on the run from French authorities. He was twice
condemned to death, in absentia, by the French judicial
system (1947 and 1950). In 1954 he became the sixth
internal leader of the CRUA-ALN. He commanded the
Kabylia wilaya. After the Soummam Congress, Krim
opposed Ramdane Abane. He quit Algeria after the Battle of Algiers to join the "external" delegation of the
FLN. During the GPRA years, he served as War Minister, Vice President of the Council of Ministers (1958),
Foreign Minister (1960), and Minister of the Interior (1961).
He was the chief FLN negotiator at Evian and was the chief
opponent of Ben Bella immediately after independence
was achieved (1962). He stayed out of politics from
1963 to 1965 when he was accused of organizing an attempted coup on Boumedienne's life. He was condemned
to death in absentia, this time by the Algerian courts,
and was assassinated in Frankfurt at the end of 1970.

KULUGHI   see KOULOUGLI

KUSAILA BEN LEMZEM AL-AWRABI (KOCEILA) (-689).
Berber chief, who led the Awraba tribe against the Arabs.
At the time of the Arab conquest, he led opposition to
Abu l'Muhadjir, Okba's successor. Kusaila was defeated
at present-day Al-Urit in 674, following which he renounced Christianity and accepted Islam. After gaining
the favor of his conquerors, he turned against them,
killing both Okba and Abu 'l-Muhadjir at Tahuda (682).
Kusaila occupied Kairawan and governed Ifrikiya the following five years. He was eventually defeated and killed
at Mems when the Caliph sent an army against him under
the command of Zubair ben Kais.

LADJOUZI, MOHAMMED TAHAR (-   ). He was active
in the PPA before the events of May 1945 and a member
of the central committee of the MTLD. He spent much
of the war years in prison, then was named prefect for
Sétif in March 1962. He won a seat in the Constituent
Assembly then worked as president of the National Society for Works and Buildings until 1974.

LAGHUAT (AL-AGHWAT). Town in an oasis of southern
Algeria about 250 miles south of Algiers.

LAHOUEL, HOCINE (-   ). Lahouel attended high
school at Skikda and joined the ENA in 1930. He was
an early leader in the PPA, Secretary General of the
MTLD from 1950 to 1951, and the chief Centralist in
the MTLD split. He joined the FLN in 1955 and represented this organization in Indonesia and in Pakistan.
Thereafter he refused all political positions. Since 1965
he has been president of the National Textile Society
and of other similar socialized enterprises.

LAÏD, MOHAMMED (1904-   ). Born at Aïn Beïda near
Constantine, he became the leading poet of the movement represented by the Association of Reformist Algerian Ulama. He wrote on religion and on politics and influenced most of the Algerian Arabic language poets who
followed him. A collection of his poems was published
in Algiers in 1967.

LAKHAL, MOSTEPHA (-   ). ALN Captain implicated
in the 1959 "plot of the colonels."

LAMINE-GUEYE LAW OF 1946. Law passed by the French
assembly in May 1946 granting French citizenship to
inhabitants of all the French overseas territories, thereby
securing equal legal status in Algeria for Algerian Muslims with European colons (settlers).

LAMOUDI, LAMINE (-   ). A member of the Ulama
Association who allowed his name to be placed on a
Communist list in the 1937 municipal elections in Algiers.
He directed the youth movement in the short-lived CMA
(Algerian Muslim Congress).

LAMOURI (-   ). Colonel from eastern sector condemned to death in 1959 for his participation in the 1958
anti-GPRA Plot of the Colonels.

LARBI, BEN REDJEM (-   ). Commander of the Sixth
Military Region (Constantine) during the Ben Bella years.

LAZIA, SMAIL (- 1944). An Algerian Communist leader
who rose to prominence when the PCA decided to "arabize" the party. He was killed in an auto accident in
1944.

LEBJAOUI, MOHAMED (-   ). Lebjaoui was a prosperous middle class Algerian merchant who was also a
friend of Albert Camus. He joined the FLN secretly in
1955, wrote propaganda for the nationalists during the
War of National Liberation and has, since independence,
published two books on that war, Vérites sur la révolution algérienne in 1970 and Bataille d'Alger ou bataille
d'Algérie in 1972. He has since emerged as a leader
in the OCRA.

LEKHIFIF (pseud.) see FILALI, ABDALLAH

LIBERTE. Supposedly a PCA French language newspaper
that was in fact the mouthpiece of the PCF delegation in
Algeria. The only regular "local" editor was Amar Ouzegane.

LITTLE KABYLIA. The area between Sétif and the Mediterranean Sea.

LOFTI, COLONEL (-   ). Killed in Wilaya V during
fire-fight with the French.

LOI CADRE. French enabling act passed by the National
Assembly in June 1956 that created the procedures
through which colonies could opt for internal autonomy.
The act also established universal suffrage and single
electorates in the colonies.

LA LUTTE SOCIALE. Communist newspaper published
in 1932 and after. It was in French and only occasionally carried translations of French articles into Arabic.

LYASSINE, MOHAMED (-   ). Minister for Heavy Industry (1979).

MACTA, DISASTER OF. Battle fought on June 28, 1835
between French forces under general Trézel and Algerian forces under Abd al-Qadir. The column of 2,000
French troops marching toward Arzew was attacked by
a large Arab force from the hills and sustained one-
fourth casualties.

AL MADANI, TAOUFIQ (1899-   ). A leading member of
the Association of Reformist Ulama, and a man rich in

Arabic and Islamic culture, he did his best to help the renaissance of Arabic culture in Algeria. He published in geography and in history, his best known work being Book on Algeria (author's translation) published in 1931. In 1968 he published a book whose title might be translated as The War of Three Hundred Years Between Algeria and Spain. He also published a play in 1950, Hannibal. He was Minister for Habous (Religious Foundations) in Ben Bella's first two governments.

MADRASAH (the place where one studies; the French used MEDERSA). There were three madāris (pl. of madrasah) in Algeria when the French began their conquest of the country in 1830. These three survived into the colonial period when they became the schools which trained students for careers as functionaries of the Islamic cult and courts. These three schools were located in Algiers, Constantine, and Tlemcen. During the colonial period, these schools were carefully supervised by the French.

MAGHRAWA. A sizable confederation of Berber tribes in the Zanata group. They originally led a nomadic existence in the area between the Chelif valley and the mountains of the Madyuna.

MAHSAS, AHMED (1923-   ). Mahsas joined the PPA during World War II, in 1942, and became a member of the party's Central Committee in 1946. He was also a member of the OS and, along with Ben Bella, was imprisoned for his participation in the activities of that clandestine organization. Also with Ben Bella, he escaped from prison in 1952 and then settled in France. For a while he was editor of L'Algérie libre, a position he used to urge MTLD members to follow neither of the two splinter groups, the Centralists or the Messalists. But since he also saw the CRUA as agents of the Centralists, he was not invited to meet with Boudiaf, Ben M'Hidi, Ben Bella, Ben Boulaid, and Didouche at their Bern meeting in the spring of 1954. In fact, Mahsas did not join the revolutionary forces until after the outbreak of the War of National Liberation. He joined the FFFLN, then left France for Cairo in 1955. He opposed the decisions of the Soummam Congress, and spent the last years of the war in Germany. He had been arrested on orders from Ouamrane, but escaped from Tunisia. After independence, he served in various official positions, the most important of which was Minister of

Agriculture and of Agrarian Reform (1963-1966). He
supported the Boumedienne Coup against Ben Bella in
June 1965. In the next year, he went into exile, briefly
joined the OCRA, then dropped that too. He is still
living in France.

MAISON DE LA CULTURE D'ALGER. A PCA club which
organized political discussions, a small theatrical group
and other social, political and cultural activities. The
Maison de la Culture d'Alger sponsored a small periodical, La Jeune Méditerrannée.

MAISON-CARREE MUTINY (January 25, 1941). Perhaps the
first rebellion in the Algerian nationalists' struggle for
independence occurred when 800 Muslim infantry and Spahis mutinied (owing to the discrimination and deprivations
to which they were subjected) and killed their French officers and NCO's. Seizing arms from a nearby armory,
the mutineers fought the French army and police for fifteen days before being suppressed. Leaders of the mutineers, Muslim NCO's, were observed raising the index
fingers of their right hands toward heaven, the Uma Islamic symbol of unity and purity, representing also a
jihad, or holy war, as well as the symbol of Messali
Hadj's nationalist organization.

MAJOR SLIMANE (alias)   see   KAID, AHMED

MAKHZAN. Privileged tribes who collected taxes on behalf
of the government; sometimes, the government itself.
From "storehouse," the modern word magazine was derived from it.

MALEK, REDHA (-   ). Algerian ambassador to Washington who had previously represented his government in
Yugoslavia, France and the Soviet Union. Before going
to Washington in 1979, he served briefly as Minister of
Information and Culture in Algiers.

MAMMERI, MOULOUD (1917-   ). A Kabyle who writes
in French, he is a first-rate novelist and playwright.
As is true of most of his contemporaries who write in
French, he has tried to explain the cultural shock suffered by Algerians in French schools and the growth and
development of Algerian nationalism. His novels are
La Colline oubliée (1952), Le Sommeil du juste (1955)
and L'Opium et le bâton (1965). This third novel is

about the war of national liberation. His plays are Le
Foehn (1962) and Le Banquet (1973). Mammeri has also
published a volume of translated poems attributed to Si
Mohand ou Mhand (1969). A short story, Le Zèbre appeared in 1957.

AL-MANAR. A review devoted to religious (and political)
     questions in North Africa. It was an organ for refor-
     mist ideas of the kind advocated by the Egyptian Muham-
     mad 'Abduh. It pushed, for example, against supersti-
     tions in Maghribi Islam and against maraboutic brother-
     hoods. These were the type of ideas that moved Ibn
     Badis to create the Association of Algerian Muslim
     'Ulama. '

MANIFESTO OF THE ALGERIAN PEOPLE. Proclamation
     of February 10, 1943 concluding that the European and
     the Algerian were distinct "without a common soul. "
     It demanded specific reforms such as the condemnation
     and end of colonialism and of the exploitation of the Al-
     gerian people by France. It called for the right of self-
     determination and a constitution for Algeria guaranteeing
     absolute liberty and equality. The document was signed
     by Ferhat Abbas, Dr. Bendjelloul, and other "conserva-
     tive" leaders. While the document made sweeping de-
     mands, it did not specifically define the relationship
     called for between France and Algeria. The Manifesto
     was presented to the Vichy government on March 31 and
     later to the Allies. A later document, the Additif, was
     much more specific in its terms. It was the first major
     document to speak of a sovereign Algerian nation and an
     Algerian state. Shortly afterward, Algeria was captured
     by de Gaulle and General Catroux, the new governor,
     rejected the document outright.

MANSOUR (pseud.) see FILALI, ABDALLAH

MANSOURA. Archeological site dating from the thirteenth
     century and the emplacement of medieval Tlemcen.

AL-MANSUR, (-1104). Ruler of the Hammadid dynasty.
     He succeeded his father, al-Nasir in 1088 and moved the
     capital to Bougie in an effort to protect it from nomadic
     attacks. Al-Mansur found himself faced with the com-
     bined opposition of the Zenata and the Almoravids. After
     the fall of Ashir, traditional stronghold of his family,
     Al-Mansur raised an army against Tlemcen and defeated

both the Almoravids and the Zenata, whom he drove into
the mountains of Kabylia.

MAOUI, ABDELAZIZ (-   ). Algerian Ambassador to
Washington until the fall of 1979. In 1965, he was Minister of Tourism in Boumedienne's first cabinet (July
1965).

MARABOUTISM. The North African cult of saints.

MARGUERITE AFFAIR. A famous incident in the department
of Oran in the spring of 1901, named after the French
settlement seized. A Muslim preacher named Yacoub
incited his followers to take over the settlement. As a
result, the subprefect was held prisoner, French property
was looted, and a rural policeman and five Europeans
were killed. The incident sparked lively debate on the
floor of the French Chamber of Deputies over its origins.
It was a cause célèbre of the conflicting colonial theories
of assimilation and association. The immediate result
was an extension of disciplinary commissions, the tribunaux répressifs indigènes. For the succeeding decade,
the affair served as public admission that the Algerian
Muslims had been injuriously ignored.

MASCARA. Town located 50 miles southwest of Mostaganem
and sixty miles southeast of Oran. A very ancient town,
it served as a garrison point for both the Almohads and
the Zayanids. Its produce markets were well-known,
and they served as an important source of revenue for
the area. The beylik of the west was located there
from 1701 to 1792, when it was moved to Oran. Thereafter it entered a period of decline.

MASPETIOL REPORT OF 1955. A study of the financial
relationship between Algeria and France issued in June
1955. The report revealed that most Algerian Muslims
had an average income of $45 a year. Only 50,000
Muslims earned as much as $502 per year. Conversely
no European earned less than $240 per year. The min-
uscule graduation of taxes, the report concluded, also
operated to the advantage of the wealthy Europeans.

MASSINISSA (240?-148 B.C.). King of Numidia. He succeeded his father Gala as chief of the Eastern Numidian
Masaesyli c. 208 B.C. His rival, Syphax of Siga, ruler

of the western Numidian Masaesyli, overthrew him with
Carthaginian assistance. Massinissa allied himself with
the Romans, aided Scipio in his conquest of Hannibal and
Syphax in 202 B. C. , and was rewarded with all of Numidia. He established his capital at Cirta and strengthened his kingdom with a formidable army and navy during his reign.

MAURITANIA ("Land of the Mauri [Berbers]"). The ancient
Latin name for an area of North Africa bounded on the
east by Algiers, on the south by the Atlas mountains,
and on the west by the Atlantic Ocean. Little is known
of its history prior to 108 B. C. when Bocchus I arose
as ruler over the tribal chiefs. He gained territory
eastward from the Numidian kingdom which was then at
war with Rome by allying with the Numidians. In 106
B. C. , Bocchus turned to the Romans and thereby secured
Roman recognition of his control as far east as the Chéliff River. Around 80 B. C. the Bogud dynasty appeared,
and by 50 B. C. the kingdom was divided along the Muluc-
cha River, the east under the rule of Bocchus II and the
west of Bogud II. As a result of Bogud's support of
Antony in the Roman civil war, Octavian awarded both
kingdoms to Bocchus. Upon the extinction of the dynasty
in 25 B. C. , Emperor Augustus awarded both kingdoms
to the Numidian prince Juba II. His successor Ptole-
maeus was executed by Caligula in 39 A. C. , and the
two kingdoms became Roman provinces under the titles
Mauritania Tingitana and Mauritania Caesariensis.

The first major uprising of the Kabyles of Mauritania Caesariensis occurred in 259, and the areas east
of Algiers continued to be under the control of local
chieftains. In 289, the Transstagnensis nomads (south
of the Shotts) also rebelled. As a result, Rome largely
abandoned Mauritania Caesariensis west of the Chéliff.
When the Vandals invaded Mauritania in 429, the collapse
of Roman authority was complete.

AL-MAZARI, MUHAMMAD ben ISMAIL (fl. 830's). With
his uncle, he served as agha of the Dawa'ir until 1830.
He continued in that post until 1833, when he submitted
to Abd al-Qadir. Under the Emir, he was agha of the
Dawa'ir and the Zmalah from 1834 to 1835. He became
agha of the Flittahs in 1835. He then collaborated with
the French against Abd al-Qadir and continued to serve
as agha of the Dawa'ire and the Zmalah after his uncle's
death in 1843.

MEDEA. A town sixty miles south of Algiers. It was built
    on the site of the Roman town of Lambdia. During the
    reign of Hasan Khair al-Din, it became capital of the
    beylik of the south. Abd-al-Qadir placed a bey there,
    who was recognized by French authorities under the
    Treaty of the Tafna.

MEDEGHRI, AHMED (1934-1974). Born in Oran, he had be-
    come a school teacher at Saida before the outbreak of
    the Revolution. He quickly took on the duties of assis-
    tant to the director of the FLN delegation in Morocco.
    He rose to the rank of major in the General Staff Com-
    mand Post-West (Morocco) before the end of the war.
    Since independence, he has been prefect for Tlemcen, a
    deputy in the National Assembly, and Minister of the In-
    terior, a position he was forced to resign in July 1964.
    He resigned when Ben Bella ordered prefects to report
    directly to him and thus bypass the Minister of the In-
    terior, Medeghri. He was one of Boumedienne's staun-
    chest supporters, and Medeghri's elimination from the
    government was directly related to the coups of June
    1965 which ousted Ben Bella from the government. He
    got his ministry back after the coup of June 1965. In
    December 1967, he also became Acting Minister for
    Finance.

MEDRACEN (KOBA MADROUS). An ancient mausoleum lo-
    cated about 35 kilometers northeast of Batna. It is
    thought to be the tomb of the Numidian king Micipsa.

MEHEMET 'ALI (-   ). Pasha of Egypt who, according
    to one French plan in 1829-1830, would have conquered
    Algeria. The Sultan in Istanbul and Great Britain opposed
    this plan of action and France decided to conquer Algeria
    herself.

MELAIKA, DJELLOUL (-   ). Vice-President of the
    Algerian National Popular Assembly.

MELLAH, ALI (- 1957). Under the name of Si Cherif,
    he tried to lead Wilaya VI (Sahara). But he was assas-
    sinated on orders of Cherif Bensaïdi who refused to have
    leaders who were not born locally. Earlier, Mellah had
    been a member of the OS, PPA, and CNRA (1956) which
    sent him to Wilaya VI.

MENDJLI, ALI (1922-   ). Born near Skikda, he was a

member of the MTLD until 1954 when he joined the FLN.
He fought in Kabylia and along the Algerian-Tunisian border, where he was in command of ALN units. He was
elected to the CNRA in 1959. A deputy in the National
Assembly, he was elected vice-president of the National
Assembly, a body that did not function regularly. In
the 1964 Political Bureau of the FLN, he was in charge
of parliamentary relations and of ideology.

MERBAH, MOULAY (-   ). A secretary in the native
judicial system of colonial Algeria, Merbah was a native
of Chellala who joined the PPA in 1945. He held various
positions in the MTLD and was always close to Messali
Hadj. Arrested in November 1954 and released in April
1955, he left Algeria and was active in the MNA in
France. Since independence, he has worked as a lawyer
in Medea.

MERCHANT MARINE. In 1979, Algeria's merchant marine
employed 5,250 sailors (including 1,000 officers) and
3,000 non-mobile agents. The merchant marine had 70
ships with a carrying capacity of 1,534,750 tons.

MESSADIA, MOHAMED CHERIF (-   ). Captain implicated in 1959 in the "plot of the colonels." Excused by
the special court appointed to try the plotters, he was
one of several young officers sent to open a southern
front which would operate from Mali and Niger. This
was an attempt by the ALN to get around the Challe-
Morice line (1960). In 1978, he was on the Board of
Directors of the FLN.

MESSALI HADJ (1898-1974). Born in Tlemcen and the son
of a shoemaker, Messali Hadj's youth was influenced by
the Derqawa brotherhood. His real name was Mesli.
He received a certificate from French colonial authorities
for completing primary school. He was drafted into the
French army during World War I and was to spend much
of the rest of his life in exile. He joined the ENA as
soon as it was launched and quickly replaced Hadj Ali
Abdelkader as this organization's leader (1926). In 1927
he attended the Brussels Congress where he met Nehru,
Sukarno, and Ho Chi Minh. While in temporary exile in
Switzerland, he met Shaykh Arslan, an early spokesman
for pan-Islamic and pan-Arabic ideologies. Back in
France, he supported the Popular Front until disagreement
with the Blum government over colonial issues led him

to separate himself and the ENA from the French left.
In the mid-1930's, other Algerian leaders tried to keep
Messali Hadj and his organization out of the Algerian
Muslim Congress.   But Messali Hadj quickly forced more
moderate leaders (Ben Badis, Abbas, Bendjelloul and the
PCA) to become more radical.   As early as 1936, Messali Hadj suggested to Algerians that they should not accept the French connection.   The next year, he created
the PPA to replace the ENA which the Blum government
had abolished.   Because of his radical political views
and activities, Messali Hadj was condemned to 16 years
of hard labor.   He was forced to reside in southern Algeria, then transferred to Brazzaville in Central Africa.
At the end of World War II, he was amnestied, returned
to Algeria, and founded the MTLD to replace the PPA
which, meanwhile, had been outlawed by the French authorities.   "Young hawks" within his party forced the
intransigent nationalist, Messali Hadj, farther and faster
than he wished to go.   The events of November 1954
eclipsed him, and he became even less effective as the
War of National Liberation progressed.   He tried to compete with the FLN by creating the MNA (in late 1954),
but his time had passed.   Messali Hadj was still in exile
in France when he died.   He was buried in his native
Tlemcen in 1974.   He had been the first twentieth-century
Algerian separatist, the most constant and intransigent
nationalist, and perhaps even the father of the idea that
Algeria should be an independent nation, not an autonomous
state within the French system, and not a colony.

MESSIMY, ADOLPHE (January 31, 1869-1935).   Assimilation-
    ist French republican politician and military specialist.
    While in the military, Messimy rose to the rank of cap-
    tain of light cavalry.   He served in the French Chamber
    as a deputy from the department of the Seine.   He was
    a rapporteur for the navy budget in 1903 and for the
    budget of the ministry of war in 1905 and 1906.   During
    the pre-World War I years, he supported full use of
    Algerian troops in the French Army.   However, though
    assimilationist, he continued to endorse Algeria's per-
    manent identity as a colony.   In 1912, Messimy presented
    a report to the Chamber proposing a series of reforms
    of the code de l'indigénat: expansion of the number of
    of Muslim seats in Algerian assemblies and an easier
    naturalization process for Algerians who could demonstrate
    French language proficiency or French professional train-
    ing.   He continued to press for similar reforms through

1914. Messimy returned to military service with the
outbreak of war and served with distinction as a general.

MEZERNA, AHMED (-   ). A member of the PNR
(Parti National Révolutionnaire) Mezerna also belonged
to the ENA from 1932 on. In August 1938, he was made
secretary of the Algiers Federation of the PPA. Repeatedly arrested and condemned by the French colonial
authorities, he nevertheless was a leader in the PPA-
MTLD organization during World War II. He sided with
Messali Hadj in the MTLD split and was in Cairo for
negotiations with the CRUA when the events of November
1, 1954 surprised him. In July 1955, he was arrested
by Egyptian authorities, apparently at the request of the
FLN leaders who did not really trust him.

MEZHOUDI, BRAHIM (-   ). Born and raised near
Tebessa, he was educated in the traditional Quranic
school, then in the madrasah of that city. He continued
his Arabic education at the Zitouna Mosque University
in Tunis, joined the PPA in the 1930's and the FLN
after the outbreak of the War of National Liberation. He
had also been a member of the Algerian Reformist Ulama
Association and after independence, he was a deputy in
the National Assembly.

MICIPSA (-118 B.C.). King of Numidia (148-118). Eldest son of Masinissa, he shared power with his brothers
Mastanbal and Gulusa until overpowering them both. He
furnished the Roman armies in North Africa with grain
and troops, allowing them to trade in his realm. His
illegitimate nephew Jugurtha--whom he adopted--succeeded
him.

AL MILI, MUBARAK (1897-1945). Born in El-Milia in Little Kabylia, he became one of the principal leaders in
the Association of Reformist Algerian Ulama and a national historian of real merit. He wrote in Arabic yet
had a view of history that is thoroughly modern. According to al-Mili, "history is the proof of the existence
of peoples, the book in which is written their power, the
place at which their conscience was resurrected, the
voice of their union, the springboard of their programs."
The title of his most important book, published in 1931,
might be translated as History of Algeria in the Past
and in the Present.

MILIANA. Town sixty miles southwest of Algiers, of im-
    portance for iron ore deposits. Miliana is built on the
    location of the Roman town of Zucchabar. From the
    fifteenth century until the arrival of the Turks, the town
    led almost a completely independent existence. Under
    Turkish rule, it was administered by the Pasha of Al-
    giers. After the French occupation of Algiers, the town
    regained its independence until being occupied in 1834
    by Abd al-Qadir. The French took control of it in 1840.

MINUCIUS, FELIS (2nd-3rd c. A.D.). Originally from Te-
    bessa, he was the author of the Latin Octavius Dialogue.

MOHAMMEDI, SAID (1912-   ). A Kabyle who worked in
    Belgium and in France during World War II, first in
    the French army, then in the army of the Third Reich.
    The Germans parachuted him into Tunisia in 1944. From
    there he proceeded to Tebessa in eastern Algeria where
    French troops captured him. Before being condemned
    to hard labor for life, he apparently tried to become a
    double agent who would serve the French secret service.
    Liberated in 1952, he reemerged as an officer in Wilaya
    III, command of which he took over in 1956. In the
    same year, he was appointed to the CNRA. In 1958 he
    was made chief of the ALN General Staff-East, a post
    he vacated to become a Minister of State in the GPRA.
    He was loyal to Ben Bella and to Boumedienne. He
    was Vice-President in Ben Bella's Second and Third
    Governments. He had been close to power under Boume-
    dienne although he apparently played no role in the June
    1965 coup.

MOKHTARI (-   ). A deputy in the Algerian Assembly
    who, in 1946, spoke against assimilation. He was a
    member of the PCA who was first promoted to member-
    ship in that group's Central Committee, then thrown out
    of the party (1949).

EL MOKRANI, MOHAMED (-   ). Principal leader of
    the Kabyle insurrection of 1870-1871. Other leaders
    were Ben Ali Cherif, Cheikh El-Haddad and Si Aziz.

EL-MOKRANI, MOHAMMED EL HADJ see AL-MUQRANI

MOKRAOUI, MUSTAPHA (-   ). Managing Director of
    SN SEMPAC (Algerian Corporation for Semolina, Flour
    Milling, Pasta and Couscous Industries) in 1979.

MONCADA, HUGO DE (-   ). Viceroy of Sicily; commanded Spanish naval forces in the 1517 expedition
against Algiers.

MONIS PROJECT. Proposal submitted before the French
Chamber of Deputies in 1911. Actually prepared by Jonnart, it called for a renewal of the powers of local Algerian officials in the communes mixtes for seven years
but reduced the extent of their jurisdiction. It rivaled
the Rozet project submitted in 1909. Both proposals
were seen as attacks on the code de l'indigénat.

MORICE LINE. Name given to a barrier erected along the
Tunisian border in 1957 by the French under the direction of the French Defense minister, André Morice. It
was intended to restrict the flow of supplies and troops
from Tunisia to the ALN and also to defend the highway
and rail system from Bône to Tebessa. Set about forty
kilometers from the Tunisian border, it was approximately
450 kilometers in length. It consisted of two rows of
electrified barbed wire on either side of a macadamized
roadway and set off by fields of antipersonnel minefields.
In 1959 the line was doubled in the north from Soux-
Ahras to Cape Roux and in the center in front of the
mine fields. An attempt in 1958 by Amirouche to cross
the line with 1,200 troups from Tunisia failed.

MOSTAGANEM. Coastal town eight miles east of the Chelif.
In the thirteenth century, the town was controlled by
the Zayanid sultans of Tlemcen. Under the Turks it was
considerably strengthened. It was occupied by the French
in 1833.

MOSTEGHANMI, AHLAM (1953-   ). She is a young poet
born in Algiers who writes in Arabic about women suf-
focated by their own society and who, of course, demands
the emancipation of females.

EL MOUDJAHID. Journal of the FLN published in Algiers
until dismantled by the French authorities, then continued
operations from sanctuaries in Rabat and in Tunis. One
of the most important contributors to El Moudjahid from
1954 on was Frantz Fanon who was also the journal's
editor from 1957-1962.

MOULAY, ABDELKADER (1924?-1971). Moulay was born
into a well-to-do family in Oran province, attended

French schools, earned his baccalaureat, then joined the
French army and attended the cavalry school at Bou
Saada. In an 18-year career, he reached the rank of
major in the French army, certainly the highest rank
ever attained by an Algerian. In 1958 he was stationed
in Germany when he and several other officers decided
to desert to the ALN. He made it to Morocco and remained with that army in exile until 1962. After independence, he joined the Ministry of Defense as "chef de
cabinet." Since March 1964 he has also been on the
General Staff, eventually rising to the position of Secretary General of the Ministry of National Defense. He
died in a helicopter accident on April 1, 1971.

MOUMDJI, ZIN EL-ABIDIN (-   ). Algerian consul-
general at Rouen (1974). He joined the Belcourt section
of the PPA and was an officer in the MTLD who did not
follow Messali Hadj blindly when the party split in 1954.
He joined the FLN in 1956, was arrested in 1958 and
not released from French prisons until 1961.

MOUNI, MOHAMMED (-   ). Author of a privately
published novel written in Arabic, The Voice of Passion,
which appeared in Constantine in 1967.

MOURTAD, ABDELMALEK (-   ). Author of a recent
novel, Fire and Light, written in Arabic and published
by the national publishing and distribution company (SNED).
Mourtad also published Blood and Tears, also in Arabic,
as a serial in the journal Al Djoumhouria.

MOUSSAOUI, SADOK (-   ). His war name was Mo-
hieddine. After independence, he was one of Benyahia's
collaborators in the Ministry of Information (1966-1971).

MOUVEMENT DEMOCRATIQUE DE LA REVOLUTION AL-
GERIENNE (MDRA). One of the several anti-Boumedienne
parties organized abroad and usually around prestigious
revolutionary leaders--in this case, Belkacem Krim.
Like most opposition parties formed outside Algeria, the
MDRA has been powerless to shake Boumedienne's hold
on power in Algeria. The MDRA was formed in 1967.

MOUVEMENT POUR LE TRIOMPHE DES LIBERTES DEMO-
CRATIQUES (MTLD). Essentially, this party was organ-
ized by Messali Hadj to continue the work of the PPA
(Parti du Peuple Algérien) after that group had been

outlawed in the French repression following the Sétif
uprising of 1945. The MTLD was itself outlawed in
1954, after the outbreak of revolution, at which time
Messali Hadj organized the MNA (Mouvement National
Algérien) as a competitor with the FLN.

AL-MUBARAK, MUHAMMAD ben ALLAL WALAD SIDI (-
1843). Member of an important family of marabouts
from Kolea. He served as Khalifa for Abd al-Qadir in
Miliana from 1837.

AL-MUBARAK, MUHI AL-DIN BEN AL-SAYYID ALI (-
1837). Member of an important family of marabouts of
Kolea. From 1831 to 1832, he assisted the French occupation forces. From 1835 to 1837, he served as khalifa of Abd al-Qadir in Miliana. He assisted the Emir
in the defeat of Musa.

MUFTI. Jurist of Islamic law.

MUHI AL-DIN, BEN MUSTAFA (1757-1833). Father of Abd
al-Qadir, influential marabout, and chief of the order
of Qadiriyah Sufi in Algeria. He aided the Moroccan
penetration of Oran province from 1830 to 1832, and
served as the Moroccan sultan's khalifa in Tlemcen (1831)
and Oran province (1832). He was influential in the
election of his son as Commander of the Believers (1832).

MUHI AL-DIN, MUHAMMAD SA'ID BEN (fl. 1835). Elder
brother of Abd al-Qadir; marabout. He assisted his
brother on a diplomatic mission to Morocco in 1838.

MUHI AL-DIN, MUSTAFA B. (1810-   ). Younger brother
of Abd al-Qadir; involved in numerous intrigues against
his older brother; left post as qaid of the Flittahs to join
Musa (1835); pardoned and named Khalifa of Medea (1837);
dismissed for incompetence (1837).

AL-MUNTAQID (THE CENSOR). A newsletter founded by Abd
al-Hamid ibn Badis in 1925 to push for reforms in Algerian Islam. The founding of al-Muntaqid is often in-
terpreted as marking the birth of Algerian reformist
movement.

AL-MUQRANI, MUHAMMED BEN ABD AL-SALAM (fl. 1830's,
d. 1853). As an opponent of Ahmad Bey, he turned to
the service of the French in 1831 and attempted to get

the support of the bey of Tunis against Ahmad. He was
imprisoned but escaped following the French occupation
of Cirta (1837). He served as Khalifa for Abd al-Qadir
in Medjana from 1837 to 1839.

MZAB. Plateau area of southern Algeria of about three
thousand square miles. It is marked by a hot and dry
climate.

M'ZABITES. Berber ethnic group living in the M'Zab (around
Ghardaiah) in the central Sahara.

NABI, BELKACEM (-   ). Minister of Energy and
Petrochemical Industries (1979).

NAHDA. Literary renaissance of the nineteenth century in
the Arab world.

NASR-ERRINE see DINET, ETIENNE

NATIONAL REVOLUTIONARY COUNCIL see COUNCIL OF
THE REVOLUTION

NAVAL BATTLE OF MERS-EL KEBIR (or Oran, July 3,
1940). Following the French defeat in June, 1940, a
portion of the French fleet took refuge at the Algerian
port of Mers-el-Kébir, near Oran. On orders of Prime
Minister Winston Churchill and the British War Cabinet,
Admiral Sir James Sommerville, Commander of the Royal
Navy's Task Force H, presented the French commander,
Admiral Gensoul, with an ultimatum: send his Kebir
fleet (2 battle cruisers, 2 battleships, 8 light cruisers,
destroyers, and submarines) to British ports, or sail to
Martinique, or else scuttle it. After agonizing negotiations, compounded by Gensoul sending a garbled and in-
complete summary of the ultimatum to his government,
the French Admiral rejected it, forcing Sommerville to
open fire on the helpless French ships still tied-up side
by side at the docks, damaging some and inflicting some
1400 French casualties. Although the British have con-
sistently rationalized the attack on their former ally
(without even the courtesy of a declaration of war) as
preventing the French fleet from joining the Germans on
the orders of Marshal Pétain's Vichy government, the
hasty attack was unnecessary, according to the French,

since the Axis had already agreed three days before to
leave the fleet in the Mers-el-Kebir port and because
the French had taken adequate measures to keep it out
of the Axis's hands. Churchill, however, needed a vic-
tory, no matter how ruthless, to convince the American
government that he was determined to stay in the war
and deliberately ignored repeated evidence that the fleet
would not collaborate with the Axis.

NAVARRO, PEDRO (-   ). Spanish commander at
Bougie (c.1510). Built the Peñon--the fort dominating
the harbor at Algiers--to enforce provisions of 1510
treaty which contained the Algerian recognition that Fer-
dinand the Catholic was sovereign over areas of Maghrib.

NEDROMA (NADRUMA). Town forty miles southwest of
Tlemcen. As early as the twelfth century, it contained
an important marketplace. During the Almoravid period
it was also a Muslim center of great significance. From
the twelfth through the fifteenth centuries Nedroma was
the country resort of the Abdalwadid dynasty. The Spanish were never able to conquer the town, and Turkish
control over it was unstable. Nedroma did not accept
the rule of Abd al-Qadir until the French posed a greater
threat.

NEKKACHE, MOHAMED (-   ). An Algerian surgeon
who was active in the MTLD before the Revolution and
who served as a medical officer attached to the General
Staff of the ALN during the War of National Liberation.
After independence, he was a member of the FNL'S Central Committee and Political Bureau. He was a Deputy
in the National Assembly, Minister of Health in Ben
Bella's first cabinet (1962), Minister of Social Affairs
in Ben Bella's second cabinet (1963), Minister of Health,
War Veterans and Social Affairs in Ben Bella's third
cabinet (1964), and he apparently retired to private practice after the Boumedienne coup of 1965.

NOUAOURA, AHMED (-   ). Colonel implicated in
1958 ALN Plot of the Colonels. He was condemned to
death.

NUMIDIA. The name under which Algeria was known when
it became a Roman province at the end of the Punic
Wars in 145 B.C.

OCCUPATION RESTREINTE.   Official French policy in Al-
    geria until 1840, whereby the French could only occupy
    the major towns of the Algerian hinterland, and exercise
    control over the remainder through native or Turkish
    rulers.   The policy was formed in 1834.

OCHIALY   see   KILIJ, ALI

L'ODJAQ.   Turkish for home (foyer in French).   In Algeria
    the term was used to refer to small units of Janissaries,
    usually a few dozen men, directed by a oda-bachi and
    officers known as buluk-bachi.   In 1830 there were 424
    odjaq in the regency of Algiers.

OFFICIAL ARAB PRESS.   Arab language journals and news-
    papers produced by the French administration of the Al-
    gerian colony, periodically, between 1830 and 1962.

OKBA BEN NAFI BEN ABD KAIS AL-KURASHI AL-FIHRI
    (-683).   Famous Arab general in the conquest of
    the Maghrib.   He was a maternal nephew of Am ben al-
    As, Arab conqueror of Egypt, who gave him command
    in Ifrikiya (663).   To prepare himself for the coming
    expedition, he founded the stronghold of al-Kairawan
    (670).   The areas he conquered remained dependencies
    of Egypt, and in 675, Okba was replaced by Abu 'l-
    Muhadjir.   The caliph eventually returned Okba to his
    governorship of Ifrikiya in 682.   This time he led armies
    into the Zab and in Tahart, where he was victorious in
    gaining tribute.   However, Okba was not able to consoli-
    date his gains by occupying the countryside.   Leading a
    small force, he was defeated at the battle of Tahuda and
    killed by Berbers under the command of Kusaila.

EL OQBI, TAYEB (1888-196?).   Born near Biskra, he was
    an eloquent, impulsive and polemical public speaker who
    was a member of Ben Badis' Association of Reformist
    Algerian Ulama.   He was suspected of having instigated
    the murder of the Grand Mufti of the Malekite rite in
    Algiers in 1936, and served some time in prison.   El
    Oqbi broke with the Ulama in the mid-1930's.

ORAN (WAHRAN).   Coastal town supposedly founded in the
    tenth century.   It originally served as a base for the
    Umaiyads but quickly fell to the Fatimids.   It served
    as an extensive source of wheat for Spain and prospered

under the Almohads and the Abd al-Wadids. Oran was
captured by Spain in 1509 and held until 1708. It was
officially surrendered to the Dey of Algiers in 1791 and
became the residence of the bey of the west until 1830.

O'REILLY, ALEXANDER (1722?-1794). Spanish general,
born in Ireland of Roman Catholic parents. Entered
Spanish army at early age. In 1757 he joined the Aus-
trian army. In 1759 he entered the French army. As
colonel, he served in the Spanish army against Portugal
(1762) and taught the Spanish army Prussian techniques.
In 1763 he became a general. He was selected to command Spanish expeditions against Algiers (1775), which
provoked much jealousy among Spanish officer corps.
With forty ships of the line and 350 other vessels, and
with 30,000 troops, he carried out a combined land and
sea assault on Algiers which failed. Casualties amounted
to 4,000. He returned to Spain, still in favor with
Charles III, and remained so until Charles's death in
1788, when he fell into disgrace. O'Reilly's expedition
was the last combined land-sea assault on Algiers during
the regency.

ORGANISATION CLANDESTINE DE LA REVOLUTION AL-
GERIENNE (OCRA). Organized by opponents of Boumedienne abroad in April 1966. The OCRA leaders are
intellectuals such as Mohand Ait al Hocine and Mohammed
Lebjaoui. This organization seems to be mildly pro-
Ben Bella and has repeatedly called for a return to constitutional practices and legality.

ORGANISATION DE LA RESISTANCE POPULAIRE (ORP).
The birth of this opposition to the Boumedienne regime
was announced in a tract distributed in Algiers on August
2, 1965. It was composed of Marxist-leaning intellectuals
who had been close advisors of Ben Bella. The two
central figures in the ORP were Mohammed Harbi and
Hocine Zahouane. They were quickly arrested in an
anti-leftist move that also led to the imprisonment of
Bachir Hadj Ali, an important ex-communist leader.
Another leading communist, Amar Ouzegane, was fired
from his position as editor of Révolution Africaine.

ORGANISATION SPECIALE (OS). Paramilitary organization
formed shortly after the passage of the Statute of 1947.
From 1947 until 1950, it accumulated military stores,
provided military training, and prepared plans for the

takeover of Algeria.   To finance these activities, one
group robbed the Oran Post Office in 1948.   In 1950,
however, the French police began uncovering the membership.   The Central Committee on the OS met and agreed
to dissolve.   Yet the organization and the training of the
group proved valuable in the Revolution, and many of
its members became leaders after independence.

OUAMRANE, AMAR (1919-   ).   Ouamrane first attracted
attention in 1945 when he tried to lead a group of Algerian sharpshooters (tirailleurs Algériens) into insurrection.   This would have been in support of the May 1945
PPA uprising at Cherchell.   He went underground in
1947 and, when the MTLD splintered, he at first sided
with Messali Hadj.   After the outbreak of November
1954, he was Krim's assistant, then commanding Colonel
of Wilaya IV.   Between 1956 and 1962, he was a member of all CNRA's.   He eventually broke with Krim and
supported Ben Bella, and was a deputy in the Constituent
Assembly (1962), then retired from public office.

OUARY, MALEK (1916-   ).   A Kabyle who writes in French,
Ouary has always been interested in his ancestors' traditions and in his milieu's songs.   He thus published a
volume of translations from Kabyle, Poéms et chants de
Kabylie (1972).   Earlier, in 1956, he had published a
novel about Kabylia, Le Grain dans la meule.

OU EL-HADJ, MOHAND (1912-   ).   Ou el-Hadj's real
name was Mokrane Beljadj, but his war name, like that
of Boumedienne, has stuck.   Before the revolution, he
had been a landowner and merchant.   He joined the ALN
in late 1955.   By 1958, he had become military assistant
to the commander of Wilaya III.   In January 1959, he
became political assistant and in April of the same year,
commander of the Wilaya.   He was promoted to colonel
in 1960 and remained in command of the Wilaya until
after independence was achieved in 1962.   During the
summer of 1962, he sided with the GPRA and fought
against the troops of the Tlemcen group.   In spite of
this, he remained in command of his men in the Kabylia
region which became the Seventh Military Region.   He
was elected deputy to the National Assembly.   In 1963,
he joined the FFS opposition party, but rallied to the
goverment in October of that year and, by April 1964,
he was named to the Political Bureau.   He joined the
Boumedienne coup against Ben Bella and became a mem-

ber of the FLN secretariat during the summer of 1965.
In 1967, he joined the anti-Boumedienne attempted coup
engineered by Zbiri. Since then, he has had no official
position and, apparently, not much political influence.
He was a kind of folk hero to the people of his native
Kabylia.

OUETTAR, TAHAR (1936-   ). Born near Sedrata, Ouettar
was, for some time, the editor of a small Arabic language journal, Ash Shab ath thagafi. He is the author
of Arabic novels published by the Algerian National Publishing and Distribution Company (SNED). Among his
books are The Ace, Ez Zilzel and The Mule's Wedding.
Another novel, The Palace and the Fisherman was seri-
alized in El Chaab. He has also published some poetry.
His first true novel was Smoke from My Heart (1961).

OULED SIDI CHEIKH. Confederation of maraboutic tribes
of Oran province that was important in the resistance
of the French conquest and which rebelled frequently
after the French had imposed themselves. Their most
important rebellion occurred in 1864.

OU-MHAND, SI MOHAND see SI MOHAND

OUSSEDIK, AMAR (-   ). Oussedik was a member of
the MTLD who quit the party in order to join the PCA
in 1946 (?). He became an editor of Alger Républicain.

OUYAHIA, ABDELKADER (-   ). Journalist who worked
for La Depêche Algérienne and La Depêche Quotidienne
for twenty-one years. In 1956, he was fired for having
had contracts with "rebels" but not turning them in to
the authorities.

OUZEGANE, AMAR (-   ). An Algerian journalist and
statesman whose first political activities were in the
ranks of the PCA. After independence, he served as
Minister of Agriculture and Agrarian Reform (1962-63)
and Minister of State (1963-64). Thereafter he was
editor of La Révolution Africaine and Minister of Tourism (1964-65). He is the author of a book, Lo Moillour
combat.

PARTI DE LA REVOLUTION SOCIALISTE (PRS). An opposition movement formed around Boudiaf. During the summer of 1964, the PRS joined with the remnants of Ait

Ahmed's FFS to form the CNDR. Among the members
of the CNDR, besides Boudiaf and Ait Ahmed, were Ben
Ahmed (Si Moussa), Hassani, and Chaabani--all leaders
who disagreed with Ben Bella. The members of the
CNDR were expelled from the FLN on July 4, 1964.

PARTI DU PEUPLE ALGERIEN. Organized in 1945 after
the Sétif uprising and the French repression that followed,
it was Messali Hadj's party for a short while. As was
true of earlier radical parties, the ENA and the NENA,
it was quickly banned, went underground, and soon had
another legal face in the form of the MTLD (Mouvement
pour le Triomphe des Libertés Démocratiques). The
most radical young hawks in the PPA organized the OS.

PASHA. Ottoman title for the ruler of the Regency of Algiers.

PELLISSIER DE REYNAUD, EDMOND (1798-1857). French
military officer. He started his military service in Algeria in 1830 on the French general staff, and became
chief of the Bureau Arabe in 1834 to the following year.
In 1837 he was appointed director of the Affaires Arabes,
and in 1839 became a member of the Commission Scientifique de l'Algérie. He served as consul at Tangiers
and Tunis from 1842. He was the author of the Annales
algériennes.

EL PEÑON. Formerly, a rocky projection in the harbor of
Algiers. It was occupied as early as 1302 by the Spaniards, who built a fortress there. This fort delayed
Khair-ed-Din's conquest of Algiers until 1529. At that
time the fort was completely destroyed and the rubble
used to construct a jetty connecting the site with the
mainland, thereby creating the port of Darse.

POLITICAL BUREAU. Proposed to the CNRA in Tripoli,
the Political Bureau was to have rules for the CNRA
between meetings of that body. At first, it was to have
been composed of Ben Bella, Ben Allal, Khider, Bitat,
Mohammedi, Ait Ahmed, and Boudiaf. The last two
refused to be members and the other five never received
the required two-thirds vote needed for investiture.
Nevertheless, the Political Bureau was allowed to serve
as arbiter during the crisis of the summer of 1962.
Once in power, Ben Bella tried to rule through this
body rather than through the regular FLN organization,

a practice that quickly led to disagreement with Khider
who eventually resigned from the government and went
into exile with the FLN funds he controlled (Summer
1963).

PORTEURS DE REDINGOTES. Young Algerians, those who
lived like Frenchmen.

PRISCIAN (-). Latin grammarian who was born in
the territory that has become Algeria. He was active
during the Vandal period of North African history.

QADI. Judge who interprets and administers the religious
law of Islam.

QA'ID HAMMU (CAID-HAMOU) (-). Reportedly
helped Emir Khaled draw up a document to be submitted
to President W. Wilson in January 1919. According to
Ibn Badis this document not only explained the situation
of Algerians but also requested an international agency
to direct the affairs of Algeria until a mandate might
be agreed on (see al-Shihab, February 1936, p. 624).

QASIM, AFNAN (-). Author of The Olive Tree
Garden (1966) and of The House of the Three and Other
Tales (1971), Arabic language novels published in Al-
geria.

QUADRIYA. Religious order or brotherhood of which Abd
al-Qadir was the leader.

RACHEDI, AHMED (-). Film director whose "Ali
in the Land of Mirages" was an Algerian entry in the
1979 Cannes Film Festival.

RACHIDI, LE see L'ISLAM and L'IKDAM

RADJEFF, BELKACEM (-). A native of Kabylia,
he emigrated to France in search of work. In May
1933 he became treasurer general of the ENA, was
arrested in 1934, tried, and sent to prison. Released
in June 1936, he continued his activities as an Algerian
nationalist. He refused to side with either the Messalists

or the Centralists in the 1954 MTLD split. Not much
is known about his activities during the War for National
Liberation. Since independence, he has worked in an
institution for war orphans.

RAHAL, MOHAMMED BEN (1856-OCTOBER 6, 1928). Born
at Nedroma of a family noted for its marabouts, he was
noteworthy for receiving his father's permission to attend
the Collège Impérial at Algiers. He replaced his father
as Agha of Trara in 1878 and served that year as a
member of the Algerian delegation at the International
Exposition at Paris. He resigned as caid in 1884 to
expand his scientific studies. He was one of two Muslims consulted by the French senatorial investigative
committee in 1891. In 1912 he was a member of the
Young Algerian delegation received by the French president. He served as a conseiller-général in 1903 and as
a délégué financier in 1920. In later years he discarded
much of his earlier French orientation.

RAHMANIYA. A religious order founded in the eighteenth
century and named for Muhammad ben Abd al-Rahman
al-Gushtuli al-Djurdjuri al-Azhari Abu Kabrain (or Qu-
brayn). A branch of the Khalwatiya, it promised special
privileges in the afterlife to its members. The two
founding zawiya are located in the Djurdjura and near
Algiers. Though the Order was initially non-political,
segments of it became anti-French during the period of
French domination. Its Grand Master Muhammad Amzian
ben al-Haddad proclaimed a jihad against the French on
April 8, 1871. That effort failed; al-Haddad surrendered
to General Saussier the following July, and his zawiya
was closed. By 1900, the Order included about 150,000
members and 170 zawiya.

AL-RAIAT AL-HAMRA. Irregular Communist publication in
French and Arabic that addressed itself to Algerian
workers in France. Copies of this publication were
occasionally smuggled into Algeria itself during the 1930's.

RAIS HAMIDOU (-   ). Algerian privateer who, in
1802, captured a forty-four gun Portuguese frigate with
some 282 men on board. It was a raid that exemplified
the daring of Algerian privateering whose existence was
due more to European inability or unwillingness to do
anything about it than to any other factor. The Algerians
captured some 1500 "Christian" slaves between 1802 and
1815.

RAKIBI, ABDALLAH (-   ). Author of <u>Souls in Revolt</u>, an Arabic language novel published in 1962.

RAMDANE, ABBANE (June 10, 1920-December 1957). Born to a family of modest means at Azouza near Fort National in Kabylia, he served for a time as a secretary in the mixed commune with headquarters at Fort National. He apparently joined the PPA at the end of World War II, gave up his job with the French administration to devote himself full time to party organization, and quickly rose to the position of party leader in the Sétif region. He was arrested in the wake of the French discovery of the OS, although he was apparently not a member of that secret para-military organization. Liberated in January 1955, he once again devoted himself to full-time political activity, this time in the FLN-ALN. He was apparently instrumental in getting members of the UDMA and of the Reformist Ulama to join the Front for National Liberation (1956). He is best known for his role at the Soummam Congress which, under his prodding, adopted a platform and administrative organization that members of the external delegation of the FLN, particularly Ben Bella and Boudiaf, disapproved. He was a member of the CNRA and of the CCE from 1956 until his assassination in December 1957. The exact causes or circumstances of his assassination are not clearly known, but it seems evident that his role at the Soummam Congress and his refusal to abandon his thesis that the internal leadership of the ALN-FLN should dominate the external delegation and the political arm of the nationalist organization should control the military made him very unpopular in several nationalist quarters. He is one of the few so-called "historical leaders" whose memory has enjoyed a good press in the Boumedienne regime.

RANDON COMMISSION. A commission established by decree of May 5, 1869 to study the political organization of Algeria. The commission's report, issued in 1870, proposed neither the end of military institutions nor a federative form of autonomy. The commission was presided over by Marshal Jacques-Louis Randon, a former governor-general of Algeria.

RASHIDIYA. A small Algerian religious order established in the nineteenth century by dissenting members of the Yusufiya Order.

RATTACHEMENTS. System whereby much of the administration of the French government in Algeria was handled,
not by the governor-general, but by ministries in Paris.
Most of these lines of authority to Paris were transferred
to the governor-general by a decree of December 31,
1896.

RAYAH. Tribes dominated by the Makhzan.

RAZEM, AISA (-   ). Director of the self-managed
farm known as "Domaine Autogéré Aomar Bouchaoui"
which, during the colonial era, was the "Domaine de la
Trappe," a 2600 acre farm famed for its vines and
wines.

REFORM ORDINANCES OF DECEMBER, 1943 AND MARCH
7-8, 1944. The chairman of the French Committee of
National Liberation, General de Gaulle, and his Governor
General of Algeria Commissioner of Muslim Affairs,
General Georges Catroux, rejected the Manifesto of the
Algerian people as well as the additif of the Muslim-
European Commission but agreed that a new relationship
was required between the Muslims and colons (settlers)
in Algeria. Although Catroux was appalled by the colons
reactionary and Vichyite attitudes, he feared Farhat
Abbas' Manifesto would subject those same colons to a
Muslim majority. Therefore, he and de Gaulle modified
the 1936 Blum-Violette plan by granting in December
1943, full French citizenship to approximately 60,000
Muslims without requiring them to surrender their status
as Muslims. In March 1944 most male Muslim adults
were granted the right to vote for a separate college
and were permitted to increase their representation in
the conseils-généraux and in municipal colleges to 40%,
a slight increase which did not endanger the colons' majority. The Association of Reformist Ulama, Messali
al Hadj, and Ferhat Abbas rejected these reforms as
insufficient and instead formed the AML. The failure
of de Gaulle's reform effort resulted in the Sétif riots
of May 8, 1945.

LA REPUBLIQUE ALGERIENNE. French language newspaper
of the UDMA. See also AL WATAN.

REVOLUTION ET TRAVAIL. Journal of the UGTA.

REVUE INDIGENE. A Parisian magazine published from 1906

to 1932. Under the editorship of Paul Bourdarie, it became famous for its appeal to the "idée indigène," the
belief that the most serious threat of French colonialism
was its attack on the dignity of the non-European. It
supported Messimy's efforts toward assimilation in Algeria.

ROCHES, LEON (1809-1901). A French diplomat who arrived
in Algeria in 1832 and became an army translator of
Arabic in 1835. From 1832 to 1837, he served as a
cavalry lieutenant. He became an advisor for Abd al-
Qadir in 1837, joined in the Algerian National Guard in
1840, then returned to the French general staff as a
translator.

RUSTAMIDS. A dynasty of the Ibadi Kharidjis located at
Tadgdempt (Tahert). The first Rustamid imam was the
Persian Abd al-Rahman ben Rustman, who had been
governor of Kairawan at the time of its capture by the
Kharadjis in 758. When the town was recaptured by the
Arabs three years later, he fled westward and established
his headquarters at Tadgdempt. In 776, the imamate
was conferred on him. He was succeeded by six members of the same family. The collapse of the dynasty in
the early tenth century has been linked to the theological
pursuits of the imams to the exclusion of politics and
their tolerance of dissident factions. Their kingdom was
absorbed by neighboring Shiites.

SAADALLAH (-   ). Author of Arabic language novel
entitled With the Winter of Eternity (1953).

SAADI, SELIM (-   ). Selim Saadi was named Minister
of Agriculture and Agrarian Reform on March 8, 1979.

SAADI, YACEF (-- -   ). Leader of the urban terrorism
organization of the ALN during the Battle of Algiers in
1956. After independence, he associated himself with
the Tlemcen Group.

SAFIR, EL BOUDALI (20th c.). Algerian author and editor
who, with Robles and others founded Forge, a literary
journal to which Algerian authors had access. To replace Forge, which was published in 1946 and 1947 only,
and with the assistance of still other authors such as

Mohammed Dib and Albert Camus, Safir was one of the
organizers of yet another journal, Soleil, which was published from 1950 to 1952. Soleil also ran into financial
problems, as had Forge.

AL-SAGHIR B. ABD AL-RAHMAN MUHAMMAD (-1856).
Served as Khalifa for Abd al-Qadir in Ziban and East
Sahara (1838-39), then continued as Khalifa in areas
under the control of Farhat b. Sa'id.

SAHARAN ATLAS. The southern portion of the Alpine mountain ranges running through Algeria. These mountains
are the western sections of the Alpine system running
through the boot of Italy, over Sicily and into North Africa. The range provides significant protection from
the Saharan winds and supports extensive grazing lands.
High-quality dates are produced in this region. Its
proximity to the coast encourages the tourist trade.

SAHLI, MOHAMMED CHERIF (-   ). Author of Le
Message de Yougourtha (1947), which, although written
in French, was a search for Algerian roots and civilization.

SAID, ABID (1933-1967). A native of Sedrata, he fought
inside Algeria until 1960 when he was put in charge of
military operations in southern Tunisia. He was Zbiri's
assistant in the Fifth Military Region in 1962 and succeeded his superior as commander early in 1963. Said
commanded ANP operations against the Kabylian rebellion
fostered by the FFS. In June 1964 he was appointed
commander of the First Military Region, with headquarters
at Blida. He committed suicide in December 1967, evidently because of his own participation in the Zbiri attempted coup. He was generally considered an excellent
field commander and apparently had considerable influence in the ANP and in political circles around Algiers.

SAIDA. A town sixty miles southeast of Mascara and 110
miles from Oran. Due to its location on the edge of
the plateau area, it has constantly been militarily significant. It served as a site for fortifications of the Romans, the Algerians, and the French.

SAIHI, MUHAMMED LAKHDAR ABDELKADER (1933-   ).
Algerian poet who writes in Arabic and whose themes
have generally dealt with the War of National Liberation

and the repressions of May 1945, but who also celebrates
the agrarian reforms of independent Algeria and denounces
the bureaucratic excess of the new government.

SALAFIYYA. Orthodox reformist movement in Islam generally following in the spirit of Muhammad Abduh's teach-
ings. In Algeria, adherents were particularly intent on
attacking maraboutic brotherhoods as well as the Young
Algerians who were influenced by French culture and
who appeared to want to become French.

SALAM IFRIKIYA. Published from 1948 to May 1950, this
cultural journal replaced the earlier As Salam which
was founded by Si Hamza Boubakeur.

SALIH REIS (-1556). He succeeded Hasan Pasha as
beylerbey of Algiers in 1552, and in his reign was noted
for the extension of Turkish dominion to Biskra and the
securing of control over the chiefs of Touggourt and
Wargla. He captured Fez in 1553, but was unable to
maintain control over it. He took Bougie in 1555. He
died on the march towards Oran in 1556.

SANHADJA. One of the large confederations of Berber
people. The Sanhadja reached its height during the tenth
to twelfth centuries. Allies of the Fatimids of Kairawan,
they fought against the Zenata confederation, which supported the Umaiyads. Their influence diminished with
the Almohad advance.

SANOUSI, MOHAMMED AL-HADI (-   ). Editor of an
anthology of Algerian poetry which appeared during the
1920's. Among the poets included in this volume published in 1927 were: Mohammed Laid, Mohammed al-
Laqani, Mohammed Said Zahiri, Amhed Ben Ghazzali,
Randan Hammoud and Ibrahim Ben Nohu.

AL-SANRAGI, IBN AL-MANSUR (-   ). Inhabitant of
Algiers who edited and produced Dū-l-Faqār, an Arabic
language reformist Muslim weekly which first appeared
in 1913 and which pushed the ideas of the Egyptian reform leader Muhammad 'Abduh.

AL-SANUSI, ABU ABD ALLAH MUHAMMAD B. YUSUF B.
UMAR B. SHU AIB (1427?-149?). Ash'ari theologian
of Tlemcen. The reviver of Islam during the fifteenth
century.

SANUSIIYYA MOVEMENT.   A Sufi order or brotherhood which
    originated in Algeria.   The Sanusiiyya order moved to
    Libya in the nineteenth century and it was a Sanussi
    leader who became king of Libya when that country
    achieved independence after World War II.

SAOUT EL-ARAB (pseud.)   see   BOUBNIDER, SALAH

SETIF UPRISING (1945).   On May 8, 1945, demonstrations
    broke out throughout Algeria.   Some were demanding
    the release of Messali Hadj from French prison while
    a few demonstrators unfurled the green and white flag
    that had been Abd al Qadir's banner.   When colonial
    authorities tried to seize these flags, the crowd went
    wild.   Shots were fired, apparently by the police.   Al-
    gerians broke up into mobs that swarmed the streets
    and attacked any Europeans they happened upon.   Before
    the day was over nearly 100 Europeans had been killed.
        The French reaction was swift and thorough.   Be-
    fore the reprisal subsided, upwards of 50,000 Algerians
    had died.   The AML (Amis du Manifeste et de la Li-
    berté) was blamed and most of the liberal Algerian leader-
    ship was arrested.   Of the more than 4500 political
    leaders who were arrested, only 2000 were ever brought
    to trial; 151 were sentenced to death and 28 were actually
    executed.   After the Sétif uprising in 1945, the growth
    of radical nationalism among Algerians quickly led to
    the War of National Liberation that broke out in November
    1954.

SHARSHAL (CHERCHELL).   A town located on the Miliana
    Massif.   Originally known as Iol by the Carthaginians,
    it became a part of the Mauretanian kingdom under Boc-
    chus II, who renamed it Caesarea in honor of his pro-
    tector Augustus (25 A.D.).   The town still contains an
    aqueduct and the walls of an amphitheater from the period
    of Roman occupation.   Sharshal suffered a great decline
    during Vandal era.   At the beginning of the eighth cen-
    tury, it was captured by the Arabs, who gave it its
    present name.   Under pressure, it began paying tribute
    to the Spanish in 1511 until Khair al-Din annexed it to
    the Regency of Algiers in 1520.   An earthquake devastated
    the city in 1738.   The French occupied it in 1832.

SHAYKH.   Chief of a Sufi order; chief of a sub-tribe.

SHIITES.   Members of the Shia sect of Islam.   Most Alger-
    ians are not Shiites but Sunnis.

SI AHMED (ALIAS)   see   DRAIA, AHMED

SI AZIZ (-   ).   Son of Cheikh el-Haddad, he was also
a leader in the 1870 Kabyle insurrection.   Condemned
to exile, he was sent to Noumea.   In 1881, he escaped
and managed to make his way to Jidda.   There he befriended the French consul and tried to gain a pardon
so he could return to Algeria.

SI BOUZID.   Alias for Benalah Hadj ould Omar.

SI CHERIF   see   MELLAH, ALI

SI LARBI   see   LARBI, BEN REDJEM

"SI MAISUM" (title given to MUHAMMAD BEN AHMAD) (c.
1820-1883).   Algerian leader in the Shadhili Order.   Born
among the Gharib tribe (between Bogari and Miliana), he
received his formal training at Mazouma, a center of
Islamic studies.   He returned to his tribesmen and established mosques at Kuran and Fikh.   After visiting
the shrine of Abd al-Rahman al-Thaalibi, he became
interested in the Shadhili Order.   Shortly after joining,
he was appointed a shaykh.   About 1865 he became Shaykh
of the Shadhiluja of central Algeria.   The French offered
him the directorship of a madrasa in Algiers, but he
declined.   Yet he remained on good terms with the French
until his death.

SI MOHAND (1845?-1907).   Si Mohand was a Kabyle poet,
most of whose work was oral but some of whose poems
were later collected and published, in a French translation.   The editor and translator was Mouloud Feraoun,
the publishers the Edition de Minuit (Poème de Si Mohand, Paris, 1960).   Mouhoud Mammeri has also translated and published some of Si Mohand's work.

SI OTHMANE (Pseud.)   see   BOUHADJAR, BENHADDOU

SIDDIQ, MOHAMMED (-   ).   Arabic language novelist
who published The Blows in 1969.

SIDI.   Honorary title used before the names of marabouts.

SIGILL.   The register of proceedings of congresses of the
Association of Algerian Muslim Ulāma.

AL-SIHAB. A journal founded in 1925 in Constantine by Abd
al-Hamid ibn Badis as an organ for the Algerian Muslim Reformist Movement. The editorial board included,
among others, Mabarak al-Mili, Tayyib al-Uqbi, Basir
al-Ibrahimi and Tawfiq al-Madani.

SITIF (or SETIF). A town located southwest of Cirta. It
is located on the ruins of the Roman city of Sitifis, the
capital of the province Mauretania Sitifiensi. It was
nearby that the Almohads defeated the Banu Hilal in 1152.
The town declined during the period of the Turkish domination following the sixteenth century.

SKIKDA. Independent Algeria's name for the city named
Philippeville by the French. It is located on the coast
of eastern Algeria between Annaba and Bejaia (formerly
Bône and Bougie, respectively).

SMALA (ZMALA). A camp of a tribe or important person,
containing families and servants. During the Turkish
Regency, the term also applied to a form of mounted
police.

SOCIETE INDIGENE DE PREVOYANCE (SIP). French colonial
institution to which Algerians could subscribe funds which
could be drawn on in times of need. The system never
worked effectively.

SONATRACH (Société Nationale pour la Recherche, la Production, le Transport, la Transformation et la Commercialisation des Hydrocarbures). Algerian government-
operated company largely responsible for development of
petroleum resources within the state. SONATRACH
maintains full control over the Algiers, Arzew, and
Skikda refineries and over domestic distribution. It
also operates facilities for the liquification of natural
gas. By 1977 Sonatrach directly controlled 77 percent
of Algerian oil production as compared with 31 percent
in 1970.

SOUFI, SALAH (1933-   ). Born in Sedrata, he was a
corporal in the French army before joining the FLN and
GPRA in 1958. He commanded troops in southern Tunisia during the War of National Liberation, and was
elected to the National Assembly in September 1962.
He was in command of the Third Military Region (Colomb

Bechar) from June 1964 to December 1965. Since the
last date he has not held important posts.

SOUIDANI, BAOUJEMAA (1922-1956). Souidani was Bitat's
second in command for the region of Algiers during the
first two years of the War of National Liberation. He
had been a member of the PPA, of the OS and of the
group of 22. After the uprising of 1945, he was particularly interested in buying and obtaining weapons, for
dealing in which he received an 18 month sentence in
1949. Out of prison, he participated in the hold-up of
the Oran post office, later killed a French police inspector, and lived underground in Boufarik until the outbreak of November 1954. He was killed while on his
way to talk to a French journalist, Robert Barrat.

SOUIYAH, HOUARI (-   ). A commercial representative from Oran who joined the central committee of the
MTLD in 1954 and promptly sided against Messali Hadj
in the Party split. As was true of so many MTLD leaders, he was arrested by the French authorities in November 1954 and liberated again in April 1955. He
quickly joined the ALN in Oran region. After independence, he was appointed prefect in Oran, was elected
to the National Assembly and became a member of the
central committee of the FLN. He has had no official
position since the June 1965 coup.

SOUMMAM. A major river which reaches the Mediterranean
Sea at Bejaia. The Soummam Valley was the site of a
famous nationalist meeting during the war years (August
1956).

SOUMMAM CONGRESS. Held in the Soummam Valley during
August 1956, this congress had representatives from all
of the revolutionary war zones, but none from the so-
called external delegation. The primary leader was Abbane Ramdane. Delegates affirmed the primacy of internal leaders and blamed external leaders for failing
to supply enough weapons to support the continuing struggle against the French. The congress also affirmed col-
legiality or group decisions and the primacy of the political arm of the FLN over the military.
       The Soummam Congress created the CNRA (Na-
tional Council of the Algerian Revolution) and the CCE
(Executive and Coordinating Committee). The CCE
made decisions between meetings of the full CNRA.

That body met again in Cairo in 1957 and in Tripoli in
1959. It was at the 1959 meeting that a provisional
constitution for the Algerian state was elaborated and
that the FLN was given official status. But it was the
Soummam Congress that established the first revolutionary institutions for Algeria.

STATUTE OF ALGERIA (1947). An Act of the French National Assembly that created an Algerian Assembly of
120 members, 60 of whom were to be Muslims. The
purpose was to give Algeria more local autonomy and
also to abandon assimilationist policies and replace these
with associationist policies. European settlers generally
opposed the change and demanded a strong Governor
General to assure themselves continued control over the
colonial administration.

SUFI. Mystics in Islam who may be Shiites or Sunnis. Su-
fis seek contact with God (Allah) through trances achieved
repeating certain phrases or specific movements repeated
over and over.

AL SUFRIYA. A major branch of Kharidjis said to have
been founded because of its opposition to the sanctioning
of the murder of one's adversaries and their families
and to the rejection of non-Kharadji Muslims as pagans.
They appeared in the Maghrib as early as 703. Shortly
thereafter, under their chief Abu Kurra, they seized
the town of Sidjilmasa from the Abbasids (739). They
eventually allied themselves with the Ibadis and were
absorbed into their ranks.

SUHAILIYA. An Algerian branch of the Shadhiliya religious
order, established in the nineteenth century.

SUNNI. Members of Islamic orthodoxy. The vast majority
of Algerians are Sunni Muslims.

SYPHAX (-203 B.C.). King of the Masaesylians of
western Numidia. At first an ally of Rome, he threw
in his lot with Carthage following his marriage to So-
phonisbe. Scipio fought him, won, and took him to Rome
as part of his triumphal parade.

TACFARINAS (-24 A.D.). Leader of a Numidian revolt

at the time of the Roman emperor Tiberius. He originally served in the Roman army, but deserted (17 A.D.).
As leader of the Mussalamians, he fought eight years
against Roman domination. He died in a battle fought
at Auzia against the Roman proconsul Dolabella.

TADALLIS (TEDELLES or DELLYS). Coastal town seventy
miles east of Algiers and four miles east of the mouth
of the Sebau River, major river of Kabylia. The site
was occupied in Roman times. The town gained some
prominence under the Hammadids. It prospered with
the arrival of Muslim refugees from Spain in the fifteenth
century. The trade languished under Turkish rule. It
was occupied by the French in 1844.

TAFNA. River of western Algeria originating near Sebdou.
The Tafna empties into the Mediterranean near Rachgoun
after crossing the Traffas massif. It was the site of
a treaty between Abd al-Qadir and French General Bugeaud on May 30, 1847. Secret provisions of the treaty
which provided--among other things--the opportunity for
Abd al Qadir to purchase arms were never implemented.

TAGDEMPT (formerly TIGRET, TAHERT). Capital of Tiaret
province and located at the southern end of the Ouarsenis
Massif. Ancient capital of the Rustamids, it was captured by Abd ar-Rahman ibn Rustam and became capital
of the Ibadiyah empire in 761. The old city was destroyed by the Fatimids in 911, but it was rebuilt subsequently. It was successively occupied by Tlemcen,
the Turks, and in 1843 the French. The modern city
was begun by the French in 1863 to the north of the old
walled town.

TAHER PACHA (-   ). Turkish diplomat dispatched
by the Grand Vizir of Istanbul in 1827 when the dey of
Algiers requested assistance against the French.

TAIFE-I RUESA (also TA'IFAT AL-RU'ASA'). The guild of
Barbary corsair captains that was the financial base of
the Regency for over three hundred years.

TALBI, AMAR (-   ). In 1979, SNED published his
Rhetorical Opinions of the Kharijites, a two volume study
of this Islamic sect.

TALEB, AHMED (-   ). As secretary of the Algerian

Muslim Congress (CMA) in Tlemcen, he attacked in November 1937, European participation in the CMA.   This
was, in other words, an attack on the Algerian Communist Party, still an essentially European party.   In 1979,
he was Minister-Advisor to President Bendjedid.

TALEB, C. (-   ).   Algerian Ambassador to Canada
(1979).

AL-TANASI, MUHAMMAD B. ABD ALLAH B. ABD AL-
DIALIL ABU ABD ALLAH. (-1494).   Historiographer
of the Zaiyanids at Tlemcen.

TAOS-AMROUCHE, MARGUERITE   see   AMROUCHE, MARIE-
LOUISE

TAYEBI, MOHAMED (1918-   ).   A native of Sidi-Bel-Abbes,
he was a merchant who became head of Zone III in Wilaya V during the War of National Liberation.   Since independence, he has been a deputy in the National Assembly, ambassador to Brazil and to Cuba, head of national security and a member of the central committee
of the FLN.   Between the coup of June 1965 and December 1967, he was a member of the FLN's Executive
Secretariat.

TEBESSA.   Town 106 miles southeast of Constantine and
twelve miles from the Tunisian border.   Synonymous
with the Roman town of Thevesta, it was the second
largest town of Roman Africa at the time of Septimus
Severus.   It was sacked by the Vandals in the fifth century.   The town was alternately captured by the Berbers,
the Arabs, then was under the control of the Aghlabids,
the Fatamids, the Zirids, the Almohads, the Hafsids,
the Turks, and the French.   After a French garrison
was established there in 1851, it attracted a large European population.

TEMAM, ABDELMALEK (-   ).   A member of the
PPA, he did not act openly because he was employed
by the French colonial administration.   As a member
of the central committee of the MTLD, he sided against
Messali in the party split of 1954, joined the FLN in
May 1955, and worked on El-Moudjahid.   Arrested in
1957, he spent the balance of the war in prison.   Liberated in 1962, he participated in the drafting of the Tripoli
program.   He also served on the commission that pre-

pared the FLN Congresses of 1962 and 1964. He has
become director of the Algerian National Bank.

LE TEMPS DE L'ANARCHIE. Period from the French land-
ing at Sidi Ferruch to 22 July 1834 when the government
in France could not decide what to do with her Algerian
conquests. In one province, native tribes attacked Turks
and Koulouglis who garrisoned Oran. The Sultan of
Morocco tried to establish claims for himself over portions of eastern Algeria. Various çoffs fought one another
in what had been the beylik of Titteri.

TENES. Coastal town 125 miles west of Algiers, occupying
the site of the Carthaginian town of Cartennae, Tenes
was built in the ninth century by Spaniards. After the
collapse of the Almohad empire, the town fell under the
control of the Ziyanids of Tlemcen. The grain trade
with Europe declined under Turkish rule. For a brief
period after 1830, the town was independent. After a
short rule by Abd al-Qadir, its inhabitants submitted
to French control in 1843.

TIDJANIYA. An Islamic Sufi brotherhood founded in the
early 19th century and which spread in the Algeria Sahara and into West and West-Central Africa. The origin
of this group was in the border area between Algeria
and Morocco.

TIFINAGH. Tuareg writing system which is similar to ancient Egyptian hieroglyphics.

TIGGURT. A Saharan town 135 miles south of Biskra. It
dominates the Wad Rir Valley. Due to its advantageous
location, it is known as the "belly of the Sahara." The
origins of the town are unknown. It was the site of a
massacre in 1871 by Bu Shusha, who executed the French
garrison there.

AL-TIHAMI, MUHAMMAD AL-SAGHIR (1799-1853). Chief
of the Ain Madhis of the Tijaniyah Sufi order (1827-44).
He refused to submit to Abd al-Qadir in 1838 but was
forced to flee from him the following year. In 1844,
he became shaykh of the Tijaniyah Sufi order.

TLEMCEN (TILISMAN). City of northwestern Algeria which
is one of the most traditionally Muslim. The site has
been inhabited since prehistoric times, probably due to

to its location as a watering spot (Berber word tilmas
meaning "spring"). Little is known of its history until
the eighth century, when Idris I built a mosque at that
location. Thereafter, Tlemcen served as a Muslim
provincial capital of importance. The modern city was
established by Yusuf b. Tashfin near the end of the
eleventh century and was expanded by the Almohads
during the following century. Under the Almoravids, it
served as a theological and legal center of training.
During the thirteenth and fourteenth centuries, Tlemcen
grew as a commercial hub for the region and capital
of the Zaiyanid dynasty. It prospered under Marinid
control. Because of its significance as a commercial
and cultural focal point, it remained an object of ag-
gression by the Turks and Spaniards during the first
half of the sixteenth century. The Turks finally secured
possession of it in 1555 under the pasha of Algiers.
During the period of Turkish occupation the city fell
into decline. From 1830 to 1833, it came under the
suzerainty of the Sultan of Morocco. The French under
Bugeaud took control over it in 1842, and it became a
commune de plein exercise in 1854 and an arrondissement capital in 1858. During 1956 the city was practically beseiged by a section of the ALN forces. After
the administrative reform of 1958 it became capital of
a department of the same name. It is located on Algeria's main east-west railroad and highway. The name
of the city was given in 1962 to the "Tlemcen group,"
the political contingent of Ben Bella, who made his
headquarters there upon entering the country.

TRANSPORTATION. Of about 82,000 kilometers of roadway
    in Algeria, 18,500 are main highways. This includes
    3,000 kilometers of asphalted road in good condition.
    Since the period of French occupation, the Algerian gov-
    ernment has constructed new roads to link the oil fields
    with the coast and has begun a segment of the trans-
    Saharan highway known as the "Road of African Unity."
    The system of 4,074 kilometers of railway is adminis-
    tered by the Société Nationale des Transports Ferrovi-
    aires (SNTF). The main rail line extends from Tunisia
    to Morocco with branches to the major ports and others
    from Algiers to Djelfa, from Oran to Crampel, Mehdia,
    and Kanadsa, and from Skikda and Annaba to Touggourt,
    Tébessa, and Khenchela. Air Algérie provides inter-
    national and domestic flights from Algeria's main airport
    Dar el-Beida. Airfields at Annaba and Oran are capable
    of providing jet air service.

TREZEL, CAMILLE ALPHONSE (1780-1860). French mili-
    tary officer. In 1833, he became chief of the French
    general staff in Algeria. The same year he was appointed
    commander at Bougie, and two years later he received
    a similar appointment at Oran. He resigned his com-
    mand in Oran after the Battle of Macta, but was promoted
    to the rank of lieutenant general in 1837. He served as
    French Minister of War from 1847 to 1848.

TRIBUNAUX REPRESSIFS INDIGENES. Tribunals set up by
    the French in Algeria as a result of the Marguerite
    affair under decrees of March 29 and May 28, 1902.
    These consisted of the justice of the peace aided by two
    local residents, one Muslim and other European, ap-
    pointed by the governor-general. Arabs could not appeal
    sentences of less than five hundred francs or six months
    imprisonment.

TROUBLE DE CONSTANTINE (AUGUST 1934). A Muslim
    mob massacred Jews and were in turn massacred by
    French "forces of order."

TUAREG or TOUAREG [singular: TARGUI] . A nomadic
    people now located in the Hoggar Mountains and the Adj-
    jer Plateau of the Sahara. Their Berber language is
    known as Tamahaq and their alphabet, Tafinagh. The
    Tuareg maintian many of their ancestral customs to the
    exclusion of Islamic tenets. They continue a number of
    matriarchal principles in family matters, and they con-
    tinue to uphold a caste system.

ULAMA. Persons trained in religious doctrine.

ULUJ ALI   see   KILIJ, ALI

UNION DEMOCRATIQUE DU MANIFESTE ALGERIEN (UDMA).
    An integrationist party formed by Ferhat Abbas in 1946
    after the failure of the AML (Amis du Manifeste et de
    la Liberté). As with all of Abbas' efforts before 1955,
    this party sought to solve Algerian problems within the
    French system, not through independence.

UNION DES ECRIVAINS ALGERIENS. This is the Union of
    Algerian Writers first created in October 1963. This
    group went into suspended animation in 1967 when Jean

Senac, the organization's secretary general resigned.
Brought to life again in January 1974, it is essentially
composed of Arabophone authors.   It is one of a dozen
professional unions controlled by the FLN.

UNION NATIONALE DES JEUNES ALGERIENS (UNJA).
Created in 1975, it did not have its constitutional congress until January of 1978.

UNION NATIONALE DES PAYSANS ALGERIENS (UNPA).
National Union of Algerian Peasants which represents
small land holders who live from their own production.
The organization's aims are to organize and educate
workers in the agricultural sector and to help the same
to defend peasant interests.

UNION POPULAIRE ALGERIENNE.   Short-lived group of
political liberals who followed Dr. Bendjelloul when he
broke with Ferhat Abbas (1940's).

UPRISING OF 1945   see   SETIF UPRISING

AL UQBI, TAYEB   see   EL OQBI, TAYEB

VANDALS.   Collective name for a group of Teutonic tribes
that occupied the area of Algeria in the fifth and sixth
century A.D.   In 428 the entire nation invaded Africa
at the request of Bonifacius, a count of Africa.   Under
the leadership of Gaiseric, they assembled in Andalusia
and sailed for the coast from there.   By May 430 only
three Roman cities had not fallen to them: Carthage,
Hippo, and Cirta.   On January 30, 435, Gaiseric signed
a treaty with Emperor Valentianian III whereby the emperor retained Carthage and its province, and the other
six provinces were surrendered to the Vandals.   In
October 439, Gaiseric attacked Carthage and captured
it.   The Vandal occupation lasted 94 years.   In an effort
to recapture the area, the emperor Justinian appointed
Belisarius to lead an expedition in June 533.   Meeting
little resistance, the general entered Carthage on September 14, 533.   After the subsequent battle of Trica-
marum, Gelimer, the Vandal ruler, was severely routed
and forced to flee to the mountains, where he eventually
surrendered.   After a minor revolt in 536, the Vandals
disappeared from Algerian history.

VICHY ALGERIA (June 1940 to November 8, 1942). Following the signature of the armistice with the Axis in June
1960, the colons (settlers) of Algeria enthusiastically
rallied behind Marshall Philip Pétain's government located at Vichy. Prearmistice European attempts to resist and continue fighting were short-lived and half-
hearted once the colons realized that the armistice did
not endanger either their personal or business interests
or their control over the Muslim majority. Although the
Muslims loyally supported the Third Republic's war effort (in sharp contrast to the colons, who saw little
reason to die for Danzig), as "subjects" and not citizens,
it made little difference to the Muslims who governed
Algeria.

The Vichy government quickly replaced the un-
reliable governor general, other personnel with suspect
loyalties, banned all political parties, and imprisoned
Muslim and European political leaders in concentration
camps, where they were subjected to frequent torture.
Catering at the same time to the European minority,
the Vichy administration deprived the Muslim population
of many of their prewar advantages and rights. Although some Muslims supported the pro-nazi Parti Populaire Français and the Parti Populaire Algérien, Muslim
resistance to the Vichy regime came from members of
the Parti Communiste Algérien (whose secretaries, Kaddour Belkaim, Ali Rabiah, and Ahmed Smaili were assassinated or executed by the Vichy government) and
from members of the French-educated évolués, such as
Ferhat Abbas. Vichy, however, rejected Abbas's repeated attempts to gain equality and citizenship for the
Muslims which prompted him to change his political
goals from that of cooperation to autonomy.

Thinking to make a concession to the Muslims,
the Vichy-controlled Algerian administration eagerly implemented the anti-Semitic laws as directed by the Marshal's government, suspending the Crémieux Decrees of
1870 thereby subjecting Algerian Jews to the same re-
strictions and discriminations suffered by the Muslims.
Actually, as Muslim nationalists pointed out, the abro-
gation of this act catered more to the colons' own anti-
Semitism than to that of the Muslims. Muslim opposition
to the Crémieux laws resulted from being denied the
equality granted to the Jews, not from wishing that the
Jews be reduced to their level.

On September 6, 1940, General Maxime Weygand
arrived in Algeria as Vichy's Delegate General in North

Africa to suppress a naissant Gaullist Free French movement in the army and administration. Vigorously ac-
complishing this task, Weygand also bribed and flattered
marabouts into supporting the Vichy regime.
        Economically, Algeria was exploited to meet de-
mands by the Nazis on France. Weygand and Vichy's
policies in Algeria were supported indirectly by the United
States government which agreed to export food and fuel
to the area to keep the North African economy from dis-
integrating. In return the Americans were granted the
right to place a dozen American vice consuls in North
Africa for intelligence operations (the Weygand-Murphy
Agreement). The Americans made little effort to work
with Algerian nationalists and their support for the Vichy-
controlled administration made a mockery of President
Franklin Roosevelt's professed war aims contained in
the Atlantic Charter.
        Although Weygand did little to build up a secret
French army in North Africa and repeatedly resisted
Allied efforts to induce him to lead the territories in
revolt against Vichy, he did resist vehemently German
efforts to obtain French North African military collaboration (the Paris Protocols). His opposition led to his
dismissal on November 11, 1941 and the installation of
a more compliant administration in line with Admiral
François Darlan's Vichy policy of collaboration. With
Vichy's blessings, the colons in Algeria were allowed to
form fascist and ultranationalist organizations while the
economic exploitation of the colony increased and overt
assistance was provided to General Rommel's army in
Libya. Increased collaboration in turn led to the formation of small European resistance units, which conspired
with the Americans to facilitate the invasions of Algeria
and Morocco in November 1942.

VOIX DES HUMBLES, LA. Anti-reformist monthly review
    published in Oran and later Constantine by the Associa-
    tion of Teachers of Native Algerian Origin (OAIOIA).
    The publication appeared from 1922 to 1933.

VOIX INDIGENE, LA (later known as LA VOIX LIBRE).
    Anti-reformist Muslim Algerian newspaper published in
    Constantine from 1929 until 1940 and from 1946 to 1952.
    It passionately defended the doctrine of assimilation.

WAKIL AL-KHARIDJ (-   ). Algerian minister of the

navy during the Turkish period of that country's history
when privateering was the business of state and the Bey
was the principal shipowner. Actually, the Wakil al
Kharidj often acted more as a foreign minister than a
naval officer since so much of the North Africa contacts
with Europeans came about because of naval activity.

WALAD AL-MUHUR, HABIB (-   ). Consul for Abd
al-Qadir in Oran (1834, 1837-39).

WANISI, ZOHOR (-   ). Author of About the Algerian
Revolution (1963) which is in Arabic and either a novel
or an historical account.

WARNIER LAW OF 1873. Act of French government which
effectively removed control over land from the Muslim
communities. Under its provisions, communal tribal
lands were made available for sale. Once sold, land
would remain under French land codes and could not return to Muslim property law even if purchased by a Muslim. The law resulted in the eviction of Muslims from
the fertile coasts to the hinterlands.

WAT'AN. Subdivisions of the Turkish beyliks or provinces.
In Algeria wat'an were theoretically ruled by a caid who
was either a Turk or a native.

AL WATAN. Arabic language newspaper representing the
views of the UDMA. It was quickly forced to cease
publication because of financial problems. The UDMA'S
French language newspaper, La République Algérienne,
however, was able to continue publication.

WATTAR, TAHAR see OUETTAR, TAHAR

WUJAQ. The military force of the Turks in the Regency of
Algiers, also known as Janissaries.

YAHIAOUI, MOHAMMED SALAH (-   ). By the end
of the War of National Liberation, which he spent fighting in Wilaya I, Yahiaoui had risen to the rank of captain. He served briefly in the FLN hierarchy, but returned to the ANP as assistant director of the Military
Academy at Cherchell. In late 1965, he was named commander of the Third Military Region (Colomb-Bechar).

He was a member of the Political Bureau of the FLN
and gave one of the keynote speeches at the 4th Party
Congress. It was this Congress which made Chadli
Bendjedid Secretary General of the FLN and sole candidate for the country's presidential elections of February
1979.

YAKER, LAYACHI (-   ). Vice-Chairman of the Algerian National Popular Assembly (1979) who, in 1970,
was appointed Minister of Commerce in Boumedienne's
cabinet.

YAZID, M'HAMMED (-   ). PPA activist who was
also secretary general of the AEMAM in 1946-1947.
He was on the central committee of the PPA when, in
1948, he was arrested, condemmed to two years in prison and ten years of exile from Algeria. This was all
punishment for acts that threatened the integrity of French
territory. In France during the early 1950's, he lived
a clandestine existence under the name of Zoubir. He
was removed from party duties on Messali Hadj's insistence, presumably because he was too conciliatory with
respect to the PCF. He naturally became a strong Centralist in the MTLD split. On November 1, 1954, he
was in Cairo. He immediately joined the FLN and became the party's representative in New York. He also
served as Minister for Information in the GPRA. After
independence, he was a deputy in the National Assembly.
Since the June 1965, Boumedienne coup, he has been
ambassador in Lebanon.

YAZOURENE, MOHAMMED (-   ). Very little is known
about Yazourene except that, after November 1, 1954,
he commanded revolutionaries in the regions between
Azazga and Akfadou. In February, 1957, he succeeded
Saïd Mohammedi at the head of Wilaya III, (Kabylia),
then left Algeria for Tunisia where he became a member of the CNRA. Closely allied with Mohammedi, he
sided with Ben Bella against Belkacem Krim.

YOUNG ALGERIANS (JEUNES ALGERIENS). The title given
in the early 1900's to identify a group of Algerian Muslims who shared a French cultural orientation. They
sought limited political reform within French Algeria,
using the model of the Young Tunisian movement. A
delegation of nine (including representatives from Constantine, Bône, Djidjelli, Biskra, Tlemcen, and Bugeaud)

under the leadership of Dr. Belkacem Ben Thami arrived
in Paris in June 1912, and it presented a manifesto to
Premier Raymond Poincaré calling for the abolition of
the code de l'indigénat, equity of taxation, increased representation in Algerian local assemblies, representation
for Muslims in some French assemblage, and automatic
French citizenship for conscripts with honorable dis-
charges. The group's call in 1912 for immediate representation of non-French Algerians in Paris was opposed on all sides of the French political scene. By
the beginning of World War I, the group numbered about
one thousand, mostly professionals. Their primary goal
in the prewar period was to gain compulsory military
service for Muslims in the belief that political rights
would follow. They did not as the postwar period revealed. The group split in 1919 over reaction to the
Jonnart Law. Those remaining in the group suffered
electoral defeat at the hands of Emir Khaled and grew
increasingly isolated from their Algerian comrades thereafter.

ZAB. Region of Algeria, an area around Biskra measuring
125 miles eastwest and 40 miles north-south, from the
Sahara to the southern Atlas. Little occupied by the
Romans, the area suffered from the Arabic invasions of
the eleventh and twelfth centuries. From the sixteenth
to the eighteenth centuries, the area was controlled by
the Bu Okkaz family. Rivalry between this family and
the Ben-Gana clan continued from the end of that period
until the French occupation in 1844.

ZAHIRI, MOHAMMED SAID (-1956). Novelist who writes
in Arabic; he wrote a number of moralistic novels such
as Customs among Algerian Women (1931) which defended
the use of the veil and Visiting Sidi Abed (1933) which
attacked maraboutism.

ZAHOUANE, HOCINE (-   ). A member of the FLN
in Algiers region during the War of National Liberation,
he was named to the Political Bureau of the FLN after
independence. As a member of the Central Committee,
he was in charge of National Orientation and Ideology
(1964).

ZAHOUANE, MOHAMMED (1913-   ). This Algerian diplo-

mat was educated at the Lyceé in Constantine, at the
Sorbonne and at New York University. After Algerian
independence was achieved, he served as director of
African, Asian, and Latin American Affairs at the Foreign Ministry (1962-63) then as director of Political Affairs (1964) in the same ministry. He was a delegate
to the United Nations' General Assembly (1964-65), then
assistant secretary general in the Organization of African
Unity. He is the author of Economic and Social Aspects
of the Algerian Revolution (1962).

ZAKARIA, MOUFDI (1913-   ). Born in the Mzab, he began publishing poems in Arabic in 1925. He is the
author of the nationalists' hymn which he composed in
1932 (Min djibalina) and of Qasaman, Algeria's national
anthem, which he wrote in 1955 while in the infamous
French prison named Barberousse. A collection of his
poems, most devoted to the War of National Liberation
and to prisoners, was published in Lebanon in 1961
under the title of The Sacred Flame.

ZAMOUM, MOHAMMED (-1958?). A Kabyle, he was
the son of a school teacher who joined the PPA and the
OS and began the War of National Liberation as director
of the Mirabeau-Dellys region. He was a member of
the CNRA and succeeded Si Mohammed (war name of
colonel Bouguerra) as leader of Wilaya IV. According
to some accounts, he was Si Mohammed.

AL ZAWAWI, MUH. AL SA'ID (-   ). An inhabitant
of Algiers of Kabyle origin who, in 1904, published a
thin book devoted to the proposition that Kabyle zawiyahs
ought to be reformed. The argument probably reflected
the influence of Muhammad 'Abduh among Algerian intellectuals around 1900.

ZAWIYAH. Properly, the corner of a building. In the Maghrib, the term has the more general meaning of a religious building or group of buildings. Today the most
important zawiyah are often associated with religious
brotherhoods.

ZAYANIDS. A Berber dynasty of kings of Tlemcen ruling
from the thirteenth to the sixteenth centuries. They
are also known as Abdalwadids.

ZBIRI, TAHAR (1920-   ). Born in the Annaba region, he

became a miner at the age of sixteen. He was an armed
participant in an ALN attack on Guelma on November 1,
1954. He was captured, imprisoned and escaped, all
in 1955. A member of the General Staff-West, he broke
through the Morice line in 1960 to take command of
Wilaya I. He was promoted to colonel in 1961 and sided
with the Ben Bella-Boumedienne group in the civil war of
1962. Although he was Ben Bella's Chief of Staff of the
ANP he personally arrested his chief on June 19, 1965.
He retained his title but never got operational control
of the ANP. In December 1967, he attempted a coup
against Boumedienne.

ZEGUINI, MOHAMED (-   ). Officer in the French
army who deserted to the ALN in 1957 (?).

ZENATA. One of the two great confederations of Berbers.
The Zenata are largely nomadic and are distinguished
by language peculiarities. Though scattered throughout
the Maghrib, they are particularly evident in the western part of the central Maghrib and the nearby Sahara.

ZENATI, RACHID (1880-1952). Author of Le Problème algérien vu par un Indigène (1938), a political treatise
which sought to move the French to grant Algerians
liberal reforms.

ZEIRIDS (or ZIRIDS). An ancient Muslim dynasty begun by
Yusuf ibn Zeiri whom the Fatimid Mouiz left in 969 A.
D. as governor in his absence. However his grandson,
al-Mansur (948-96) asserted his independence, and the
dynasty soon divided into two lines, one at Fez and the
other at Kairowan and Tunis. Weakened by internal dis-
sensions, struggles against the Saharan Berbers and the
Normans of Sicily, they were finally overwhelmed by the
Almoravids in the eleventh century.

ZERDANI, ABDELAZIZ (-   ). Director of Le Peuple,
the French language newspaper of the FLN in Algiers.

ZERDOUM, KASSEM (-   ). A fellow student of Boumedienne's in Cairo who was caught by the French authorities in Oran province; he was apparently tortured
and killed during the War of National Liberation.

ZERGUINI, MOHAMED (-   ). Minister for Postal and
Telecommunication Services in President Bandjedid's
cabinet of March 8, 1979.

ZIGHOUD, YOUSSEF (-1957).   Leader of the North Con-
    stantine wilaya killed in combat in 1957.

ZIRID   see   ZEIRIDES

ZIYARAH.   Pilgrimage to a religious shrine or tomb of a
    marabout.

ZOUBIR (pseud.)   see   YAZID, M'HAMMED

ZURRAH B. SIDI UMAR B. AL-DOUBAH (1789-   ).
    Mother of Abd al-Qadir; marabout.

SELECTED BIBLIOGRAPHY

Introduction

For complete bibliographies on books about Algeria published in English, readers should turn to Richard I. Lawless, A Bibliography of Works on Algeria Published in English Since 1954 (University of Durham, Center for Middle Eastern and Islamic Studies, 1972), and Algerian Bibliography: English Language Publications, 1830-1973 (London and New York: Bowker, 1974). For works in French, the most useful works are the yearly bibliographies which appear in the Annuaire de l'Afrique de Nord published in Paris by the Centre National de la Recherche Scientifique for the CRESM (Centre de Recherches et d'Etudes sur les Société Mediterranéenes) at Aix-en-Provence.

Instead of being repetitive of excellent and recent works, I have prepared a bibliography that stresses the most important books in English published prior to 1973, and as complete a listing as possible for the period since 1973. The same basic principle of selection has also been applied to articles. To simplify consultation of this selected bibliography, I have divided the entries into the following sub-headings:

> Bibliographies
> Bibliographical Articles
> General References
> Economics
> Geography, Geology
> History
> Politics
> Social Conditions, Population
> Recent Articles

The selection and the organization used in composing the bibliography will, I am sure, make it a more useful first reference.

Bibliographies

Adams, H. D. Selective Bibliography of Hispano-Islamic Art in Spain and Northern Africa. New York: New York Institute of Fine Arts, 1939.

Africa: Directory of Labor Organizations. Washington, D. C. :

United States Department of Labor, Bureau of Labor Statistics, 1962.

Africa Research Bulletin. [Series A: Political, Social and Cultural. Series B: Economic Financial and Technical.] Exeter, England: Monthly, 1963+.

Ajaegbu, Hyacinth I. (comp). African Urbanization: A Bibliography. London: International African Institute, 1972.

Alman, Miriam (ed). United Kingdom Publications and Theses on Africa 1967-68. London: Standing Conference on Library Materials on Africa, Frank Cass, 1973.

Aspects of Agricultural Policy and Rural Development in Africa-North and North-East Africa: An Annotated Bibliography. Oxford: Commonwealth Bureau of Agricultural Economics, 1971.

Azzouz, Azzedine, and others. Selected Bibliography of Educational Materials: Algeria-Libya-Morocco-Tunisia. 10 vols. Tunis, Tunisia: Agence Tunisienne de Public Relations, 1967-1976. [Sponsored by the National Science Foundation, and the Office of Education (DHEW), Washington, D. C.].

A Bibliography of African Government 1950-1966. Compiled by Aldefer, H. F. Narberth, Pa.: Livingston Publishing Co., 1967.

Bibliography on Algeria. Compiled by Aldefer, H. F. Tangiers: Documentation Centre, African Training and Research Centre in Administration for Development (CAFRAD), 1971.

Bibliography on Land Tenure in Africa. Rome: Rural Institutions Divisions, Food and Agricultural Organization of the United Nations.

Bibliography on the Maghreb. Tangiers: Documentation Centre, African Training and Research Centre in Administration for Development, 1971.

Bratton, Michael (comp). American Doctoral Dissertations on Africa 1886-1972. Waltham, Mass.: African Studies Association, Research Liaison Committee, Brandeis University, 1973.

Competing Values in the Modern Arab World: A Bibliography of Books and Articles in the English and French Languages. Beirut: Centre International Pour le Monde Arabe Moderne, Université St. Joseph, 1971.

Conover, Helen F. (comp). French North Africa (Algeria, Morocco, Tunis) a Bibliographical List. Washington D. C.: Division of Bibliography, Library of Congress, 1942.

_____. North and North-East Africa: A Selected Annotated List of Writings, 1951-1957. Washington, D. C. : Library of Congress, 1957.

Dictionary of African Biography, 2d ed. London: Melrose Press, 1971.

European Economic Communities. Statistical Office. Foreign Trade Statistics: Associates Overseas Areas. Brussels: 1959-1965.

_____. Overseas Associates: Statistical Bulletin. Brussels. 5 annual issues, 1965+.

Friedland, William H. Unions, Labour and Industrial Relations in Africa. Ithaca, New York: Centre for International Studies, Cornell University, 1965.

Hambly, Wilfred. Bibliography of African Anthropology, 1937-1949. Chicago: Chicago Natural History Museum, 1952.

Hogg, Peter (ed). The African Slave Trade and Its Suppression: A Classified and Annotated Bibliography. London: Frank Cass, 1972.

Hoover Institution. US and Canadian Publications and Theses on Africa 1961-1966. Stanford, Calif. : Hoover Institution Press, 1967.

Howard, H. N. , Ehrman, Edith, Hale, Mathleen and Morehouse, W. Middle East and North Africa: A Bibliography for Undergraduate Libraries. Williamsport: Occasional Publications 14, Foreign Area Materials Centre, 1971.

International African Institute. Africa. (Bibliog. section. Quarterly, 1929+).

John, Janheinz. Who's Who in African Literature. Tübingen: Horst Erdman Verlag, 1972.

Lawless, Richard I. Algerian Bibliography: English Language Publications, 1830-1973. London and New York: Bowker, 1974.

_____. A Bibliography of Works in English on Algeria Published since 1954. Occasional Paper Series No. 1, Durham, England: Centre for Middle Eastern and Islamic Studies, University of Durham, 1972.

Legum, Colin (ed). Africa Contemporary Record. London: Rex Collings, 1968+.

Matthews, Daniel G. (ed). A Current Bibliography on African Affairs. Washington, D.C. : African Bibliographic Centre, 1970.

Matthews, N. and Wainwright, M. Doreen. A Guide to Manuscripts and Documents in the British Isles Relating to Africa. London:

Oxford University Press, 1971.

Near East and North Africa: An Annotated List of Materials for
   Children. New York: Information Centre on Children's Cultures,
   U.S. Committee for UNICEF, 1970.

Pearson, J. D. (comp). Index Islamicus 1906-1955: A Catalogue of
   Articles on Islamic Subjects in Periodicals and Other Collective
   Publications. Cambridge: W. Heffer & Sons, 1958.

_____. Index Islamicus Supplement: 1956-1960. Cam-
   bridge: W. Heffer & Sons, 1962.

_____. Index Islamicus: Second Supplement, 1961-1965.
   Cambridge: W. Heffer & Sons, 1965.

Pearson, J. D. and Walsh, Ann. Index Islamicus: Third Supplement,
   1966-1970. Cambridge: W. Heffer & Sons, 1972.

_____. Index Islamicus: Fourth Supplement, Part 1:
   1971-1972. London: Mansell Information/Publishing Ltd. , 1973.

Playfair, Sir. R. Lambert. A Bibliography of Algeria from the
   Expedition of Charles V in 1541 to 1887. Royal Geographical
   Society. Supplementary papers 11 (1889), pp. 127-430.

_____. Supplement to the Bibliography of Algeria from
   the Earliest Times to 1895. London, 1898.

Rural Development in Africa: A Bibliography. Madison, Wisconsin:
   Training and Methods Series No. 17, Land Tenure Centre, University of Wisconsin, 1971.

_____. Madison, Wisconsin: Training and Methods Series
   No. 17, Supplement 1, Land Tenure Centre, University of Wisconsin, 1973.

Segal, Ronald. Political Africa: A Who's Who of Personalities and
   Parties. New York: Praeger, 1961.

Selected Bibliography on Local Government. Tangiers, Morocco:
   African Training and Research Centre in Administration for Development, 1972.

A Selected Functional and Country Bibliography for Near East and
   North Africa. Washington D. C. : U. S. Dept. of State, Foreign
   Service Institute Centre for Area and Country Studies, 1971.

Selim, George Dimitri (comp). American Doctoral Dissertations on
   the Arab World 1883-1968. Washington D. C. : Near East Section,
   Orientalia Division, Library of Congress, 1970.

Standing Conference on Library Materials on Africa. United Kingdom Publications and Theses on Africa. Cambridge: Heffer, 1963+.

Sweet, Louise and O'Leary, Timothy. Circum-Mediterranean Peasantry: Intoductory Bibliographies. New Haven: Human Relations Area File Press, 1969.

Trade Unions in Africa (A Select Bibliography 1960-62). Washington, D. C. : Special Bibliographic Series: Labour in Africa, 1,
1 (Trade Unions), African Bibliographic Centre Inc. , 1963.

United Nations. Economic Commission for Africa. Foreign Trade
Statistics of Africa. Series A: Direction of Trade. New York;
May 1962.

_____. Economic Commission for Africa. Foreign Trade
Statistics of Africa. Series B: Trade by Commodity. New York;
Semi-annual, 1960+.

United States. Agency for International Development. Statistics
and Development Division. Africa: Economic Growth Trends.
Washington, D. C. ; Annual, 1969+.

Whitney, James Lyman. Catalogue of the Spanish Library and of
the Portuguese Books Bequeathed by George Ticknor to the Boston
Library, Together With the Collection of Spanish and Portuguese
Literature in the General Library. Boston, 1879.

Zell, Hans, ed. African Books in Print. London: Mansell Infor-
mation/Publishing Limited, 1975-.

_____. and Silver, Helene (eds). A Reader's Guide to African
Literature. New York: Africana Pub. Co. , 1971.

Bibliographical Articles

"The Algerian Literature of France," North British Review, 30
(February 1859), pp 1-21.

Attal, Robert. "A Bibliography of Publications Concerning North
African Jewery," Isaiah Sonne Memorial Volume.

"Bibliography on the Climatology of the North-West Africa," Meteorological Abstracts and Bibliography, 3:1 (January 1952).

Burke, E. "Recent Books on Colonial Algerian History," Middle
Eastern Studies, 7:2 (May 1971), pp. 241-250.

Cooke, J. "The Army at Vincennes: Archives for the Study of
North African History in the Colonial Period," Muslim World,
61:1 (January 1971), pp. 35-8.

Creswell, K. A. C. "A Bibliography of Muslim Architecture in North

Africa (excluding Egypt)," Suppl. Hespéris, 41 (1954), 54 p.

Halpern, Manfred. "Recent Books on Moslem-French Relations in Algeria," Middle East Journal, 3:2 (April 1949), pp. 211-215.

_____. "New Perspectives in the Study of North Africa," Journal of Modern African Studies, 3:1 (1965), pp. 103-114.

Heggoy, A. A. "Books on the Algerian Revolution in English: Translations and Anglo-American Contributions." African Historical Studies, 3:1 (1970), pp. 163-8.

_____. "The Sources for Nineteenth-Century Algerian History: A Critical Essay," Muslim World, 54:4 (October 1964), pp. 292-99.

_____. "Some Useful French Depositories for the Study of the Algerian Revolution," Muslim World, 58:4 (October 1968), pp. 345-7.

_____. "On Oral Sources, Historians and the Fichier de Documentation," African Studies Review, 14:1 (April 1971), pp. 113-120.

Liebesney, Herbert J. "Literature on the Law of the Middle East," Middle East Journal, 3:4 (October 1949), pp. 461-6.

Rivlin, Benjamin. "A Selective Survey of the Literature in the Social Sciences and Related Fields on Modern North Africa," American Political Science Review, 48:3 (September 1954), pp. 826-48.

General References

Abun-Nasr, Jamil, M. A History of the Maghrib. New York: Cambridge University Press, 1971.

Amin, Samir. The Maghreb in the Modern World: Algeria, Tunisia, Morocco. Baltimore: Penguin, 1971.

Barbour, Neville (ed). A Survey of Northwest Africa (The Maghrib). New York: Oxford University Press, 1962.

Berque, Jacques. French North Africa: The Maghreb Between Two World Wars. New York: Praeger, 1967.

Brown, Leon Carl (ed). State and Society in Independent North Africa: The James Terry Duce Memorial Series, Washington, D. C. : The Middle East Institute, 1966.

Gordon, David C. Self Determination and History in the Third World. Princeton: Princeton University Press, 1971.

Hermassi, Elbaki. Leadership and National Development in North
    Africa. Berkeley and Los Angeles: University of California
    Press, 1972 (paperback ed. , 1975).

Julien, Charles-André. History of North Africa: Tunisia, Algeria,
    Morocco From the Arab Conquest to 1830 (trans. by John Petrie;
    ed. by C. C. Stewart). London: Routledge and Kegan Paul, 1970.

Knapp, Wilfred. Northwest Africa: A Political and Economic Sur-
    vey. London: Oxford University Press, 1977.

Laroui, Abdallah. The History of the Maghrib: An Interpretive
    Essay (trans. from the French by Ralph Manheim). Princeton:
    Princeton University Press, 1977.

Middle East and North Africa 1977-78: A Survey and Reference
    Book. 24th edition. London: Europa Publications, 1978.

Nyrop, Richard F. Area Handbook for Algeria. Washington, D. C. :
    Government Printing Office, 1972.

Oxford Regional Economic Atlas of the Middle East and North Africa.
    Oxford: Oxford University Press, 1960.

Economics
(See Amin under "General References")

Algeria, Ministère de l'Information et de la Culture. Direction de
    la Documentation et des Publications. Algeria in Numbers:
    1962-1972. Algiers: SNED, 1973.

The Algerian Market. Paris 1969 [Special issue in English of Mar-
    chés Tropicaux et Méditerranéens]

Algerian Oil Policy: Events, Studies, Declarations. 2 vols. , Al-
    giers: Sonatrach, 1972.

Arab Economist: Monthly Survey of Arab Economies.

Blaire, Thomas, L. The Land to Those Who Work It: Algeria's
    Experiment in Workers' Management. New York: Doubleday and
    Co. , 1970.

Brant, E. D. Railways of North Africa: The Railway System of the
    Maghreb. Newton Abbot: David and Charles, 1971.

Clegg, Ian. Workers' Self-Management in Algeria. Baltimore:
    Penguin Books, 1971.

Foster, Phillips, W. Research on Agricultural Development in
    North Africa. New York: Agricultural Development Council,
    1967. [American Universities Research Program Monograph No. 2.]

Gasteyger, C. et al. Europe and the Maghreb. Paris: Atlantic
Institute, 1972.

Labour Survey of North Africa. New Series 60; Geneva: International Labour Organisation, Studies and Reports, 1963.

Lightblan, Y. Oil in the North African Economy in Independent
North Africa. Washington, D. C. : The Middle East Institute,
1966.

Pawera, J. C. Algeria's Infrastructure: An Economic Survey of
Transportation, Communication and Energy Resources. New
York: Praeger, 1964.

Middle East Economic Digest. London, 1957-[weekly]

Quarterly Economic Reviews: Algeria Morocco. London: Economist Intelligence Unit, 1948-[Annual Supplements]

Rossignoli, B. The Banking System in Algeria. Milan: Cassa de
risparmio delle provincia Lombarde, 1973.

Trebour, Madeleine. Migration and Development: The Case of Algeria. Paris: Development Center O. E. C. D. , 1970.

United Nations Economic Commission for Africa. Summaries of
Economic Data: Algeria, 1973. Addis Ababa, 1975.

Warren, Cline J. and Santmyer, Carolee. Agriculture in Northern
Africa. Washington, D. C. : Dept. of Agriculture, 1965.

Zartman, I. William. The Politics of Trade Negotiations Between
Africa and the European Economic Community: The Weak Con-
front the Strong. Princeton: Princeton University Press, 1971.

Georgraphy / Geology

Fage, J. D. An Atlas of African History. London: E. Arnold,
1958.

Gardi, Réné. Blue Veils, Red Tents: The Story of a Journey
Across the Sahara (trans. from French by Edward Fitz-Gerald).
London: Hutchinson and Toronto: McGraw-Hill, 1953.

_____. The Sahara (trans. from French by Ewald Osers).
London: George Harrap, 1969.

Johnson, Douglas, L. The Nature of Nomadism: A Comparative
Study of Pastoral Migrations in Southwestern Asia and Northern
Africa. Chicago: Department of Geography, University of Chi-
cago, 1969.

193   Bibliography

Lawless, R.I., and Blake, G.H. Tlemcen: Continuity and Change
in an Algerian Islamic Town. London and New York: Bowker,
1976.

Oxford Regional Economic Atlas of the Middle East and North Africa.
London: Oxford University Press, 1960.

Stevens, Jon. The Sahara Is Yours: A Handbook for Desert Travellers. London: Constable, 1969.

Thomas, Benjamin E. Trade Routes of Algeria and the Sahara.
Berkeley and Los Angeles: University of California Publications
in Geography, 1957.

History

(See under General References, entries for Abun-Nasr, Amin, Barbour, Berque, Julien, Laroui, and Knapp)

Barnby, H.G. The Prisoners of Algiers: An Account of the Forgotten American-Algerian War, 1785-1797. London: Oxford
University Press, 1966.

Braudel, Fernand. The Mediterranean and the Mediterranean World
in the Age of Philip II. 2 vols. London: Collins, 1973.

Clayton, Vista. The Phantom Caravan or Abd el Kader, Emir of
Algeria (1808-1883). Hicksville, New York: Exposition Press,
1975.

Confer, Vincent. France and Algeria: The Problem of Civil and
Political Reform 1870-1920. Syracuse, N.Y.: Syracuse University Press, 1966.

Danziger, Raphael. Abd-al-Qadir and the Algerians: Resistance
to the French and Internal Consolidation. New York and London:
Holmes and Meier, 1977.

Daumas, E. (General). The Ways of the Desert (with Commentaries
by the Emir Abd-el-Kader) (trans. from the French by Sheila M.
Ohlendorf). Austin, Texas: University of Texas Press, 1970.

Fisher, Godfrey. Barbary Legend: War, Trade, and Piracy in
North Africa 1415-1830. Oxford: Clarendon Press, 1957.

Gallagher, Charles F. The United States and North Africa: Morocco,
Algeria and Tunisia. Cambridge, Mass.: Harvard University
Press, 1963.

Gordon, David C. North Africa's French Legacy: 1954-1962. Harvard Middle Eastern Monograph 9. Cambridge: Centre for Middle Eastern Studies, 1962.

Gordon, David C.   The Passing of French Algeria.   London: Oxford University Press, 1966.

Heggoy, Alf Andrew.   Insurgency and Counter-Insurgency in Algeria. Bloomington, Indiana: Indiana University Press, 1972.

Henissart, Paul.   Wolves in the City: The Death of French Algeria. New York: Simon and Schuster, 1970.

Hess, Andrew.   The Forgotten Frontier.   Chicago: University of Chicago Press, 1978.

Hopkins, J. F. P.   Medieval Muslim Government in Barbary Until the Sixth Century of the Hijra.   London: Luzac, 1958.

Horne, Alistair.   A Savage War of Peace.   New York: Viking, 1978.

Le Tourneau, Roger.   The Almohad Movement in North Africa in the 12th and 13th Centuries.   Princeton: Princeton University Press, 1969.

Mellen, Joan.   Filmguide to the Battle of Algiers.   Bloomington, Indiana: Indiana University Press, 1973.

Ruedy, John D.   Land Policy in Colonial Algeria: The Origins of the Rural Public Domain.   Berkeley and Los Angeles: University of California Press, 1967.

Spencer, William.   Algiers in the Age of the Corsairs.   Norman: University of Oklahoma Press, 1976.

Valensi Lucette.   On the Eve of Colonialism (trans. by Kenneth J. Perkins).   New York and London: African Publishing Co. , 1977.

Williams, Ann.   Britain and France in the Middle East and North Africa.   London: MacWilliam, 1968.

Politics

(See Barbour and Knapp under General References)

Al-Fasi, 'Alal.   The Independence Movements in Arab North Africa (trans. from Arabic by Hazem Zaki Nuseibeh).   Washington, D. C. :   American Council of Learned Societies, 1954.   [Near Eastern Translation Program No. 8.]

Ahmad, Eqbal.   Politics and Labour in Algeria.   New York: African Studies Assoc., 1967.

Alwan, Mohamad.   Algeria Before the United Nations.   New York: Robert Speller & Sons, 1959.

Bedjaoui, Mohammed. Law of the Algerian Revolution. Brussels: International Association of Democratic Lawyers, 1961.

Behr, Edward. The Algerian Problem. New York: Norton, 1962.

Brace, Richard and Brace, Joan. Algerian Voices. Princeton, N. J. & London: Van Nostrand Company, 1965.

_____. Ordeal in Algeria. Princeton, N. J. : D. Van Nostrand Company, 1965.

Fanon, Frantz. A Dying Colonialism (trans. from French by Haakon Chevalier). New York: Grove, 1967.

_____. Toward the African Revolution. Harmondsworth: Penguin Books, 1970.

Gellner, Ernest, and Micaud, Charles. Arabs and Berbers: From Tribe to Nation in North Africa. London: Duckworth, 1973.

Jackson, Henry F. The FLN in Algeria. Party Development in a Revolutionary Society. Westport, Connecticut: Greenwood Press, 1977.

Lazreg, Marnia. The Emergence of Classes in Algeria: A Study of Colonialism and Socio-Political Change. Boulder, Colorado: Westview Press, 1976.

Moore, Clement Henry. Politics in North Africa: Algeria, Morocco, and Tunisia. Boston: Little, Brown & Co. , 1970.

Ottaway, David and Marina. Algeria: The Politics of a Socialist Revolution. Berkeley and Los Angeles: University of California Press, 1970.

Quandt, William. Algerian Military Development: The Professional- ization of a Guerilla Army. Santa Monica: Rand Corporation, 1972.

_____. Palestinian and Algerian Revolutionary Elites: A Comparative Study of Structures and Strategies. Santa Monica: Rand Corporation, 1972.

_____. Revolution and Political Leadership: Algeria, 1954-1968. Cambridge: MIT Press, 1969.

Zartman, I. William. Government and Politics in Northern Africa. New York: Praeger, 1963.

Social Conditions, Population

(See Gellner under Politics and Berque under General References)

Bleeker, Sonia. The Tuareg Nomads and Warriors of the Sahara.
New York: Morrow, 1964.

Bourdieu, Pierre. The Algerians (trans. by Alan C. M. Ross).
Boston: Beacon Press, 1962.

Brett, Michael, ed. Northern Africa: Islam and Modernization.
London: Frank Cass, 1972.

Cabot Briggs, Lloyd. Tribes of the Sahara. Cambridge: Harvard
University Press, 1960.

Carl, Louis and Petit, Joseph. Mountains in the Desert. Garden
City, N. Y.: Doubleday & Co., 1954.

Fuchs, Peter. The Land of the Veiled Men (trans. by Brice Faw-
cett). New York: Citadel Press, 1956.

Furlongue, Geoffrey. The Lands of Barbary. London: John Mur-
ray, 1966.

Gordon, David C. Women of Algeria: An Essay on Change. Cambridge: Harvard University Press, 1968.

Halpern, Manfred. The Politics of Social Change in the Middle
East and North Africa. Princeton: Princeton University Press,
1963.

Hirschberg, H. Z. The Jews in North Africa. Jerusalem: The
Jewish Agency, 1957.

_____. North African Jewry. Tel Aviv: Women's Inter-
national Zionist Org. Coll., History Round the Clock, 1957.

May, Jacques M. The Ecology of Malnutrition in Northern Africa:
Libya, Tunisia, Algeria, Morocco, Spanish Sahara, Ifni and Mauritania. New York: Hafner, 1967.

Mernissi, Fatima Beyond the Veil. Cambridge, Mass.: Schenk-
man, 1975.

Miner, Horace M. and Vos, G. C. Oasis and Gasbah: Algerian
Culture and Personality in Change. Ann Arbor: University of
Michigan, 1960.

Norris, H. T. The Tuaregs: Their Islamic Legacy and its Diffusion in the Sahel. Warminster, Wilts: Aris and Phillips, 1975.

Stephens, R. W. Population Factors in the Development of North
Africa. Washington, D. C.: George Washington University Press,
1960.

Trimingham, J. Spencer. The Influence of Islam Upon Africa.
London: Longmans and New York: Praeger, 1968.

Recent Articles

Abdelsayed, Fr. Gabriel. "Islam and State in Mediterranean Africa."
Africa Report, 21 (March-April, 1976), pp. 42-45.

Abercrombie, T. J. "Algeria: learning to live with independence,"
National Geographic, 144 (August 1973), pp. 200-33.

Abrams, L. and Miller, D. J. "Who Were the French Colonialists?
A Reassessment of the Parti Colonial, 1890-1914," The Historical
Journal, 19: 3 (September 1976), pp. 685-726.

Abu-Haidar, Farida. "A Survey of the Algerian Novel Written in
French," Maghreb Review, 2 (January-February 1977), pp. 19-
21.

Abu-Laban, Baha and Abu-Laban, Sharon McIrvin. "Education and
Development in the Arab World," Journal of Developing Areas,
10 (April 1976) , pp. 285-304.

Accad, Evelyn. "Interrelationship Between Arab Nationalism and
Feminist Consciousness in North African Novels Written by Women," Ba Shira 8, 2 (1977): pp. 3-12.

"African Development Bank Lends $6 Million to Algeria," Trans-
lations on Africa, (Washington, D. C.), June 16, 1972, pp. 1-2.

"Algeria: A Special Report," The Times Supplement, (London) November 1 and 2, 1974.

"Algeria: Agricultural Co-operation," International Labour Review,
103, (June 1971), pp. 585-586.

"Algeria Aims at Industrialization," Petroleum Economist (London),
February 1975, pp. 51-53.

"Algeria: Lean Years Ahead," Africa Confidential (London), May
9, 1975, pp. 1-3.

"Algeria: The Maghreb and Africa," Africa Confidential (London) ,
March 16, 1972, pp. 1-2.

"Algeria: A New Social Security Scheme," International Labour
Review, 105 (March 1972), pp. 295-298.

"Algeria: U. S. Relations," Africa Confidential (London), May 1973, pp. 4-6.

Andrew, C. M. and Kanya-Forstner, A. S. "French Business and the French Colonialists," The Historical Journal, 19: 4 (December 1976), pp. 981-1000.

Baechler, Jean. "Revolutionary and Counter-Revolutionary War: Some Political and Strategic Lessons from the First Indochina War and Algeria," Journal of International Affairs, 25 (1971), pp. 70-90.

Baker, I. "Cathcart's Travels: American Sailor's Captivity, 1785-95," American Heritage, 26 (June 1975), pp. 52-60.

Beckett, Paul, "Algeria vs. Fanon: The Theory of Revolutionary Decolonization, and the Algerian Experience," Western Political Quarterly, 26 (March 1973), pp. 5-27.

Benabdelkrim. "The Agrarian Revolution in Algeria," World Marxist Review, 19 (October 1976), pp. 118-126.

Ben-Dor, Gabriel. "Civilianization of Military Regimes in the Arab World," Armed Forces and Society, 1:3 (May 1975), pp. 317-327.

Bennoune, Mahfoud. "The Introduction of Nationalism into Rural Algeria, 1919-1954," Maghreb Review, 2 (May-June 1977), pp. 1-12.

_____. "The Origin of the Algerian Proletariat," Dialectical Anthropology (Amsterdam), 1:3 (May 1976), pp. 201-24.

Boals, K. and J. Stichm. "Women of Liberated Algeria," Center Magazine, 7 (May 1974), pp. 74-6.

Bostock, Anya. "Women of Algiers," New Left Review, 83 (January 1974), pp. 50-56.

Bouhouche, A. "The French in Algeria: The Politics of Exportation and Assimilation," Revue d'Histoire Maghrebine, (June-July 1978), pp. 238-60.

Brett, Michael. "The Colonial Period in the Maghrib and its Aftermath: The Present State of Historical Writing," Journal of African History, 17:2 (1976), pp. 291-305.

_____. "Islam in the Maghreb: Its First Formulation," Maghreb Review, 2 (May-June 1977), pp. 18-22.

Brown, L. Carl. "The United States and The Maghrib," Middle East Journal, 30 (Summer 1976), pp. 273-290.

Brown, R. W. "Africa's Giant Oilfields," Africa Report, 20 (March 1975), pp. 50-54.

Colombel, Pierre. "Old Frescoes Show Sahara Once Had Pleasanter Climate," Smithsonian, 6 (July 1975), pp. 68-75.

Colonna, F. "Cultural Resistance and Religious Legitimacy in Colonial Algeria," Economy and Society (London), 3:3 (August 1974), pp. 233-252.

Cooke, James J. "The Colonial Origins of Colon and Muslim Nationalism in Algeria--1880-1920," Indian Political Science Review, 10 (January 1976), pp. 19-36.

Damis, John. "The Free-School Phenomenon: The Cases of Tunisia and Algeria," International Journal of Middle East Studies, 5 (Summer 1974), pp. 434-449.

Day, Alan. "Algeria Blunts Giscard's Sword," Middle East (London), April 1975, pp. 28-29.

de Gramont, Sanche. "Frantz Fanon: The Prophet Scorned," Horizon, 14 (Winter 1972), pp. 32-37.

Delaval, Bernard. "Urban Communities of the Algerian Sahara," Ekistics, 38 (October 1974), pp. 252-58.

"Economic Prospects in Algeria," Arab World, 44 (Summer 1975), pp. 16-17.

Elvin René. "Holidays on a Pirate Coast," Geographical Magazine, 46 (February 1974), pp. 162, 164.

Emembolu, G. E. and Pannu, S. S. "Africa: Oil and Development," Africa Today, 22 (October 1975), pp. 39-47.

Fitzgerald, E. Peter. "Civil Authority, Local Governments, and Native Administration in Colonial Algeria, 1834-1870," French Colonial Studies, 2 (1978), pp. 23-48.

_____. "The District Commissioner of Colonial Algeria, 1875-1939," Proceedings of the French Colonial Historical Society, 3 (1978), pp. 163-77.

Furlonge, Geoffrey. "Relations Between Britain and North Africa," Maghreb Review, 1 (October-December 1976), pp. 3-5.

Gallissot, R. "Precolonial Algeria," Ecomony and Society, 4 (1975), pp. 418-45.

Gellner, Ernest. "The Unknown Apollo of Biskra: The Social Base of Algerian Puritanism," Government and Opposition, 9 (Summer 1974), pp. 227-310.

_____. "Urban Life in Pre-Colonial North Africa,"
British Journal of Sociology, 27 (March 1976), pp. 1-20.

Gendzier, Irene L., "Psychology and Colonialism: Some Observa-
tions," Middle East Journal, 30 (Autumn, 1976), pp. 501-515.

Good, Kenneth, "Settler Colonialism: Economic Development and
Class Formation," Journal of Modern African Studies, 14 (December 1976), pp. 597-620.

Gran, P. "On Modern Maghrebi History," Revue d'Histoire Maghrebine, (January 1979), pp. 57-60.

Gretton, John. "A Desert State That Vanished," Geographical Magazine, 49 (December 1976), pp. 155, 156, 159, 160.

Griffin, K. "Algerian Agriculture in Transition Toward Socialism,"
in Griffin, K. Land Concentration and Rural Poverty. London:
Holmes and Meier, 1976.

Guellal, Cherif. "Algeria's Oil Strategy," Africa Report, 20 (Summer 1975), pp. 41-44.

Hale, Gerry. "City and Sect in the Algerian Sahara," Geographical
Review, 62 (January 1972), pp. 123-124.

Heggoy, Alf Andrew. "Arab Education in Colonial Algeria," Journal
of African Studies. 11:2 (Summer 1975), pp. 149-160.

_____. "On the Evolution of Algerian Women," African
Studies Review, 17, (Summer 1974), pp. 449-456.

_____. "They Write in French Not in Arabic: Some
Thoughts on North African Authors," The Indiana Social Studies
Quarterly, 30:2 (Autumn 1977), pp. 98-102.

_____, and Zingg, Paul J. "French Education in
Revolutionary North Africa," International Journal of Middle East
Studies, 7 (1976), pp. 571-578.

Hennebelle, Guy. "Arab Cinema," Middle East Research and Information Project, 52 (November 1976), pp. 3-12.

Hess, Andrew. "Consensus or Conflict: The Dilemma of Islamic
Historians," American Historical Review, 81 (October 1976), pp.
788-799.

Hitchcock, Veronica. "Land of Emperor and Bey," Country Life,
158 (October 1975), pp. 1134-1138.

Hooker, M. B. "French Colonial Laws: Colonial Policy and Islam
in Algeria," in Hooker, M. B., Legal Pluralism: An Introduction
to Colonial and Neo-Colonial Laws. Oxford: Oxford Univ. Press,
pp. 203-16.

Ilevbare, J. A. "The Impact of the Carthaginians and the Romans on the Administrative System of the Maghreb." Journal of the Historical Society of Nigeria, 7:2 (June 1974), pp. 187-197; 7:3 (December 1974), pp. 385-402.

Johnson, Marion. "Calico Caravans: The Tripoli-Kano Trade After 1880," Journal of African History, 17:2 (1976), pp. 95-117.

Kearney, V. S. "Algeria: Third World in Microcosm," America, 130 (June 1, 1974), pp. 433-35.

Keenan, Jeremy. "An Era Ends for Tuareg Nomads," Geographical Magazine, 44 (April 1972), pp. 465-471.

_____. "Power and Wealth Are Cousins: Descent, Class and Marital Strategies Among the Kel Ahaggar (Tuareg-Sahara)," Africa (London), 47:3 (1977), pp. 242-52.

_____. "The Tuareg Veil," Middle Eastern Studies, 13 (January 1977), pp. 3-13.

Lawless, Richard. "The Lost Berber Villages of Eastern Morocco and Western Algeria," Man [new series], 7 (March 1972), pp. 114-121.

_____. "Programs and Problems in the Development of Maghreb Agriculture," Maghreb Review, 1 (October-December 1976), pp. 6-11.

_____. "Evoluting a Central Place Hierarchy: A Report on Research at Tlemcen," Maghreb Review 2 (July-August 1977), pp. 8-13.

Lawson, Kay. "An Algerian Community Amid Political Change: Review Article," Africa Today, 22 (January-March 1975), pp. 91-92.

Lazreg, M. "Bureaucracy and Class: The Algerian Dialectic," Dialectical Anthropology (Amsterdam), 1:4 (September 1976), pp. 295-305.

Lee, R. D. "Autonomy and Dependence in French Algeria: Four Approaches to a Case Study," Revue de l'Occident Masulman et Méditerranéen, 2 (1977), pp. 141-70.

Lewis, William H. "North Africa: Struggle for Primacy," Current History, 76 (March 1979), pp. 119-21, 131.

Magnus, Ralph. "Middle East Oil and the OPEC Nations," Current History, 70 (January 1976), pp. 22-26, 38.

Martin, Guy. "Fanon on Violence and the Revolutionary Process," African Insight, 2 (1974), pp. 14-19.

McCormack, Robert. "Airlines and Empires: Great Britain and the 'Scramble for Africa' 1919-1939," Canadian Journal of African Studies, 10:1 (1976), pp. 87-105.

McLachlan, K. S. and Burrell, R. M. "The Role of Algerian and Libyan Oil and Natural Gas in Western Energy Supply," in Burrell, R. M. and Cattrell, A. J. , Politics, Oil and the Western Mediterranean, Beverly Hills: Sage, 1973, pp. 37-63.

Moore, R. B. "Note on Racism in History," Freedomway, 14 (November 1974), pp. 347-349.

Mortimer, Mildred. "The Feminine Image in the Algerian Novel of French Expression," Ba Shira, 55 (July-September 1977), pp. 391-402.

Mortimer, Robert A. "Algeria and the Politics of International Economic Reform," Orbis, 21 (Fall 1977), pp. 671-700.

_____. "Boumedienne Redesigns His Regime," Africa Report, 22 (July-August 1977), pp. 14-18.

Murphy, Dermot F. "Colonial and Post Colonial Language Policy in the Maghreb," Maghreb Review, 2 (March-April 1977), pp. 1-9.

Nellis, John R. "Socialist Management in Algeria," Journal of Modern African Studies, 15 (December 1977), pp. 529-554.

Newberry, Daniel. "Tagarub Through Education," Middle East Journal, 30 (Summer 1976), pp. 311-321.

Nurse, R. J. "Critics of Colonialism: JFK and Algerian Independence," Historian, 39 (February 1977), pp. 307-326.

Perinbam, Marie. "Fanon and the Revolutionary Peasantry: The Algerian Case," The Journal of Modern African Studies, 11:3 (1973), pp. 427-445.

Perkins, Kenneth J. "The Bureaux Arabes and the Colons: Administrative Conflict in Algeria, 1844-1875," Proceedings of the French Colonial Historical Society, 1 (1976), pp. 96-107.

_____. "Pressure and Persuasion in the Policies of the French Military in Colonial North Africa," Military Affairs, 40 (April 1976), pp. 74-78.

Posnansky, Merrick and McIntosh, Roderick. "New Radiocarbon Dates for Northern and Western Africa," Journal of African History, 17:2 (1976), pp. 161-195.

Post, Ken. "The Alliance of Peasants and Workers: Some Problems Concerning the Articulation of Classes (Algeria and China),"

Working Papers of the Center for Developing Area Studies, McGill University, 8 (1975) pp. 1-17.

Quandt, William B. "Can We Do Business With Radical Nationalists? Algeria: Yes!" Foreign Policy, 7 (Summer 1972), pp. 108-131.

Rake, Alan. "Algeria: Africa's Fastest Moving Economy," African Development (London), September 1973, pp. 13-14.

Ralston, Richard David. "Fanon and His Critics: The New Battle of Algiers," Culture et Développement, 8:3 (1976), pp. 463-492.

Ravenson, Jon. "Algeria: From Beaches to Desert," Africa Report, 17 (June 1972), pp. 26, 28.

Ridgeway, J. "Gas Battle of Algiers," Ramparts, 10:184 (March 1972).

Rosenberg, Adrea M. "The Middle East Slave Trade," Middle East Review, 9 (Winter 1976/1977), pp. 58-62.

Schliephake, Konrad. "Changing the Traditional Sector of Algeria's Agriculture," in Land Reform/Food and Agricultural Organization of the United Nations, 1 (1973), pp. 19-28.

Seddon, David. "Primitive Rebels in the Pre-Colonial Maghreb," Maghreb Review, 1 (October-December 1976), pp. 18-20.

——————————. "Tribe and State: Approaches to Maghreb History," Maghreb Review, 2 (May, June 1977), pp. 23-40.

Shlaim, Avi. "The Maghreb Countries and the EEC," Maghreb Review, 1 (August-September 1976), pp. 10-13.

Sivan, Emanuel. "Anti-Colonialism at the Age of the Popular Front: Algerian Communism 1935-1939," Asian and African Studies (Jerusalem), 11 (Winter 1977), pp. 337-374.

——————————. "Colonialism and Popular Culture in Algeria," Journal of Contemporary History, 14 (January 1979), pp. 21-53.

——————————. "The Kabyle: An Oppressed Minority in North Africa" in Veenhoven, W. A. (ed.) Case Studies on Human Rights and Fundamental Freedoms, Vol. 1, The Hague, (1975), pp. 261-279.

——————————. "L'Etoile Nord-Africaine and the Genesis of Algerian Nationalism," Maghreb Review, 3 (January-April 1978), pp. 17-22.

——————————. "Leftist Outcast in a Colonial Situation: Algerian Communism, 1927-1935." Asian and African Studies (Jerusalem), 10:3 (1975), pp. 209-257.

_____. "Slave Owner Mentality and Bolshevism: Algerian Communism, 1920-1927," Asian and African Studies (Jerusalem), 9:2 (1973), pp. 154-195.

Smith, Tony. "The French Colonial Consensus and Peoples' War. 1946-1958," Journal of Contemporary History, 9 (October 1974), pp. 217-247.

_____. "The French Economic Stake in Colonial Algeria," French Historical Studies, 9:1 (Spring 1975), pp. 184-189.

_____. "The Political and Economic Ambitions of Algerian Land Reform, 1962-1974," Middle East Journal (Washington), Summer 1975, pp. 259-178.

Sutton, Keith. "Agrarian Reform in Algeria: The Conversion of Projects into Action," Afrika Spectrum (Hamburg), 9:1 (1974), pp. 50-68.

_____. "Population Resettlement--Traumatic Upheavals and the Algerian Experience," Journal of Modern African Studies, 15 (June 1977), pp. 279-300.

_____. "The Progress of Algeria's Agrarian Reform and Its Settlement Implications," Maghreb Review, 2 (January-April 1978), pp. 10-16.

Talbott, John. "French Public Opinion and the Algerian War: A Research Note," French Historical Studies, 9 (Fall 1975), pp. 354-361.

_____. "The Myth and Reality of the Paratrooper in the Algerian War," Armed Forces and Society, 3:1 (Fall, 1976), pp. 69-86.

_____. "Terrorism and the Liberal Dilemma: The Case of the 'Battle of Algiers'," Contemporary French Civilization, 2 (Winter 1978), pp. 177-190.

Thompson, William. "Planning Studies in Developing Countries: Kuwait, Kenya and Algeria," Royal Town Planning Institute Journal, 61 (April 1975), pp. 150-154.

Uzoigwe, G. N. "Spheres of Influence and Doctrine of the Hinterland in the Partition of Africa," Journal of African Studies, 3:2 (Summer 1976), pp. 183-223.

Van Dyke, Stuart. "Response to Rebellion: The Algerian French and the February 6, 1956 Crisis," French Colonial Studies, 2 (1978), pp. 97-112.

Von Sivers, Peter. "Insurrection and Accommodation: Indigenous

Leadership in Eastern Algeria, 1840-1900," International Journal of Middle East Studies, 6 (July 1975), pp. 259-275.

Wall, Irwin M. "The French Communists and the Algerian War," Journal of Contemporary History, 12 (July 1977), pp. 521-544.

Weiner, J. B. "New Approaches to the Study of the Barbary Corsairs," Revue d'Histoire Maghrébine, (January 1979), pp. 205-208.

Williams, Maurice J. "The Aid Program of the OPEC Countries," Foreign Affairs, 57 (January 1976), pp. 308-324.

Wolff, Ursula. "Report from Algeria's Mzab," Africa Report, 21 (March 1976), pp. 50-52.

_____. "Algeria's Unearthly Cities," Travel, 147 (February 1977), pp. 54-59, 90.

Wright, Frank. "Frantz Fanon: His Work in Historical Perspective," Black Scholar, 6 (July 1975) , pp. 19-29.

Younger, Sam. "Ideology and Pragmatism in Algerian Foreign Policy," World Today, 34 (March 1978), pp. 107-114.

Zartman, I. W. "Elites of the Maghrib: A Review Article," International Journal of Middle East Studies, 6 (October 1975) , pp. 495-504.

Zebadia, A. "Note on West African Literatural Contribution to North African History," Revue d'Histoire Maghrébine, (January 1979), pp. 209-210.

_____. "Some Unedited Documents in Algiers National Library," Afrika Zamani, (December 1977), pp. 173-176.

Zingg, Paul J. "The Cold War in North Africa: American Foreign Policy and Postwar Muslim Nationalism 1945-1962," The Historian, 39:1 (November 1976), pp. 40-61.

_____. "One Dimensional History: Review of United States-North African Historiography Since Algerian Independence," ASA Review of Books, 1 (1975), pp. 147-156.

Zlatorunsky, A. "Algeria's Horizons," International Affairs (Moscow), (November 1973), pp. 80-85.

Zoller, Adrien-Claude. "Algerian Nationalizations: The Legal Issues," Journal of World Trade Law, 6 (January:February 1972), pp. 33-56.

FRENCH GOVERNORS IN COLONIAL ALGERIA

Governors

Louis Auguste Victor de Bourmont, comte de Ghaisnes#	1830
Bertrand Clauzel#	1830-1831
Pierre Bethezène#	1831-1832
Anne Jean Marie René Savary, duc de Rovigo#	1832-1833
Théophile Voirol#	1833-1834
Jean Baptiste Drouet, comte d'Erlon*	1834-1835
Bertrand Clauzel*	1835-1837
Charles Marie Denys Damrémont, comte de*	1837
Sylvain Charles Valée, comte*	1837-1841

Governors-General

Thomas Robert Bugeaud de la Piconnerie, duc d'Isly*	1841-1847
Louis Christophe Léon Juchault de La Moricière	on interim
Marie Alphonse Bedeau	1847
Henri Eugène Philippe Louis d'Orléans, duc d'Aumale	1847-1848
Louis Eugène Cavaignac	1848
Nicolas Anne Théodule Changarnier	1848
Gerald Stanislas Marey Monge, comte de Peluse	1848
Viala Charon, baron	1848-1850
Alphonse Henri d'Hautpol, comte	1850-1851
Aimable Jean Jacques Pelissier, duc de Malakoff	1851
Jean Louis César Alexandre Randon, comte	1851-1858

Ministers

Napoléon Charles Paul Bonaparte	1858-1859
Justin Napoléon Samuel Prosper de Chasseloup-Laubat	1859-1860

Governors-General

Aimable Jean Jacques Pelissier, duc de Malakoff	1860-1864
Edouard Charles de Martimprey	1864

#served under the title Commander-in-Chief of the Army of Africa
*served under the title Governor-General of French Possessions in
North Africa

Marie Edme Patrice Maurice de MacMahon, duc de
  Magenta   1864-1870
François Louis Alfred Durrieu   1870
Jean Walsin Esterhazy   1870
Alexandre Charles Auguste du Bouzet   1870-1871
Arsène Mathurin Louis Marie Lambert   1871
Louis Henri de Gueydon   1871-1873
Antoine Eugène Alfred Chanzy   1873-1879
Jules Philippe Louis Albert Grévy   1879-1881
Louis Tirman   1881-1891
Jules Martin Cambon   1891-1897
Lozé (named but refused post)
Louis Lépine   1897-1898
Edouard Julien Laferrière   1898-1900
Célestin Auguste Charles Jonnart   1900-1901
Amédée Joseph Paul Revoil   1901-1903
Maurice Varnier   1903
Célestin Auguste Charles Jonnart   1903-1911
Charles Lutaud   1911-1918
Célestin Auguste Charles Jonnart   1918-1919
Jean Baptiste Eugène Abel   1919-1921
Jules Joseph Théodore Steeg   1921-1925
Henri Dubief   1925
Maurice Viollette   1925-1927
Pierre Louis Bordes   1927-1930
Jules Gaston Henri Carde   1930-1935
Georges Le Beau   1935-1940
Jean Charles Abrial   1940-1941
Yves Charles Chatel   1941-1943
Bernard Marcel Peyrouton   1943
Georges Albert Julien Catroux   1943-1944
Yves Chataigneau   1944-1948
Marcel Edmond Naegelen   1948-1951
Roger Etienne Joseph Leonard   1951-1955
Jacques Emile Soustelle   1955-1956

Resident Ministers

Georges Albert Julien Catroux   1956
Robert Lacoste   1956-1958

Delegates-General

Raoul Salan   1958
Paul Albert Louis Delouvrier   1958-1960
Jean Morin   1960-1962
Christian Fouchet   1962

Based on lists in David P. Henige, Colonial Governors from the
Fifteenth Century to the Present (Madison: University of Wisconsin

Press, 1970); Charles-André Julien, Histoire de l'Algérie contempor-
aine: La Conquête et les débuts de la colonisation (1827-1871) (Paris:
P. U. F. , 1964); and Charles-Robert Ageron, Les Algériens musulmans et la France (1871-1919) (Paris: P. U. F. , 1968).

CRUA MEMBERS
(Algiers, April 1954)

("Historical Leaders")
Ait Ahmed, Hocine.
Ben Bella, Ahmed.
Ben Boulaid, Moustefa
Ben M'Hidi, Mohamed Larbi.
Boudiaf, Mohamed.
Bitat, Rabah.
Didouche, Mourad.
Khider, Mohamed.
Krim, Belkacem.

MEMBERSHIP OF THE COMMITTEE OF TWENTY-TWO

Badji, Mokhtar
Belhadj, Abdelkader (Kobus) (?)
Belouizdad, Athmane
Ben Abdelmalek, Ramdane
Ben Alla, Hadj (?)
Benaouda, Mostefa
Ben Boulaid, Mustapha*
Ben M'hidi, Larbi*
Ben Tobbal, Lakhdar
Bitat, Rabah*
Bouadjadj, Zoubir
Bouali, Said
Bouchaib, Ahmed
Boudiaf, Mohammed*
Boussouf, Abdelhafid
Didouche, Mourad*
Habachi, Abdesalem
Mellah Ali, (colonel Si Cherif)
Merzougui, Mohammed
Nechati, Mohammed
Suidani, Boudjemaa
Zighout, Youssef

Names followed by (?) are members about whom there may be some
question. Names followed by * are the historical leaders; see CRUA
list, above.

MEMBERS OF THE FIRST CNRA
(August 1956)

Full Members	Alternate Members
Abane, Ramdane*	Benaouda, Mostepha Amar (?)*
Abbas, Ferhat	Ben Tobbal, Lakhdar*
Ait Ahmed, Hocine	Ben Yahia, Mohammed
Ben Bella, Ahmed	Boussouf, Abdelhafid
Ben Boulaid, Mustapha	Cherif, Mahmoud*
Benkhedda, Benyoussef	Chihani, Bachir
Ben M'Hidi, Larbi*	Dhilès, Slimane (?)
Bitat, Rabah	Idir, Aissat (?)
Boudiaf, Mohammed	Francis, Ahmed
Dahlab, Saad	Lebjaoui, Mohammed (?)
Khider, Mohammed	Mahsas, Ahmed
Krim, Belkacem*	Mehri, Abdelhafid
Debaghine, Lamine	Mellah, Ali*
Al Madani, Tewfik	Mezhoudi, Brahim*
Ouamrane, Amar*	Mohammedi, Said*
Yazid, M'Hammed	Temmam, Abdelmalek
Zighout, Youssef*	Thaalbi, Tayeb

Names followed by (?) are men who, according to William B. Quandt
[Revolution and Political Leadership. Cambridge: MIT Press, 1969.
p. 281], were probably members but whose membership has not
been established beyond the shadow of a doubt. Names followed by
(*) are those who attended the Soummam Congress that elected members to the CNRA.

CCE MEMBERS
(Cairo, September, 1957)

Abbane, Ramdane.
Abbas, Ferhat.
Bentobbal, Lakhdar.
Boussouf, Abdelhafid.
Cherif, Mahmoud.
Debbaghine, Lamine.
Krim, Belkacem.
Mehri, Abdelhamid.
Ouamrane, Amar.

FIRST GPRA MEMBERS
(September 1958)

Abbas, Ferhat, President.

Krim, Belkacem, Vice President in Charge of Armed Forces

Ben Bella, Ahmed
Ait Ahmed, Hocine   Vice Presidents who
Bitat, Rabah   were in French
Boudiaf, Mohamed   prisons at the time.
Khider, Mohamed

Debbaghine. Lamine, Minister for Foreign Affairs.
Cherif, Mahmoud, Minister for Arms and Supplies.
Bentobbal, Lakhdar, Minister of the Interior.
Boussouf, Abdelhafid, Minister for Liaisons and Communications.
Mehri, Abdelhamid, Minister for North African Affairs.
Francis, Ahmed, Minister for Economic Affairs and Finance.
Yazid. M'Hammed, Minister for Information.
Ben Khedda, Youssef, Minister for Social Affairs.
El-Madani, Tewfik, Minister for Cultural Affairs.

Khene, Lamime
Oussedik. Omar   Secretaries of State.
Stambouli, Moustefa

SECOND GPRA
(Tripoli, January 1960)

Membership was the same as the First GPRA, but with the following
changes:

Krim, Belkacem, added Ministry of Foreign Affairs to his other duties.
Mohammedi. Said, Minister of State.
Mehri, Abdelhamid, Minister for Social and Cultural Affairs.

Eliminated from the First GPRA were:

Debbaghine, Lamine (Foreign Affairs).
Cherif, Mahmoud (Arms and Supplies).
El-Mandani, Twefik (Cultural Affairs).

Resigned from the First GPRA:

Ben Khedda, Benyoussef (Social Affairs).

THIRD GPRA
(August 1961)

Ben Khedda, Benyoussef, President and Minister for Finance.
Krim, Belkacem, Vice President and Minister of the Interior.
*Ben Bella, Ahmed, Vice President.
*Boudiaf, Mohamed, Vice President.

*Ait Ahmed, Hocine, Minister of State.
Ben Tobbal, Lakhdar, Minister of State.
*Bitat, Rabah, Minister of State.
*Khider, Mohammed, Minister of State.
Mohammedi, Said, Minister of State.
Boussouf, Abdelhafid, Minister for Armaments and General Liaisons.
Yazid, M'Hammed, Minister for Information.
Dahlab, Said, Minister of Foreign Affairs.

*Honorary members who were actually in French prisons between
1958 and 1962.

BEN BELLA'S FIRST GOVERNMENT
(September 1962)

	Cabinet Post
Ben Bella, Ahmed	President
Bitat, Rabah	Vice President
Bentoumi, Amar	Justice
Medeghri, Ahmed	Interior
Boumedienne, Houari	National Defense
Khemisti, Mohammed	Foreign Affairs
Francis, Ahmed	Finance
Ouzegane, Amar	Agriculture
Khobsi, Mohammed	Commerce
Khelifa, Laroussi	Industry and Energy
Boumendjel, Ahmed	Reconstruction, Public Works
Boumaza, Bachir	Work and Social Affairs
Benhamida, Abderrahmane	Education
Nekkache, Mohammed	Health
Mohammedi, Said	War Veterans
Bouteflika, Abdelaziz	Youth and Sports
al Madani, Tewfik	Religious Foundations (Habous)
Hadj Hamou, Mohammed	Information
Hassani, Mohammed	Posts and Telecommunications

BEN BELLA'S SECOND GOVERNMENT
(September 1963)

	Cabinet Post
Ben Bella, Ahmed	President
Boumedienne, Houari	Vice President and Defense
Mohammedi, Said	Vice President
Ouzegane, Amar	Minister of State
Hadj Smain, Mohammed	Justice
Medeghri, Ahmed	Interior
Bouteflika, Abdelaziz	Foreign Affairs
Boumaza, Bachir	Economy

Mahsas, Ahmed	Agriculture
Boumendjel, Ahmed	Reconstruction
Nekkache, Mohammed	Social Affairs
Belkacem, Cherif	National Orientation
al Madani, Tewfik	Religious Foundations
Zaibek, Abdelkader	Posts and Telecommunications
Kaid, Ahmed	Tourism
Batel, Sadek	Undersecretary, Youth Sports

BEN BELLA'S THIRD GOVERNMENT
(December 1964)

	Cabinet Post
Ben Bella, Ahmed	President, Minister of Finance, Information, and Interior
Boumedienne, Houari	Vice President and Defense
Mohammedi, Said	Vice President
Cherif, Abderrahmane	Minister Delegated to Presidency
Bedjaoui, Mohammed	Justice
Bouteflika, Abdelaziz	Foreign Affairs
Mahsas, Ahmed	Agriculture
Dellici, Nourredine	Commerce
Boumaza, Bachir	Industry and Energy
Hadj Smain, Mohammed	Reconstruction and Housing
Boudissa, Safi	Work
Nekkache, Mohammed	Health, War Veterans and Social Affairs
Belkacem, Cherif	Education
Batel, Sadek	Youth and Sports
Heddam, Tedjini	Religious Foundations
Zaibek, Abdelkader	Posts and Telecommunications
Amrani, Said	Administrative Reform
Ouzegane, Amar	Tourism
Ghozali, Ahmed	Undersecretary for Public Works

MEMBERS OF THE POLITICAL BUREAU OF THE FLN
BEFORE THE BOUMEDIENNE COUP OF 1965

	Concurrent Position

First Political Bureau
(August 1962)

Ben Bella, Ahmed	President
Khider, Mohammed	Secretary General, FLN
Bitat, Rabah	Vice President
Ben Alla, Hadj	Vice President of Assembly
Mohammedi, Said	Minister of War Veterans

Second Political Bureau
(April 1964)

Ben Bella, Ahmed	President
Ben Alla, Hadj	President of the Assembly
Mohammedi, Said	Vice President
Boumedienne, Houari	Vice President and Defense
Mendjli, Ali	Vice President of Assembly
ou el Hadj, Mohand	
Mahsas, Ahmed	Minister of Agriculture
Benmahjoub, Omar	Deputy
Nekkache, Mohammed	Minister of Social Affairs
Bouteflika, Abdelaziz	Minister of Foreign Affairs
Boumaza, Bachir	Minister of National Economy
Medeghri, Ahmed	Minister of Interior
Zbiri, Tahar	Chief of Staff of ANP
Chaabani, Mohammed	Commander Fifth Military Region
al Hocine, Ait	President of Amicale in France
Zahouane, Hocine	
Youssef, Khatib	Deputy

FIRST BOUMEDIENNE CABINET
(July 12, 1965)

Boumedienne, Houari, President and Minister of Defense.
Bitat, Rabah, Minister of State.
Medeghri, Ahmed, Minister of the Interior.
Bouteflika, Abdelaziz, Minister of Foreign Affairs.
Kaid, Ahmed, Minister of Finance.
Abdesslam, Belaid, Minister of Industry and Energy.
Mahsas, Ali, Minister of Agriculture.
Delleci, Nourredine, Minister of Commerce.
Bedjaoui, Mohamed, Minister of Justice.
Taleb, Ahmed, Minister of Education.
Haddam, Tedjimi, Minister of Public Health.
Zerdani, Abdelaziz, Minister of Labor and Social Affairs.
Ali Yahia, Abdennour, Minister of Public Works.
Smain, Mohamed Hadj, Minister of Reconstruction and Housing.
Ben Hamouda, Boualem, Minister of Mujahidin (Veterans).
Ben Mahmoud, Abdelkrim, Minister of Youth and Sports.
Saadouni, Larbi, Minister of Religious Affairs.
Zaibek, Abdelkader, Minister of Postal and Telecommunications
    Services.
Boumaza, Bachir, Minister of Information.
Maaoui, Abdelaziz, Minister of Tourism.

Changes in Boumedienne's First Cabinet:

Smain was dismissed April 5, 1966.   Reconstruction and Housing
    Ministry was merged with Public Works.

Mahsas was dismissed September 22, 1966. Ali Yahia replaced him
  at Ministry of Agriculture 2 days later and was himself replaced
  at Public Works by Lamine Khene.
Boumaza fled Algeria on October 8, 1966. Mohamed Ben Yahia replaced him as Minister of Information on October 24, 1966.
Zerdani and Ali Yahia resigned December 15, 1967. On March 7,
  1968, Zerdani was replaced by Mohamed Said Mazouzi at the
  Ministry of Labor and Social Affairs while Mohamed Tayebi took
  over for Ali Yahia as Minister of Agriculture.

CABINET CHANGES, 1965-1978

1966: Bitat, Rabah, Minister of Transportation

1967: Ali Yahia, Abdenour, Minister of Agriculture
       Ben Yahia, Mohammed, Minister of Information
       Khene, Lamine, Minister of Public Works

1970: Belkacem, Cherif, Minister of Finance
       Tayebi, Mohamed, Minister of Agriculture
       Yaker, Layachi, Minister of Commerce
       Said Mazouzi, Mohamed, Minister of Labor & Social Affairs

1973: Belkacem, Cherif, Minister of State
       Bitat, Rabah, Minister of Transportation
       Mahroug, Smail, Minister of Finance
       Ben Yahia, Mohamed Seddik, Minister of Higher Education
          & Scientific Research
       Taleb, Ahmed, Minister of Information & Culture
       Benhamouda, Boualem, Minister of Justice
       Boumedienne, Houari, Minister of National Defense
       Messaoudene, Said Ait, Minister of Post & Telecommunica-
          tions
       Benmahmoud, Abdelkrim, Minister of Primary & Secondary
          Education
       Boudjellab, Dr. Omar, Minister of Public Health and Popula-
          tion
       Zaibek, Abdelkader, Minister of Public Works
       Kassim, Mouloud, Minister of Traditional Education & Re-
          ligious Affairs
       Guennez, Mahmoud, Minister of War Veterans
       Fadel, Abdallah, Minister of Youth & Sports
       Khodja, Kamel Abdallah, Secretary of State for Planning
       Arbaoui, Abdallah, Secretary of State for Water & Irrigation

1975: Abdelghani, Mohamed Ben Ahmed, Minister of Interior

Appendices 216

BOUMEDIENNE CABINET, 1978

Hadj Yala, Mohamed, Minister of Commerce
Lacheraf, Mustapha, Minister of Education
Ghozali, Sid Ahmed, Minister of Energy & Petrochemistry
Ben Yahia, Mohamed Sedik, Minister of Finance
Liassine, Mohamed, Minister of Heavy Industry
Rahal, Abdellatif, Minister of Higher Education
Aouchiche, Abdelmadjid, Minister of Housing and Construction
Malek, Redha, Minister of Information & Culture
Ben Habyles, Abdelmalek, Minister of Justice
Amir, Mohammed, Minister of Labor
Abdesselam, Belaid, Minister of Light Industry
Zergoini, Mohamed, Minister of Postal Services & Communications
Messaoudene, Said Ait, Minister of Public Health
Benhamouda, Boualem, Minister of Public Works
Akbi, Abdelghani, Minister of Tourism

MEMBERS OF THE POLITICAL BUREAU OF THE FLN
(1979)

Bendjedid, Chadli
Bitat, Rabah
Bouteflika, Abdelaziz
Belhouchet, Abdallah
Draia, Ahmed
Bencherif, Ahmed
Yahiaoui, Mohamed Salah
Tayebi, Larbi
Affane, Djilali

Abdelghani, Mohamed Benahmed
Belaid, Abdelesselem
Benhamouda, Boualem
Mazouzi, Mohamed Said
Benyahia, Mohamed Seddik
Amir, Mohamed
Kasdi, Merbah
Ibrahimi, Ahmed Taleb

GOVERNMENT OF ALGERIA
March 8, 1979

Bendjedid, Chadli, President of the Republic and Secretary General
    of the Party
Abdelghani, Ahmed Ben Ahmed, Prime Minister, Ministry of Interior
Bouteflika, Abdelaziz, Minister, Advisor to the President
Taleb Ibrahimi, Ahmed, Minister, Advisor to the President
Benhabyles, Abdelmalek, Secretary General of the Presidency
Benyahia, Mohamed Seddik, Minister of Foreign Affairs
Saadi, Salim, Minister of Agriculture and Agrarian Reform
Ghozali, Sid Ahmed, Minister of Hydraulics
Ghazali, Ahmed Ali, Minister of Public Works
Nabi, Belkacem, Minister of Energy and Petrochemical Industry
Ait-Messaoudene, Said, Minister of Light Industries
Lyassine, Mohamed, Minister of Heavy Industry
Hadj Yala, M'Hamed, Minister of Finance

Brahimi, Abdelhamid, Minister of Planning and National Development.
Bouhara, Abderazak, Minister of Health
Brerhi, Abdelhak, Minister of Higher Education and Scientific Research
Kharroubi, Mohamed, Minister of Education
Oumeziane, Mouloud, Minister of Labor and Vocational Training
Akbi, Abdelghani, Minister of Commerce
Zerguini, Mohamed, Minister of Post and Telecommunications
Aouchiche, Abdelmadjid, Minister of Housing, Construction and Urban Development
Messaadia, Mohamed Cherif, Minister for War Veterans
Boualem, Baki, Minister for Religious Affairs
Houhou, Djamal, Minister for Sports
Allahoum, Abdelmadjid, Tourism Ministry
Goudjil, Salak, Transportation Ministry
Soufi, Lahcene, Ministry of Justice
Mehri, Abdelhamid, Information and Culture Ministry
Houhat, Ahmed, Secretary of State for Fisheries
Brahmia, Brahim, Secretary of State for Forestry and Reforestation
Hamdani, Smail, Secretary General of the Government

STATE CORPORATIONS

Actualités Algériennes (Office des): Weekly newspaper and news-reels.

AGENOR (Agence Nationale pour la Transformation et la Distribution de l'Or et autres Métaux Précieux): Gold and Other Precious Metals Exploration and Distribution Agency.

AIR ALGERIE: National Flag Air Carrier.

ALTOUR--Société Nationale Algérienne de Tourisme et d'Hôtellerie: National Society for Tourism and Hotels.

ANEP--Société Nationale d'Edition et de Publicité: Publishing and Advertising Corporation.

BAD--Banque Algérienne de Développment: Algerian Development Bank.

BCA--Banque Centrale d'Algérie: Central Bank of Algeria

BEA--Banque Extérieure d'Algérie: Foreign Trade Bank of Algeria.

BNA--Banque Nationale d'Algérie: National Bank of Algeria.

APS--Algérie Presse Service.

CAAR--Caisse Algérienne d'Assurances et de Réassurances: Algerian Insurance and Reinsurance Company.

CADAT--Caisse Algérienne d'Aménagement du Territoire: Bank for the Improvement of Algeria.

CCR--Compagnie Centrale de Reassurance: Central Reinsurance Company.

CNAT--Centre National d'Etudes et d'Animation de l'Enterprise des Travaux: National Center for Public Works-Studies and Imple-mention.

CNRC--Centre National du Registre du Commerce: National Center of Trade Registration.

CNAN--Compagnie Nationale Algérienne de Navigation: National Shipping Corporation.

CNEP--Caisse Nationale d'Epargne et de Prévoyance: National Savings and Provident Bank.

CNMA--Caisse Nationale de Mutualité Agricole: Agricultural Insurance and Credit Union.

COMEDOR--Comité d'Aménagement d'Alger: Algiers Urban Planning Agency.

COMEX--Institut National Algérien du Commerce Extérieur: Chamber of Commerce and Trade Promotion.

CNI--Commissariat National à l'Informatique: National Commisariat for Data Processing.

CPA--Credit Populaire d'Algérie: People's Credit Bank of Algeria.

DNC/ANP--Direction Nationale des Coopératives de l'Armée Nationale Populaire: National Headquarters of the Army Cooperatives (Civil Engineering).

ECH-CHAAB PRESS--Société Nationale: Daily Arabic Newspaper and Printer.

ECOTEC--Bureau National des Etudes Economiques et Techniques: National Office of Economic and Technical Studies.

EL-MOUDJAHID: Daily French Language Newspaper.

EMA--Société Nationale des Eaux Minérales Algériennes: National Mineral Water Society.

ENC--Entreprise Nationale de Commerce d'Outils de Quincallerie et d'Equipment Ménager: National Enterprise for Hardware, Household Utensils, Office Machines.

ENEMA--Etablissement National Pour l'Exploration Météorologique et Aéronautique: National Organization for Meteorological and Aeronautical Exploration.

ENERIC--Entreprise Nationale d'Etudes et de Réalisations des Infrastructures Commerciales: National Organization for the Study and Construction of Commerical Infrastructures.

INAPI--Institut Algérien de Normalisation et de Propriété Industrielle: Algerian Institute for Patents and Trademarks

INC--Institut National de Cartographie: National Cartographic Institute

INRAA--Institut National de la Recherche Agronomique d'Algérie:
National Institute of Agronomic Research for Algeria.

Institut National des Cultures Industrielles: National Institut for
Industrial Crops.

OAIC--Office Algérien Interprofessionel des Céréales: Algérien
Interprofessional Grains Board.

OAP--Office Algérien des Pêches: Algerian Fisheries Office.

Office de l'Aviation Civile: Civil Aviation Board.

OFLA--Office des Fruits et Légumes d'Algérie: Algerian Fruits
and Vegetables Board.

ONAB--Office National des Aliments du Bétail: National Animal
and Poultry Feeds (Import) Board.

ONACO--Office National de Commercialisation: National Marketing
Board (Food and Basic Agricultural Products).

ONAFEX--Office National des Foires et Expositions: National Board
for Trade Fairs and Exhibitions.

ONALAIT--Office National du Lait et des Produits Laitiers: National
Board for Milk and Dairy Products.

ONALFA--Office National de l'Alfa: National Esparto Grass Office.

ONAMA--Office National du Matériel Agricole: National Office for
Agricultural Equipment Marketing.

ONAMHYD--Office National du Matériel Hydraulique: National Hy-
draulic Equipment Board.

ONAPO--Office National des Produits Oléicoles: National Olive
Products Board.

ONAT--Office National Algérien du Tourisme: National Tourism
Office.

ONCIC--Office National Pour le Commerce et l'Industrie Cinémato-
graphiques: National Film Board.

ONCN--Office National de Construction Navale: National Naval Construction Board.

ONCV--Office National de Commercialisation des Produits Viti-
vinicoles: National Board for Viniculture Products.

INM--Office National de la Météorologie: National Meteorological
Office.

ONP--Office National des Ports: National Port Authority.

ONTF--Office National des Travaux Forestiers: National Forestry Office.

PCA-Pharmacide Centrale Algérienne: Algerian Central Pharmaceuticals and Medical Equipment Board.

LA REPUBLIQUE--EL Djoumhouria-Presse-Société Nationale Daily French Language Newspaper

RTA--Radiodiffusion Télévision Algérienne: Algerian Radio and Television Broadcasting Corporation,

SAA-Société Algérienne d'Assurance: Algerian Insurance Society.

SAP--Société Agricole de Prévoyance: Agricultural Planning Society (Imports and Distribution of Seeds).

SNAT--Société Nationale de l'Artisanat Traditionnel: National Handicrafts Society.

SNB. TRAPAL--Société Nationale du Bâtiment et de Travaux Publics d'Alger: National Building and Public Works Society of Algiers.

SNB. TRAPCO--Société Nationale du Bâtiment et des Travaux Publics de Constantine: National Building and Public Works Society in Constantine.

SNC--Société Nationale de Comptabilité: National Accounting Society.

SN. COTEC--Société Nationale de Commercialisation des Textiles et des Cuirs: National Textile and Leather Products Marketing Society.

SNED--Société Nationale d'Edition et de Diffusion: National Publishing and Distribution Company.

SNERI--Société Nationale d'Etudes et de Réalisations Industrielles: National Industrial Development and Implementation Society.

SNERIF--Société Nationale d'Etudes et de Réalisations de l'Infrastructure Ferroviaire: National Rail Construction Society.

SNIC--Société Nationale des Industries Chimiques: National Society for Chemical Industries.

SNLB--Société Nationale des Industries du Liège et du Bois: National Cork and Wood Products Society.

SNMC--Société Nationale des Matériaux de Construction: National Construction Materials Society.

SN METAL--Societé Nationale de Constructions Métaliques: National
Metal Constructions Society.

SNNGA--Société Nationale "Les Nouvelles Galéries Algériennes":
Board of the National Department Stores.

SN REAH--Société Nationale de Recherche d'Eau et d'Aménagement
Hydraulique: National Water Research and Hydraulics Society.

SN REGMA--Société Nationale de Promotion, de Réalisation et de
Gestion des Marchés de Gros: National Society for Wholesale
Promotion and Management.

SNS--Société Nationale de Sidérurgie: National Iron and Steel Company.

SN SEMPAC--Société Nationale de Sémouleries, Meuneries, Pates
Alimentaires et Couscous: National Board for Foods Made From
Grains.

SNTA--Société Nationale des Tabacs et Allumettes: National Tobacco
and Matches Monopoly.

SNTF--Société Nationale des Transports Ferroviaires: National
Railways Company.

SNTR--Société Nationale des Transports Routier: National Trucking
Company.

SNTV--Société Nationale des Transports de Voyageurs: National
Intercity Buses Company.

SOGEDIA--Société de Gestion et de Développement des Industries
Alimentaires: National Food Industries Company.

SONACAT--Société Nationale de Commercialisation et d'Application
Technique: National Electrical Appliances Marketing Company.

SONACOB: Société Nationale de Commercialisation des Bois et
Dérivés: National Society for Wood and Wood Products Marketing.

SONACOME--Société Nationale de Construction Mécanique: National
Mechanical Industries Society.

SONAGHTER--Société Nationale des Grands Travaux Hydrauliques et
d'Equipement Rural: National Irrigation Society.

SONAMA--Société Nationale de Manutention: National Stevedoring
Society.

SONAREM--Société Nationale de Recherches et d'Exploitation Min-
ières: National Society for Mining and Large Scale Quarrying.

SONATHERM--Société Nationale Algérienne de Thermalisme: National Health Spas Society.

SONATIBA--Société Nationale de Travaux d'Infrastructure et du Bâtiment: National Building Construction Society.

SONATITE--Société Nationale des Travaux d'Infrastructure des Télécommunications: National Telecommunication Equipment and Construction Company.

SONATMAG--Société Nationale de Transit et de Magasins Généraux: National Freight Forwarding and Warehousing Company.

SONATRACH--Société Nationale de Transport et de Commercialisation des Hydrocarbures: National Oil and Gas Corporation.

SONATRAM--Société Nationale de Travaux Maritimes: National Port Construction Corporation.

SONELEC--Société Nationale de Fabrication et de Montage du Matériel Eléctrique et Electronique: National Electrical and Electronic Equipment Corporation.

SONELGAZ--Société Nationale de l'Electricité et du Gaz: National Electricity and Gas Corporation.

SONIC--Société Nationale des Industries de la Cellulose: National Cellulose Industries-Paper Corporation.

SONIPEC--Société Nationale des Peaux et Cuirs: National Hides and Leather Society.

SONITEX--Société Nationale des Industries Textiles: National Textiles Corporation.

TNA--Théâtre National Algérien: Algerian National Theatre.

INDEX

Abbas, Ferhat 11, 12, 13, 14, 15, 17, 48, 76, 88, 94, 105, 145, 161, 176
Abd al-Qadir, ben Muhji al-Din al Hasani ix, 7, 8, 10, 46, 47, 53, 55, 57, 65, 70, 72, 74, 76, 89, 90, 98, 100, 102, 103, 107, 112, 117, 118, 122, 123, 130-133, 142, 143, 147, 150, 151, 152, 158, 162, 163, 170, 172, 178
Abd alQadir el Djilani 128
Abdelkader, Hadj Ali 125
Abduh, Muhammad 57, 103, 123, 140, 164
About the Algerian Revolution (Zohor Warnisi) 178
Abu Abd Allah, Sherif 55
Abu Thabit 55, 56
Abu Yakub 56
Abu Zaiyan ix, 1, 66
Abu Zakariyya al-Djanawuni, Yaliya 96
Abucaya, Simon 15
The Ace (Tahar Ouettar) 156
L'Action (newspaper) 99
Adherbal 127
Adjoul Adjoul, Ben Abdelhafid 93, 114
Adventures of a Hero (film) 62
Affreville 80
African Charter 52
L'Afro-asiatisme (Malek Bennabi) 79
Aghalids 81
AGTA (Assoc. Général des Travailleurs Algériens) 67
Ahmad Bey 96, 150
Ahmed Ben Mostapha, goumier (Caid Ben Cherif) 74
Ahmed Dey 45, 46
Ain Beida 84, 136
Ain Kerma 81
Ain Mahdi 172
Ain M'Lila 75
Ait Ahmed, Hocine 16, 17, 54, 84, 111, 119, 157
Ait al Hocine, Mohamed 154
Alaska 3
Al-Alawi, Abu al-Abbas Ahmad

b. Mustafa 70
Alawi dynasty 53
Alexandria 118, 121, 131
Alger Républicain (newspaper) 80, 83, 111, 129, 156
Algeria Between Yesterday and Today (A. Benhedouga) 79
Algerian Assembly 16, 17, 48, 51, 58, 67, 72, 73, 75, 83, 107, 109 see National Popular Assembly.
Algerian Grand Literary Prize 77
Algerian Peoples Union 51
Algerian Shadows (A. Benhe-douga) 79
Algerian Socialism 17, 97, 120 see Soummam Congress, Tripoli Program, Charter of Algiers....
Algerian Statute 67
L'Algérie française vue par un indigène (Cherif Benhabyles)
L'Algérie libre (newspaper) 138
L'Algérie sous l'égide de la France (Said Faci) 106
Algiers Municipal Council 107
Ali al-Rabal 46
Ali Khodja 46
Alleg, Henri 60
Allied Invasion of Algeria x, 176, 177
Almohad 63, 64, 96, 113, 117, 123, 141, 154, 164, 167, 171, 173
Almoravid 113, 123, 140, 141, 173
ALN (Armée de la Libération Nationale) 14, 15, 16, 53, 63, 69, 72, 75, 78-80, 83, 85, 88, 103, 113, 129, 132, 135, 136, 144, 147, 149, 152, 155, 160, 168, 173, 182
Le Alouettes Naives (Assia Djebbar) 102
The Ambitious One (Arar Moham-med al-Ali) 61
Ambrose 69
Amirouche 148
AML (Amis du Manifeste et de la Liberté) 12, 161, 165, 174